THE AMERICAN PHILOLOGICAL ASSOCIATION
AMERICAN CLASSICAL STUDIES

Deborah Samuel, Editor

Number 9

EROS SOPHISTES
Ancient Novelists at Play

by
Graham Anderson

GRAHAM ANDERSON

EROS SOPHISTES
Ancient Novelists at Play

SCHOLARS PRESS

Published by
Scholars Press
101 Salem St.
P.O. Box 2268
Chico, CA 95927

EROS SOPHISTES
Ancient Novelists at Play

GRAHAM ANDERSON

c c

Library of Congress Cataloging in Publication Data

Anderson, Graham.
   Eros sophistes.

   (American classical studies ; no. 9)
   (ISSN 0278-5943)
   Bibliography: p.
   Includes index.
   1. Classical fiction—History and criticism. I. Title.
II. Series.
PA3040.A48   883'.01'09 81-16573
ISBN 0-89130-547-5   AACR2

Manufactured in the U.S.A.

EROS SOPHISTES: ANCIENT NOVELISTS AT PLAY

CONTENTS

EROS SOPHISTES: ANCIENT NOVELISTS AT PLAY

PREFACE

War es nicht eine Art Ironie des Schicksals, dass
der jugendliche hero-worshipper sich mit einer
Litteraturgattung befasste, in der höchstens
Mittelmässigkeiten, 'Individuen, die nur als
Gattungswesen Bedeutung haben', zu Worte kommen?

Otto Crusius on Erwin Rohde

Many aspects of the ancient novel have received attention in
the past century, but the main aim of scholars since Rohde's *Der*
griechische Roman und seine Verläufer (1876) has been to interpret
the surviving works in terms of their ever-elusive origins. As a
result there has been a significant lack of interest in treating
them as literature. One of the most controversial and crucial
aspects of literary interpretation is how serious - or otherwise -
such products were intended to be. There is a conventional and
widely-held view that the Greek novel at least is a sub-literary
genre intended to provide indiscriminate trash for an undiscriminat-
ing audience; and its more sophisticated practitioners still
suffered from a lack of literary taste and judgement despite their
admitted skills. It is the stereotyped sentimental plot that has
been largely responsible for bringing the novel into disrepute.
I have tried to explore the various ways in which novelists
diversified that plot with charm, wit, humour, or even outright
burlesque. That is not to be mistaken for a thesis that the novels
are 'funny' rather than 'serious'; it is rather the beginning of
an exploration into the novelists as individuals, finding their
own ways of turning a pair of lovers into literature.

Writers of the so-called 'comic' novel have proved still more
difficult to interpret. Petronius has been read in recent years
as an earnest moralist, Apuleius as no more than a facile enter-
tainer; and opposite views of both are still being advanced with
equal vigour. Even the most rudimentary appreciation of these
texts cannot be attempted until we can be sure how the author
could have expected them to be read; and we must be prepared to
ask whether the terms 'ideal' and 'comic' prejudge the works they
have characterised for so long.

Over the past twenty years the problem has become more urgent.
Since Merkelbach's *Roman und Mysterium* appeared in 1962, many
scholars have been concerned with supporting or denying the
possibility of serious religious symbolisms that will explain the
novel itself, and its prominent use of religious paraphernalia.
In arguing that religion is often used in a literary and facetious
way, I have tried to show that the novels are usually intelligible
in their own terms, or those of their authors.

My chief problem in the present study has been one of scale.
To some extent this has been determined by the state of scholarly
opinion on each individual novelist. For most of the ideal novels
I have accepted the sentimental and 'serious' aspects of the plot
as universally recognised; my task has been to adduce just
enough evidence to show how any given writer deviates from the
plain pattern of love-and-adventure. Lightness of touch is
notoriously difficult to characterise, but I have consciously
tried to avoid an exhaustive catalogue of humorous effects; these
have however so often been ignored, denied, condemned or explained
away by scholars in the past that I have felt it necessary to
demonstrate the consistency of any given author's practice. In
determining the texture of documentation, I have relied, as Longus
did, on *sophrosyne* in a matter which admits of little. In the
case of Petronius and Apuleius the balance between comic and
serious has been much more thoroughly explored; I have only felt
the need to broaden the perspective of discussion at a few points
in a field much more familiar to most classical scholars.

The first draft of this study was substantially completed
by the summer of 1976, just before the conference on the Ancient
Novel held in honour of the centenary of Rohde. Since then
several items have appeared which overlap with my own: I have
recorded my independent agreement rather than indebtedness where
appropriate. Many have suffered in the cause of this work. I am
grateful to Deborah Samuel of the American Philological Association
and Scholars Press, who put up with its delays and vicissitudes;
to Eve Hurste, who transmuted my so-called typescript into camera-
ready copy; and to all those on whom I tested my ideas at various
stages, especially to Ewen Bowie, Ken Dowden, J. N. O'Sullivan,
Peter Parsons, Gerald Sandy, Jack Winkler, and Stephanie West. I
wish to record a debt of much longer standing to my old teacher
Henry Chalk, tragically killed earlier this year before his own
work on Longus had reached its final fruition. And I am grateful
to Bryan Reardon, who saw and heard this *pathos erotikon* at many

stages; he has been its Polycharmus and Calasiris combined, as
well as its chastising and rescuing deity; the prolixity and
perversity that remain are my own. Finally I am grateful to
Margaret, who survived a worse ordeal than any heroine of the
novel: the production of this book.

Keynes College   Graham Anderson
University of Kent at Canterbury   September 1981
England

Postscript: While this study was in press what appear to be the
origins of the novel have at last been confirmed.   I report my
findings provisionally in an addition note; the arguments presented in the text are not affected.

CHAPTER ONE

PLAYFUL FICTION: THE TRADITION AND THE PROBLEMS

Rohde's survey[1] of the Greek novels,[2] now over a century old,
was built on three assumptions: they were late, they were bad,
and they were serious. The first assumption was disproved as
early as 1893;[3] the other two have been allowed to stand, and
between them they have fostered the notion that the novels are
merely a degenerate form of *something*. B. E. Perry showed that
the assumption that the novels were bad had itself been related
to the assumption that they were late.[4] But while he found some
humour in Chariton, and others have suspected it in Achilles and
Longus, the third assumption, that the novels are serious, has
persisted and proliferated. Since Merkelbach's *Roman und Mysterium*[5] it has been tempting to find the requisite degree of
seriousness in religious allegory, if it cannot be maintained by
other means. I wish to show on the contrary that a high proportion of the extant novels are concerned with a much more elusive treatment of love. Out of five fully extant 'ideal' novels
only one is almost unrelievedly serious; in another sentimental
melodrama is handled in a skilfully lighthearted way; in a third
it is wryly twisted, if not perverted; while in the last two the
authors have cultivated a sophisticated and ingenious balance
between humour and idealism which is easier to illustrate than to
define.

Failure to recognise this aspect of the novelists' craft
has been a serious omission in the past. It is difficult to
proceed with confidence in the interpretation of any work of
literature, let alone a whole genre, without knowing whether the
author meant it to be comic or serious, or neither or both. It
is too often because one assumes that the novels are serious that
one assumes they are ludicrously incompetent and therefore despic-
able; they must then be either laughably crude or tastelessly
oversophisticated, and one assumption will go on generating
another. But if all this is unhinged, the aesthetic achievements of the novelists may be due for revaluation: and some may
be rehabilitated in the same way, and perhaps to the same degree,

σπουδογέλοιον

as Ovid has been in the last few decades. There may also be more
to come: if standard situations in the extant novels are handled
in a playful or ambiguous manner, then some of the new fragments
may also appear in a different light.

It is useful to study this aspect of the novel against the
general literary environment of the genre. Here we have a versa-
tile literary mechanism capable of absorbing a wide range of situations and authors - not always in the most reverent way. It is
necessary to recognise the playful handling of melodramatic
themes in the many genres which fostered the growth of the novel
(whatever their relative roles in its formation); and in the
literary diversions in Imperial literature which so often use
the same material in different moulds. If a writer is imitating
a genre with a certain scope for σπουδογέλοιον, he has at least
the option of annexing, developing or exaggerating its repertoire
of such effects at the same time. Second-century sophists never
tire of including Platonic pleasantries, whether they aim to
imitate, exploit, improve or subvert their original author. When
almost all the supposed ancestors of the novel offer *some* balance
between comic and serious, the potential range of nuances direct-
ly accessible to the novelists is very large, and no single
writer is likely to be able to use all of them. Nor, it should
be stressed, is he in any sense obliged to use any. He can of
course employ standard jokes taken over from a model only incidentally if he chooses; but if he does much more than that, he
has then to take the conscious decision whether to write a deliberately comic or playful work, or one in which wit or humour will
at least affect the reader's interpretation of the plot as a
whole. The literary physiognomy of a novelist will depend to
some degree on his approach to this problem.

The most suitable starting-point for scholarship on the novel
is still Epic. It has long been recognised that the *Odyssey* was
particularly influential in our extant example;[6] and the *Odyssey*
rather than the *Iliad* offers outlets for humour which the novelists themselves were able to reproduce.[7] A long action of travel
and separation has plenty of scope for entertaining falsehood.
Odysseus himself cultivates elaborate *pseudos* not only for the
needs of the moment, but as a sophisticated entertainment in its
own right.[8] And there is also room for a lighthearted look at
the amorous ploys of Nausicaa or Calypso,[9] though such themes are
secondary to that of the cunning folk-hero. It is not till the

Hellenistic period that they come into their own, and Rohde
rightly emphasised the part played by Alexandrian poetry in the
genesis of the novel.[10] Sophisticated amusement is an essential
part of this literature, both in its attitude to traditional
mythology and in its presentation of erotic themes.[11] The standard Hellenistic picture of Eros himself invites humorous treatment:[12] Moschus' first Idyll is a convenient index of the sort
of variations available on the δόλιον βρέφος, and it is easy
enough for Longus to turn the runaway archer into a shepherd or
a pirate on the same frivolous and charming scale. Hellenistic
poetry also plays with the innocence or pathos of the victims of
love: Europa's seaborne exploits offered opportunities for playful and ironic amusement,[13] which the Second Sophistic was to
cultivate in turn: Lucian and Achilles Tatius both have recourse
to the scene.[14]

A decisive step for the future development of the ideal
novel is the incorporation of a Hellenistic love-theme into an
Epic of travel and adventure: what Rohde sought somewhere in the
hinterland of Antonius Diogenes had been available much earlier
in Apollonius Rhodius.[15] The *Argonautica* offers frequent humorous
touches in what purports to be a work of Epic scale and conception, whose latter half comes close to the shape of the ideal novel
itself. The Epic machinery has to be heaved into position by a
tiny Eros, bribed by a worldly Aphrodite.[16] And love is presented in a significant partnership with themes of religion and
sorcery: a seer can now concern himself with the divination of
love.[17] Nor is Apollonius absolutely committed to the wonders
that confront the heroes: even goddesses are terrified when the
Argo rides in mid-air![18] Not every novelist will be committed
to his elaborate displays of paradoxography either. Moreover the
resolution of Apollonius' love-theme turns on a trick with a
chastity test: Arete warns Jason to marry Medea before he is
forced to hand her back to her father as a virgin.[19]

Here, then, we have a light treatment of three characteristic ingredients of the novel within a single work: sophisticated
and equivocal treatment of love, wonder and religious machinery.
Euripides' *Helen* is no less rewarding:[20] it is significant that
his most obviously tragicomic play should also have the very plot
nearest to the standard outline of the novel. It is still more
significant that the most playful and ambiguous elements in the
Helen recur as standard repertoire in the novel itself. Menelaus

himself has the air of an anti-hero;[21] there are elaborate games
with double identity and deception (including a *Scheintod*);[22] and
the couple escape by means of an elaborate sacrificial hoax.[23]

   All such features will find their counterpart even in the
very limited sample of extant novels. And the *Helen* itself anti-
cipates the crucial problem which scholars of the novel have
still to face: how many touches of this kind - in plot, character
or detail - does it take to turn a serious work into a comic
fantasy, or even downright burlesque? The question has been ve-
hemently debated with regard to the *Helen* itself:[24] if it is not
outright parody (if only of Euripides himself), then at least it
can claim to offer more than a suspicion of ambiguity. A novel
patterned after the *Helen* will not turn out like Xenophon of
Ephesus. Nor, indeed, will one modelled on the *Iphigenia in Tau-
ris*, a close second to the *Helen* in this respect. Its potential
for sheer burlesque is clearly realised in the *Charition* Mime; we
can look for similar developments in the novel.

   Historiography can also claim a major share in the shaping
of the novel,[25] and appears to be still less promising than Tragedy as a source of wit or humour. But in fact the key text,
Xenophon's *Cyropaedia*, has a number of surprises in store. In
spite of the often austerely military subject-matter, and the
absence of a main erotic theme, the author has made a point of
including a number of humorous diversions - and of saying in a
number of cases that a remark actually caused laughter. Many of
the main heads under which the humour of the novels can be
classified are here already. Araspes despises Eros, and becomes
his victim;[26] while Eros himself is a disease or an ἄδικος
σοφιστής.[27] There is also room for amusing military slapstick,[28]
smiles at childhood misunderstandings,[29] and humour at symposia,
including Cyrus' own posing as a marriage-broker.[30] Xenophon's
witticisms are of markedly varied character and quality, but are
undoubtedly intentional and set out to provide diversion to a
degree no imitator could fail to notice. Within the bounds of
more conventional historiography, Herodotus and Ctesias provided
early sanction for a mixture of the trivial, scandalous and
exotic.[31] Such a formula carries with it the temptations of
entertaining forgery: Cicero cites Crassus' accusation that Memmius had eaten Largus' arm - an act supposedly authenticated by
the bogus inscription LLLMM (*Lacerat Lacertum Largi Mordax
Memmius*) on all the walls of Tarracina - and duly interpreted by

an old man on the spot![32] Any novelist is free to transfer this
kind of history to Scythia or Babylon and play on his reader's
credulity still more.[33] The result need not turn out as mere
degenerate historiography; but the novelist is at liberty to
revel in precisely that - for sophisticated or comic ends.

Unlike the other genres so far mentioned, New Comedy had
evolved in the context of comic entertainment as such.[34] The
standard plot of the ideal novel owed a number of its complica-
tions and contrivances to this form, especially in the resolu-
tions; the humorous effects connected with plot-structure also
overlap. Both genres offer opportunities for mistaken identity
and the multiple irony arising out of it, or for the compounding
of the same situations several times within the same plot. Iamblichus demonstrates the same kind of complication with double
identity as Plautus' *Menaechmi*,[35] while combinations of absurdly
complicated plot and religious deception are repeatedly favoured
by the novelists.[36]

New Comedy also specialised in humour at the expense of
character types, both in themselves and when their designs and
expectations are frustrated by the course of events. Some of the
types overlap; there is little to separate Labrax in the *Rudens*
from Chariton's Theron. There may be fewer *milites gloriosi* in
the extant novels, and the angry Athenian father pursuing the
same girl as the hero will be supplanted by the King of Persia;
but the cunning slave is still available, now doubled by the royal
eunuch; and it need not be due to ineptitude that the heroes of
the novels are as much at a loss as the young lovers of Comedy
itself.

The school reading-lists which found room for Menander
accepted Plato on the same terms - as a literary classic in his
own right.[37] Novelists and their readers alike could be expected
to know both the *Symposium* and the *Phaedrus*. Both texts represent Plato's literary elegance and humour at its most whimsical
and refined;[38] both are largely concerned with love, and extensively imitated in many other genres. Apart from the metaphysical
myths from Socrates and Diotima, they furnish a number of features
for the novelist's repertoire. These include the ironic manipu-
lation of amorous rhetoric:[39] lovers in the novels find themselves
sooner or later in the dock, purveying or rebutting similar absurdities. Socrates himself provides gentle mockery of a number of
features of traditional piety,[40] and is not above concocting a

suspect temple-legend.[41] The novelist who encounters these literary touches in the standard set text on the psychology of love
will have a ready-made arsenal.

So much for the main literary forms in the novelists' repertoire. It might be noticed that not all the classical models
cited are in fact typical of their respective genres: the *Odyssey*,
Helen, *Cyropaedia*, *Phaedrus* and *Symposium* have all a more consistently humorous or diversionary character than Epic, Tragedy,
Historiography or Philosophic Dialogue normally allowed. This
fact has too often been left out of account by those who accuse
the novelists of inept imitation or literary impropriety.

But one literary influence far outweighs the consequences of
any single genre. The bulk of the extant ideal novels lean
heavily on the resources of rhetoric to achieve their effects and
extend their material to any length. In theory the art of per-
suasion was a serious business with a serious end. In practice
it was one of the most obvious outlets for humour, literary diversion and teasing ambiguity - all the more so in the Second
Sophistic period, with the predominance of epideictic oratory.
The plots of the novels often offer the means to embody as much
of this rhetorical diversion as possible. The place of laughter
in rhetorical practice had been established as early as Gorgias,
who did not draw the line at a mock-defence of Helen. He also
recognised that the orator must be able to laugh at his opponent's
serious arguments, and defeat his opponent's laughter with seriousness.[42] Nor should we assume that all ancient connoisseurs
of rhetoric were as easily deceived as students in the schools.
There was a substantial consensus of educated opinion that declamation could be as unbelievably silly as we ourselves are
accustomed to suspect.[43] The Elder Seneca and others imply that
bombast would produce laughter the moment it was perpetrated in
the adult world outside. It was very easy to create deserted
lovers or outraged priestesses who protested just a little too
much: the paradox *inpudicitia officium* was capable of bringing the
house down when abused by one of Seneca's acquaintances.[44]

Two rhetorical techniques demand special mention both for
their comic potential, and for the fact that they are so often
ignored in discussion of the novel. The first is λέξις
ἐσχηματισμένη, highly valued in Philostratus for its difficulty:
the speaker has to say the opposite of what he means and sustain
the illusion.[45] It is of course conceivable that such an exercise

can employ irony without being funny; but it can also be regular-
ly used to provide elegant amusement, as in Lucian's *Phalaris* or
De Dea Syria.[46]   The second game is 'adoxography', in which trivial material is handled in a refined and mock-serious way.[47]
Such a technique is not confined to praising flies or singing the
merits of fevers; it can be used to describe lovers' ailments,[48]
or even to prove the soul's divinity - with reference to the
physiology of love at first sight![40]   And it can make Eros ruler
of the universe, or turn the parasite Gnathon into a μέγας
σοφιστής.[50]

    But it is the pair of lovers which forms the central focus
of the ideal novels, and it is important to stress the effect of
applying rhetorical wit and humour to their situation.   Plutarch
includes the moods of the lover among the subjects which normally
occasion laughter, as readily as baldness or snub noses:[51]   Plato,
New Comedy, Hellenistic poetry or Roman Elegy will provide ample
proof on any part of the subject: first blushes, impious offences
against Eros, lovers' oaths and the like; there is a well-
established repertoire of standard smiles.[52]   If the lover's
plight can be made amusing in itself, it will be all the more so
when combined with incongruous rhetoric: a *miles gloriosus*
trying to impress his love,[53] or a door describing the *exclusus
amator*'s lament,[54] is not likely to be wholly serious; no more is
Agathon describing Eros in the language of Gorgias.[55]   Learned
and scholarly approaches to love will have a similar effect in
the wrong hands: the sublimest moments of the *Symposium* and
Phaedrus are incongruous in the pseudo-Lucianic *Amores*, where the
relative delights of homosexual and heterosexual sex are clinic-
ally compared in a lighthearted and lascivious *adoxon* - with
plenty of reference to Platonic mixture of comic and serious.   We
should be equally sceptical when real-life young lovers in Achilles start Platonising in compromising postures; and learned digressions on symptoms, cures, or the efficacy of deities and
magicians in love-affairs can be used to threaten the plots of a
love-story in a pretentious and incongruous way.   An alliance of
love, scholarly rhetoric,[56] and first-person narrative has little
chance of remaining wholly serious; it is as hard to ignore such a
combination in Achilles Tatius as it is in Petronius.

    We can illustrate such techniques outside the novel from
Ovid, who exploits the humorous incongruity between love and Epic
or didactic literature, and knows how to carry his religious

learning lightly; the whole conception of the *Ars Amatoria* or the
attitude of *expedit esse deos* will throw light on the attitudes
of Achilles Tatius.[57] Other sophistic literature will also be
useful: Philostratus' *Heroicus* and *Imagines* or Dio Chrysostom's
Euboicus[58] show us the kind of nuances in which a cultivated
writer will present imaginative and romantic subject-matter outside the novel proper. A more comprehensive sample is offered by
Lucian, long established as the professional wit of his age.[59]
Toxaris and *Quomodo historia conscribenda sit* offer sophisticated
games with suspect narrative; *Philopseudes* and *de Dea Syria* extend the frolics into the field of oriental superstition; while
the *Dialogi Marini* offer delicate paraphrases of lovers' naivety
itself. Taken together the *parerga* of Imperial rhetoric explore
almost all the territory travelled by the *Liebespaar* and their
authors.

   It is perhaps worthwhile to ask why the whole question of
humour or wit in the novel has generated so little interest in
the past. The preoccupation with origins is partly responsible:
however often Rohde's main thesis has been contested, his opinion
of the achievements of the novelists has died very hard; it was
not till 1930 that Perry pointed out the link between his judgement on Chariton and the conviction that such products were the
work of *Graeculi* of the fourth and fifth centuries.[60] But such
initiatives have been isolated.[61] For much of the last two decades scholars have been concerned with a headlong quest for
serious meaning in the novels. Merkelbach extended a discarded
theory of religious origins and argued for reading them as actual
mystery texts;[62] others have seen religious elements as at least
a genuine reflection of late antique piety and religious psychology. But the mere presence of religious institutions as such is
too often allowed to pass for either commitment to religion or
mere rhetorical decoration. We have to ask why initiates are so
busy making fun of the mysteries, parodying initiation, or dis-
crediting the clergy. We cannot explain the presence of comic
elements as mere diversion 'allowed' in works of religious inspi-
ration:[63] and we are not dealing with the messenger in *Antigone*
or the nurse in the *Choephori*, but something like the bogus
ritual in the *Helen*.[64]

   In 1965 Fritz Wehrli attempted to argue a unity of origin
for both ideal and comic novel in popular narrative themes.[65]
There would have been burlesque material in this original stratum,

in due course taken over to suit the narrative needs of writers
as diverse as Petronius and the ideal novelists. This would explain the substantial overlap between for example Achilles,
Chariton, and Petronius in the ubiquitous community of uniquitous
material.[66] There are a number of important insights here:
Wehrli admits that the handling of miracles in the novelists
shows a *herrschende Rationalität*:[67] he acknowledges the substantial comic element in the extant ideal examples, and is the only
scholar to my mind to relate it to a theory of origins. But the
theory he adopts is too narrow: he does not see these writers as
sophists working on classical themes because they *are* classical,
as well as for their own sake.[68] Nor does he view each novel
systematically as a whole, so that he does not consider the cumulative impact of amusing effects, the individuality of their
authors, or the balance between comic and serious in each. The
problems are only beginning to define themselves.

No-one who works with humour can ignore the questions of
definition and the risks of subjectivity involved. I am concerned throughout with establishing what humorous or playful effects
any given author intended for the appreciation of his more discerning readers; and I believe that so much can be done reasonably objectively. We cannot define the discerning reader too
closely, and should not try: there is always someone who does not
see the joke. If Lucian and Aristides ever attended the same declamations, it is hard to imagine that they both laughed in the
same places.[69] And even the liveliest of ancient comic writers
could miscalculate their effects and their audiences, as Aristophanes was forced to admit by his revision of the *Clouds*. It is
also worth bearing in mind that in the second century A.D. not
everyone was *meant* to see every joke; we now know something of
Lucian's most erudite literary fraud,[70] and we should perhaps
bear it in mind when reading Heliodorus' account of the evil
eye.[71] In the end commonsense is the final criterion; but that
is no more than is necessary in reading any other kind of literature.

The terminology of humour ancient and modern is as perversely flexible as the subject itself: Fowler wisely did not risk a
definition, translator of Lucian though he was.[72] Among ancient
terms it is easy enough to contrast γέλοιον and χαρίεν, but impossible to chart with precision the middle ground between them;
nor can we expect in either language to schematise all related

terms.[73] I have found it more illuminating to say 'Longus smiles
at his characters' or 'Heliodorus plays with his themes' rather
than to determine whenever either of them crosses the non-exist-
ent line between wit and humour. Discussions of sophistication
or diversion in the context of large surveys of rhetoric are probably the worst starting-point, next to psychological speculation
on the nature of the laughable:[74] Aristotle and Cicero do not
necessarily prescribe the appropriate canon for Ovid or Herodas,[75]
let alone a whole genre for which no ancient critical discussion
survives; and Plutarch would scarcely have been suitably quali-
fied to savour Achilles Tatius.

        Nor is there a satisfactory treatment, ancient or modern, of
Greek notions of σπουδογέλοιον;[76] given the nature and scope of
the subject, there is never likely to be. Each writer had to
find his own balance between the two elements, and the term con-
ceals problems rather than solves them. There is no satisfactory
treatment either of sick humour in antiquity.[77] Ancient critics
were not quick to appreciate deliberate bad taste destined to
produce a calculated and refined humorous effect, with no moral
or didactic message and no trace of human sympathy. Yet such a
concept is useful when dealing with declamations on Cynegirus'
severed hand or the artistic cruelties of Phalaris, and there is
a place for it when Clitophon laments over the detachable limbs
of Leucippe; even in Heliodorus Cnemon thanks a girl's corpse for
being the messenger of her doom.

        I have deliberately avoided examining ancient literature
along guidelines set by modern theories of humour, often formulated without reference to antique texts. My object is not to
find a single explanation of why we laugh, but merely to determine by any means available what ancient readers would have been
able and expected to find laughable or amusing in a work of prose
fiction. To this end the mention of a few rhetorical devices
which can be *made* comic by their context is worth a good deal of
psychological and semantic introspection. But it is still worthwhile to note that a substantial number of the illustrations
below would certainly have appeared as uproariously funny to
Bergson, for example, as they do to me.[78] In fact almost all the
illustrations offered in *Le Rire* could have been drawn just as
readily from Heliodorus: robbers robbed, comic disguise, redupli-
cation of events, plot-within-plot, type-characterisation:[79] and
above all, the treatment of the reader as spectator and of

dramatic actors as mere marionettes.[80] It is worth noting that
his last point, which Bergson regarded as typical of the 'mechanical' essence of comedy, is the very feature of the novel which
Rohde found incompetent and unacceptable.

But the nature and terminology of wit or humour are not the
only problems; the most difficult is to determine and interpret
the balance between comic and serious - or their nearest equi-
valents - in the context of each individual author. Where there
is clearly *some* serious content in the novel, its relationship to
the comic has still to be questioned. Is it there for variety
and contrast, or mere private *jeu d'esprit*? Has it been contrived to be incongruous, and subsequently undermined? Or has it
arisen because the writer did not know what he was doing? There
are no abstract criteria and no theoretical formulae for answering such questions, still less in a genre where they have so
seldom been asked. I have made a point of basing my arguments
instead on parallel passages in the same novelist, in other
novelists, or in sophistic and related literature; and I have
tried to pay due attention to the context of a passage, or to
the cumulative effect of a number of similar passages in a single
author. All this will leave room for disagreement; that is no
more than is likely in any discussion of humorous intent.[81] But
as long as other problems in the interpretation of the novel are
affected by the reader's reactions to the presence or absence of
humour or wit, then such an examination will be both necessary
and worthwhile. A century after Rohde it is more than overdue.

CHAPTER TWO

NEW COMIC MELODRAMA, *ANABASIS EROTOS*: CHARITON

It is convenient to begin with Chariton's *Chaereas and
Callirhoe*. Not only is this most probably the first of the extant ideal novels; it also shows us how the most straightforward
and unpretentious love story can accommodate playful embellish-
ments of various sorts. Moreover it has usually been regarded as
a link with romantic historiography, and has accordingly been
read as a serious melodrama.[1] But it is clear that the author
also owes much to New Comedy, especially since the publication of
fragments of Menander's *Sicyonius*: play and novel alike use the
motif of the young woman captured by pirates and sold into slavery in Caria, where she is to be bought by a rich Greek.[2] Of
course Chariton is not obliged to treat New Comic motifs in a New
Comic way; but such a point of contact alters the balance of external evidence, and we must consider whether this novel is not
just melodrama, but a historical New Comedy in prose, or a New
Comic re-writing of history.

The plot as it stands is self-evidently melodramatic and
pathetic. Here as in all the ideal novels we have potentially
tragic or 'exciting' material: presumed death of lovers, capture
by unscrupulous pirates, and separation of hero and heroine.[3] We
have Reardon's myth of the isolation of individual characters
with whom the reader can identify.[4] But Chariton is also an able
writer with adequate rhetorical and dramatic technique. We have
to ask whether he has simply wallowed in a sentimental plot, or
whether he has so offset it by comic nuances that some qualification is necessary.

He is able to handle even the most poignant moments of his
plot with a lightly humorous touch. The most pathetic moment for
Callirhoe, sold into slavery in Asia, is the decision whether to
lose her child by her husband Chaereas, or to bring it up as the
child of her master Dionysius.[5] A simple author writing for
simple people might have settled for making the most of her agoni-
sing decision.[6] But Chariton organises a twist in the plot which
counterbalances the pathos of the situation with humour. He

divides the decision into two: first Callirhoe has to determine
whether to have the child or lose it; after her debate she dreams
that Chaereas entrusts the child to her, and decides to have it
for his sake.[7] Her confidante Plangon then presents her with the
alternatives of marrying Dionysius or losing the child. Chariton
presents the crisis as a three-sided debate among the interested
parties: the child inside, Chaereas represented by a picture
clasped to her bosom - and Callirhoe herself. She votes to die,
the child to live - so that Chaereas now has the casting vote.[8]
His portrait votes in favour of keeping the child - or rather has
already voted - and so Callirhoe offers to marry Dionysius.
There is no need to decide here between melodrama and comedy.
The idea of the debate itself is not intrinsically comic and could
have served as the basis for poignant tragedy; even the notion of
the unborn child casting its vote might be dismissed as mere
Hellenistic conceit- and Callirhoe's social ambitions for the
child might be explained as observation of human nature (she
wants it to return in triumph from Miletus to Syracuse).[9] But it
is difficult to ignore a third detail of this unusual episode.
When Callirhoe registers Chaereas' casting vote in the debate,
she commits him to a position he had never taken. He had asked
her to preserve the child for her sake, before there was ever any
question of marrying Dionysius; despite the correct assumption
that she is still alive, Callirhoe blithely shifts the moral
dilemma on to Chaereas ('You are Dionysius' best man, Chaereas').[10]
Dionysius' dilemma over Callirhoe is expressed equally blithely:
Aphrodite had been devising political machinations, and Eros
regarded his *sophrosyne* as *hybris*.[11] This is all melodrama; but
it is melodrama with a lighthearted twist, or the human side of
New Comedy.

    Such, then, is Chariton at his most serious. But let us
look at his preoccupations. He is most consistent in his interest
in character and motivation, and the good-humoured handling of
it.[12] The emotional range, as well as the names of several of the
characters, belongs to New Comedy. It is a mistake to regard
Chaereas as an ineptly handled hero:[13] he is simply the New Comic
young lover, whose inept infatuation is a matter of sympathetic
observation and amusement: at the very sight of Callirhoe he is
like a wounded war hero, ashamed to fall, unable to stand;[14] and
it is only when he agrees to fight in order to commit suicide
that he recovers her.[15] His chief rival Dionysius of Miletus is
sensitively and less conventionally handled, as the sincere

devotee of Callirhoe, innocently entangled in a bigamous marriage.
But his function and character give him much in common with those
New Comic fathers who so often find themselves in competition
with their sons. For all his μεγαλοψυχία, he is pompous as well
as lovelorn: he can sneer at his servant Leonas for comparing
Callirhoe to Aphrodite; the moment he himself sets eyes on her,
he beats him for not recognising the goddess herself.[16] Moreover
Dionysius suffers throughout from lover's insecurity and self-
interest, not even allowing a monument to Chaereas near the temple of Aphrodite where he himself first saw her.[17] And in the
end he remains the dupe of love: left with Callirhoe's child, but
abandoned by her, he still almost persuades himself that she is
in love with him: οὕτω κοῦφόν ἐστιν ὁ Ἔρως καὶ ἀναπείθει ῥᾳδίως
ἀντερᾶσθαι.[18]

     Chariton is able to develop the implications of his one-
dimensional minor characters with the same degree of amusement
and sympathy. He notes the patience of Polycharmus, who has to
organise the rest of the fleet's return because Chaereas is preoccupied with Callirhoe.[19] He also enjoys the masterly villain
as much as the deceived gentleman. The pirate Theron is above
all a professional thief: still πανοῦργος in extreme circumstances, he steals water from his dying fellow-pirates, but considers
the act 'a neat piece of professional work' (τεχνικόν τι).[20] Un-
sure of his rescuers, he is careful to pose as a corpse; but the
moment he revives he remembers his villainy and begins his lying
with a tall story about his fictitious voyage from Crete.[21] The
suitors are just as delightfully and professionally evil: the
tyrant of Agrigentum points out as an objective fact that they
obtain their tyrantships by underhand villainy (πανουργίᾳ) rather
than by force. He therefore asks his fellow rulers to elect
him(!) head of their band: Chariton has created a democratic
assembly of tyrants.[22]

     The most consistent source of amusement in his characters is
their self-interest. The King of Persia persuades himself that
it would be nothing less than impiety not to be interested in
Callirhoe - an argument also used by Clitophon in Achilles.[23]
Theron is swayed by commercial considerations, and believes it
would be more just for Callirhoe's funeral wealth to belong to
the living; while his band see no need for such fine rationalisa-
tions, regarding themselves as φρόνιμοι rather than ἀνόητοι.[24]
Chariton often plays with the petty self-interest of crowds, a

matter much more easily presented in the novel than in New Comedy
itself. Preparations for the first trial in Persia are compared
to the excitement and partisanship before the Olympic Games:[25]
the whole of Babylon is a court, for the entertainment of all
except the participants.[26] He outlines the arguments used by the
various social interests before both trials, and assigns them
specious arguments comically at odds with their real motives;[27]
Callirhoe herself is made to appear for no other reason than that
everybody wants to see her.[28] Crowd scenes are often contrived
to be futile: after all the bustle of the search for Callirhoe,
it is not human effort, but chance, which leads the Syracusans to
her.[29]

      This interest is naturally applied to the habits of whole
peoples. Chariton smiles at the Syracusan assemblies, held at
the slightest excuse; at their curiosity about the love-affair
itself; and of course about the return of Chaereas' ship.[30] He
also smiles at their proneness to flattery. Theron dissolves
their impressionable assembly by invoking their clemency, and
nearly gets away with it.[31] Chariton manipulates national pre-
judice to produce humorous effect from the most commonplace material.   It is the Sicilian pirate Theron who delivers a verdict on
the Athenians: apart from being litigious and talkative, from his
own professional point of view they are inquisitive and have
archons worse than tyrants[32] - so that he must make for the
τρυφῶντες καὶ ἀπράγμονες of Ionia instead.[33] The Greeks themselves can also be presented from self-interested Persian points
of view, with equally transparent bias.[34]

      Perry began to explore Chariton's techniques of irony,[35] and
his instances could be multiplied. Games with ignorance begin
with the love-affair itself, since the crowd in Syracuse sweep
the couple into marriage without their own knowledge; irony is
still at work after the plot has come to a halt, when an officious
adjutant tries to marry the pair all over again.[36] Chariton plays
with such devices repeatedly throughout. The plot itself revolves
round the continued ignorance of Dionysius, first that Callirhoe
is married to Chaereas, then that he is alive and that his rival
Mithridates can produce him;[37] and finally that Callirhoe loves
Chaereas and not himself.[38] Such ignorance can just as easily be
exploited for the needs of sentimental melodrama: but Chariton
nearly always provides something more: he can make his ironies
into epigrams (Χαιρέαν ἔτι ζῶντα πενθοῦσα);[39] he can arrange them

into elaborate sequences, as when Dionysius goes through all the
preliminaries of suicide for Callirhoe when we know she has decided to marry him;[40] or he can construct elaborate doublets, such
as the temple-keeper's descriptions of hero and heroine to each
other.[41] Chariton is particularly fond of using irony to illu-
mine his characters by undermining their complacent assumptions.
He will arrange sudden appearances which the reader and one of the
characters knows will have a devastating effect on another:
Callirhoe is produced to Dionysius, Stateira, or the court at
Babylon, always with the same result.[42] He contrives rhetorical
tirades when the reader knows that they are completely unjusti-
fied: Chaereas bewails the impossibility of finding Callirhoe
amid the vastness of Asia - as he lands at the temple on her new
husband's estate; or Chariton carefully describes the mourning
for each of his *Liebespaar* in turn, before pointing out that they
are alive.[43] It is Dionysius who is the most frequent victim,
because of his pompous and preemptive assumptions: he prepares a
suitable rhetorical pathos so as to use his son as an advocate
against Chaereas - not knowing that the child is his rival's.[44]

In particular Chariton uses his technique of dramatic irony
to set up elaborate deceptions which characters then carry out
with panache for their own ends. Of course there are the conventional first kiss trick and the many excuses to see Callirhoe;[45]
at a more sophisticated level Leonas and Artaxates know their
masters' love affairs and further their own favour by playing up
to them;[46] while Mithridates takes special care to delay Chaereas' appearance in court to the last possible moment, and produces him with an elaborate flourish of innocence when the audi-
knows he himself had designs on Callirhoe.[47]

Character-presentation and irony between them account for
much of the comic dimension in Chariton, and both operate as they
would have done in New Comedy itself. But here the plot is also
given a carefully defined historical background.[48] Love and
fourth-century politics are allowed to mix in a blithely incongruous way. Tyrants not only have their democratic assemblies
and neglect their régimes to spend time devising slanders against
Chaereas' marriage; they also lose their traditional privilege of
satisfying their lusts at will, and have to undergo the conventional labours of love, only to be effortlessly outdone by the
hero.[49] Hermocrates, the foremost statesman in Syracuse, gives
his consent to his daughter's wedding 'for reasons of state' -

namely that the crowd sympathises with his rival's son's infatuation for her.   Chariton marries off his Romeo and Juliet by Act of
Parliament.[50]   For equally trivial reasons of state Artaxerxes
insists on arbitrating between Greek private citizens, though indignant at playing the role of an old matchmaker:[51] this gesture
is advanced as an act of gratitude to Hermocrates for defeating
the Athenians - but is really to further his own acquaintance with
Callirhoe.[52]   She for her part is able to justify the deception of
Dionysius for political purposes: the Syracusan assembly are
naturally delighted to know that a Syracusan child will soon be
influential in Miletus,[53] so that the heroine's deception of her
husband of convenience becomes a master-stroke of international
diplomacy.[54]   And Hermocrates' way of playing the demagogue is
simply to bring his daughter into the assembly.[55]

Against this background Chariton can adapt the usual meta-
phors of *militia amoris* to the political conditions of fifth-
century Syracuse: love is now a φιλόνεικος in a democratic repub-
lic, a demagogue in the Syracusan assembly, a πολυπράγμων in the
affairs of Dionysius of Miletus, or a conspirator against the
King of Persia.[56]   The triumphs of love accordingly outdo the
Syracusan victory in Thucydides: on Chaereas' return the city is
full of Persian spoil in peacetime instead of Attic poverty in
war;[57] while even the villain Theron had outdone the Athenians
by abducting Hermocrates' daughter.[58]   It is no surprise for a
celebrated phrase of Pericles' funeral speech to be adapted to the
effeminate Tyrians: καταφρονήσει μετ᾽ ἀλαζονείας, οὐ φρονήματι μετ᾽
εὐβουλίας χρώμενοι.[59]   Chariton's history belongs to the annals of
milites gloriosi.

In comparison with Achilles or Heliodorus, he is not conspicuous for his use of themes of religion or superstition.   As the
writer of an erotic *Hellenica*, this particular new Xenophon had
other concerns.   But it is useful to note the sort of religious
motifs which do occur, and how they are used.   In the first place
the mysteries only appear as an incidental allusion, (and not an
entirely dignified one): even the nights at Eleusis or the Olympic Games fail to produce as much enthusiasm as Callirhoe's
trial.[60]   There are smiles at superstition as such: the heroine
can be mistaken for a nymph or a goddess,[61] or even a ghost.[62]
But religious institutions are not used for purposes of display:
there are no ecphrases of religious processions and no parades of
Zauberapparat; instead religion supplies frequent opportunities

for deception. Everyone in Miletus hurries to set eyes on Callirhoe, but all pretend it is to worship the goddess.[63] The king
institutes a bogus religious festival to further his designs on
her,[64] beginning with a sacrifice to Eros and Aphrodite;[65] the
point is not lost on Dionysius.[66] Or when Mithridates has Chaereas alive, he pretends he is raising a corpse and being rewarded
for past goodness and devotion: θεοὶ βασίλειοι ἐπουράνιοί τε καὶ
ὑποχθόνιοι, βοηθήσατε ἀνδρὶ ἀγαθῷ πολλάκις ὑμῖν εὐξαμένῳ δικαίως
καὶ θύσαντι μεγαλοπρεπῶς.[67] In fact he too has been acting purely
out of self-interest, with his eye on the heroine.[68] The gods are
also used to throw light on Chaereas and Dionysius. Both husbands
think that some god must be the ἀντεραστής,[69] drawing appropriate
mythological comparisons for their rivals;[70] while Dionysius beats
his servant for *not* mistaking Callirhoe for Aphrodite: the piety
of this sanctimonious seigneur is conditioned by amorous motives.[71]

      Chariton is not a conspicuously rhetorical writer by compari-
son with Achilles or Heliodorus. But it is useful to note his
performance on a number of rhetorical topoi which recur in the
genre as a matter of course.[72] It is consistently difficult to
insist on distinctions between rhetorical paradox used for merely
ornamental purposes and rhetorical wit: but either will reinforce
and enhance the light-hearted sense of *jeu d'esprit* of a work already comically nuanced in other ways. Chariton accordingly produces a novelty shipwreck,[73] with its own private rough weather,
foundering on a calm sea;[74] or a paradoxical symposium, when
Dionysius finds out that Callirhoe was married after all, so that
the party becomes a σκυθρωπὴν ὑπόθεσιν.[75] There is a comic army
of pirates, with Theron as general;[76] and of course a string of
paradoxes concerned with the *Scheintod* scenes, with Dionysius
accused of raising the dead whenever he wants to commit adultery,
or Callirhoe lamenting 'first you buried me in Syracuse, then I
buried you in turn in Miletus...and neither of us has the body'.[77]
Chariton can also use the conventional topoi of love as yet
another means to reveal and smile at the pretentiousness of his
characters: Dionysius is ready to take his oath of loyalty to
Callirhoe, if possible by going up to Zeus and taking hold of him;
he is made to swear by the sea instead.[78] Chaereas for his part
would go up into the air if he could, but since he cannot fight
the enemy in the air, settles for doing so on land.[79]

      But Chariton's forte is in playing with trials. He includes
familiar rhetorical manoeuvres, as when Chaereas accuses himself

of Callirhoe's murder,[80] or Dionysius arbitrates a suit between
Love and Reason;[81] he can even have his Persians improvise a
beauty contest between Callirhoe and Rhodogyne.[82]   But even in the
main trial, for all its melodramatic momentum, he still finds room
for a light touch. Instead of indulging in overloaded rhetoric,
he opts at the final impasse for the kind of quickfire exchange
typical of an Old Comic agon: 'I was first' 'My case is stronger';
'I didn't let go my wife' 'But you buried her'; 'Show me the di-
vorce certificate' 'I'll show you her tomb'; 'Her father gave her
to me' 'She gave herself to me'; 'You're unworthy of Hermocrates'
daughter' 'You are Mithridates' slave'; 'I demand Callirhoe' 'I'm
not giving her up'; 'You've got someone else's property' 'You
killed your own'; 'Adulterer' 'Murderer'.[83]   Chariton has duly
provided the delightful entertainment he sent his courtroom audience to find. He is also capable of the standard melodramatic
tirade, but he can undercut it with his usual irony. Even when
rehearsing his case Dionysius is already carried away: 'What do
you say, paedagogus? We are not allowed into the palace; what
dreadful tyranny! They shut out the son who comes as ambassador
from father to mother'.[84]   The seigneur has done his homework in
the declamation-school; we have already noted that the child is
not his.

     Finally, Chariton's handling of the plot itself: he remains
unshakeably loyal to the sentimental ideals and values implied in
the basic outline of the ideal novel. But that does not prevent
him from enjoying the mechanism with the occasional smile. Love
contrives that the couple meet at a narrow bend - just to make
sure they don't miss each other![85]   Or Providence provides calm
weather for Callirhoe's voyage, but miseries and death for Theron
and the pirates, all with quite mechanical precision;[86] and when
all the permutations of erotic intrigue are brought to an impasse - Chariton simply allows Tyche to start a war.[87]   Finally
he breaks the dramatic illusion with an assurance: at the beginning of book VIII all the melodramatic incidents are over - as his
readers will be delighted to know.[88]   This amounts to an amused
aside: 'so much for the shock-horror, now for the happy ending',
and implies a craftsman's elegant awareness of his superiority to
the plot.[89]

     In the end it is difficult to find the right terminology for
Chariton: the unpretentious simplicity and economy of the narrative disguises the author's considerable dramatic and rhetorical

skill;[90] it is reasonable to accept that he is a good deal less
naive than his characters, and that his audience could have extended a good deal beyond the adolescents and poor in spirit re-
served for him by Perry. It seems fair to imply the term 'comic'
somewhere in one's description of the text. Nor is it too far
from Chariton's amorous tyrants to the chorus of amorous peers
in *Iolanthe*, or from the antics of the trial in Babylon to *Trial
by Jury*. The balance of comic elegance and indulgent sentimentality in W. S. Gilbert offers a useful comparison: we could do
worse than call *Chaereas and Callirhoe* Hellenistic Operetta.

CHAPTER THREE

PLATO *EROTICUS*: ACHILLES TATIUS

In Chariton's version the sentimental myth is preserved more
or less intact: the author is prepared to believe in make-believe,
and encourages his reader to do so. Not so Achilles Tatius, in
whose hands the myth is exposed to refined and ingenious criticism, if not outright sabotage.[1] One episode embodies a number of
characteristically humorous elements, and serves to make Achilles'
intentions clear beyond any doubt. The last book opens with a
slanging match between Clitophon and Thersander: twice the latter
strikes the hero, but a third time accidentally hurts his own
hand against his rival's teeth.[2] The teeth avenge the injury
done to the nose, as the hero observes to the reader; Clitophon
adds that he pretended to Thersander not to have noticed the
incident, but immediately turned the whole affair into a rhetorical farce (ἐτυρρανήθην τραγῳδῶν 'I played a stage tyrant');[3] and
his bloody nose becomes τραύματα, ὡς ἐν πολέμῳ καὶ μάχῃ.[4] Since
at this point he has slept with Thersander's wife, but knows that
his own fiancée is out of Thersander's clutches, he can well
afford some melodramatic gestures. Another example: the beautiful Melite is trying to persuade Clitophon to consummate his
marriage with her aboard ship;[5] he has only rhetoric with which
to defend himself against the blandishments of this enthusiastic
widow of Ephesus. In a serious novel one might feel entitled to
expect all the arguments proper to a *propempticon* or an εἰ
γαμητέον - but not Clitophon's version: does Melite want a marriage bed that won't stand still?[6]

Achilles has undermined the sentimental plot itself by his
handling of the chastity standard so prominent in Xenophon of
Ephesus or Heliodorus. Of course the heroine Leucippe emerges
unscathed in the end; but Durham has drawn attention to a fact
easily lost sight of amid so many machinations - that the first
two books out of eight are devoted to getting her into bed with
Clitophon - and not unwillingly either.[7] The same attitude under-
lies Achilles' handling of the details: Leucippe's mother makes
an absurd lament over her daughter's chastity, when it is still
intact.[8] Most ridiculous of all, Clitophon does not sleep with

Melite under the impression that Leucippe is dead, but the moment
he realises that both she and Melite's own husband Thersander are
still alive. Of course neither of the 'lost' loves fears a breach
of faith under such circumstances.[9] Leucippe herself makes the
most melodramatic stand at the end of book VI,[10] but it should not
escape the reader that at the corresponding point in the previous
book, Clitophon had been faced with the same situation and had
given in without the slightest regret - as he was at pains to
stress, with a suitably gnomic flourish: τὸ δ' ἀπερίεργον εἰς
Ἀφροδίτην ἥδιον μᾶλλον τοῦ πολυπράγμονος· αὐτοφυῆ γὰρ ἔχει τὴν
ἡδονήν.[11]

Achilles is more than a perverse *praeceptor amoris*: his real
individuality lies in what we might call medical paradoxography.
It is well known that he kills Leucippe three times, in the first
place by public disembowelment.[12] We can best appreciate the wry
implications of this if we compare Xenophon of Ephesus' handling
of a similar situation. His pirates bury their heroine in a
trench with two wild dogs; but at that point he respectfully stops
short and finds an ingenious way of keeping the dogs at bay.[13]
Achilles however goes through with the whole business of dismemberment, to the extent of playing a cruel trick on the reader and
another on the hero, when Menelaus pretends to reassemble and sew
up the corpse in two stages: Leucippe is brought back to life,
still apparently disembowelled, and only after that bizarre halfway stage is the divine cure completed.[14] This is sick humour at
its most scholarly: for Achilles the sacrificial altar is an
operating-table. And no sooner is the heroine delivered from her
physical death than he brings her a mental one, by inducing a coma
from a rival's love-potion.[15] This gives Clitophon time to specu-
late on whether she has normal dreams or those of a madwoman,
though of course he does not fail to comment on a little indecent
exposure in the midst of her struggles.[16] Achilles is chief sur-
geon and consultant psychiatrist in his own erotic clinic, dis-
secting his patients body and soul in front of the reader.

Nor is his voyeurism confined to the body tissues of the
heroine: there is further scope in the ecphrases that comment on
the action. He can dwell at length on the contours of Europa's
body, and how thinly they are concealed; to a similar picture of
Andromeda he has lovingly added a vicious monster.[17] So in the
warning dreams of Clitophon and Panthea: Calligone is severed from
the waist downwards, Leucippe from the groin upwards.[18] The first
actual disembowelment is suitably prefaced by an ecphrasis of

Prometheus' liver.[19] Such an author revels as much as Ovid in
the picture of Tereus and Procne, and cannot resist retelling it
with more detail for the benefit of Leucippe.[20] He has already
spared no detail of the fate of Cleinias' lover, dragged to death
in a thicket by a runaway horse.[21] Mangled corpses with a sexual
connexion are a speciality of Achilles; we are close to the world
of Ovid's Pasiphae, sacrificing her heifer rivals with unconceal-
ed satisfaction.[22] Achilles' sheer delight in cruelty extends
even to the details of Perseus' sword - one half pointed, the
other curved, to thrust and cut in one operation.[23]

    His handling of the sensuous side of the lovers is also
deliberately perverse. He can trivialise medicine with love, and
inflate love with medical bombast,[24] concentrating his attention
on the kiss: there is a long ecphrasis on its physiology,[25] and a
learned syncrisis between homosexual and heterosexual varieties;[26]
while Clitophon fears that even kisses can be the object of adultery.[27] After all that he describes his own adultery with Melite
in only a few words.[28]

    Achilles clearly sees himself as a Plato *eroticus*, and much
of the first two books as an anti-*Phaedrus*. When Clitophon has
produced his enormous ecphrasis of the erotic garden, complete
with plane-trees, he leaves the reader in no doubt that the scene
is set for seduction: βουλόμενος εὐάγωγον τὴν κόρην εἰς ἔρωτα
παρασκευάσαι.[29] Achilles inserts a virtuoso flourish of erotic
psychology, not to illustrate the recognition of lovers, but to
describe Leucippe's emotions when her mother catches her in bed,
in the act but before it, so to speak.[30] For the great syncrisis
between 'Lysias' and Socrates he substitutes a travesty, comparing
the advantages of boys and women as lovers.[31] And when Melite
claims that Clitophon will not consummate his marriage with her,
she adapts a remark from Alcibiades' confession to οὕτως ἀνέστην
ὡς ἀπὸ εὐνούχου.[32]

    The other erotica are rhetorical in an amusing way: subject
and treatment are kept deliberately at variance, to the detriment
of both. One image sums up the matter. When Clitophon is making
his first overtures to Leucippe, Love is an αὐτοδίδακτος σοφιστής;
by the time he has his affair with Melite, it has become an
αὐτοσχέδιος as well, and provides suitably specious arguments at
a time when he has least cause to give in.[33] Once love is established as a sophist, then all the other details fall into place.
Few of the characters could escape the same charge: the contents

of major soliloquies are absurd. Cleinias hears that his boy-
friend is to marry, and launches into an εἰ γαμητέον with patently ridiculous arguments, from the misery of bridegrooms to the
fate of Penelope's suitors.[34] In the eyes of a committed homosexual the fact that the bride is ugly can go to the bottom of
the list.[35]

    Achilles is also able to qualify the most bombastic lovers'
rhetoric with bathetic effects. Among the extant novelists only
he is capable of saying that since the tongue does not avail to
plead before barbarians - he will have to present his funeral
dirge as a mime![36] The lament he goes on to produce is ridiculous
enough on its own terms: how much more so when he reminds us it
was in silence? There is a wryly inappropriate touch in the syncrisis over the body of Charicles.[37] The latter's father laments
that his son will not marry (in fact the fate he had most dread-
ed); while his lover Cleinias curses himself and the horse which
caused the accident. There is a similar debate between *epitaphioi*
in Lucian's *de Luctu*, between a father and the corpse of his son
answering back.[38] Achilles explicitly calls the whole affair a
mourning competition.[39]

    Insinuations about virginity were a favourite topos in the
Controversiae.[40] Thersander has the opportunity to make the most
trenchant sarcasms against Leucippe when the reader knows they
are untrue (εὐνοῦχοί σοι γεγόνασιν οἱ λησταί; φιλοσόφων ἦν τὸ
πειρατήριον; οὐδεὶς ἐν αὐτοῖς εἶχεν ὀφθαλμούς;).[41] The priest's
attack on Thersander displays similar rhetorical indulgence, and
is easily equal to the insinuations in the most uninhibited pam-
phlets of Lucian. Achilles emphasises its comic intent by pointing out that the speaker imitated Aristophanes, master of sexual
double entendre.[42] Nor is the incongruity of the contents likely
to be missed: it is delivered by a priest of Artemis.

    Achilles also reserves his worst sabotage for the clichés of
the standard melodramatic plot. It is not just a matter of finding more and more absurd novelties: he sets out to present them
in a cynical way. No self-respecting novelist will fail to arrange for his heroine to be abducted, in most cases more than
once. But the first instance in *Leucippe and Clitophon* is rather
different. It is not the heroine who is kidnapped, but the hero's
(by now) unwanted fiancée.[43] But it is one thing to be captured
on sight in a chance encounter with pirates, another to be taken
by arrangement without having been seen at all. The villain

abducts Leucippe by repute, captures the wrong woman Calligone,[44]
decides his mistake is not so bad after all, and reforms accordingly.[45] Achilles has twisted one convention after another.

Storms, shipwrecks and eccentric battles are the essential
theatrical props of the novel. Here he makes it his business to
contrive the most grotesque mixture, and in so doing seems to
stray across the borderline between melodrama and sheer farce.
The fight with the *boukoloi*, with its infantry battles on water
and shipwreck on land, might still be seen as nothing more than
rhetorical paradox:[46] but not so the three major shipwreck scenes.
We have passengers doing a marathon round the deck to balance the
ship, or fighting a naval action against the crew, perched in mid-
air in the life-boat.[47] But the real Heath-Robinson invention
comes when Achilles combines shipwreck, stage-simile and sea-
fight in one: the pirates take on a merchant ship's company led
by an actor, bravely fighting with dummy weapons.[48]

The *Scheintod* is also an obvious opportunity for burlesque,
though one might suppose that the sophisticated parodist has to
work very hard to produce anything more ludicrous than what his
victims have already written.[49] To my mind Achilles makes it
quite clear that he has done just that. It is not just the horror
of the episode which is amusing - any melodramatic sacrifice can
produce the same effect; it is the number of contrivances required
to 'explain' the operation, and the excessive paraphernalia he
has attached to it. Achilles describes the mock-sacrifice of Leucippe in a matter of lines. It takes several pages to account for
all the ingredients of the deception - complete with shipwreck and
chest washed ashore, not to mention the mechanics of the stage-
dagger with its retractable blade.[50] The ritual itself has also
to be contrived: it just happened that two of the hero's friends
had already infiltrated the pirates, all the more easily since one
of them, Menelaus, happened to be a native of the district;[51] it
just happened that the pirates had a law requiring the newest re-
cruits to perform the sacrifice,[52] and that an oracle required her
to wear a sacrificial robe ideally suited to concealing the girdle
of sheepgut arranged to explode on the impact of the false dagger![53] If this is not ludicrous enough, Achilles himself comments
indirectly on the *Scheintod* convention: when Melite is making her
final attempt to seduce Clitophon, she makes the wish that if he
only gives in to her once, may Leucippe never die again, not even
falsely![54] Even the heroine's desperate rival is resigned to the
fact that she is accident-prone but indestructible. It is only

after the three *Scheintod* scenes, however, that Achilles is able
to excel himself. Although the second and third are something of
an anticlimax after the ingenuity of the first, they afford Clitophon the unique lament that his beloved's body is subject to a
law of diminishing returns: first he was left with the whole corpse, next with the body and no head, third time round with nothing
at all.[55] *Non ignoravit vitia sua, sed amavit.*[56]

As to the contents of Achilles' paradoxography, he has not
simply provided mechanical book-learning by copying out handbook
information derived from Ctesias or Megasthenes. He has produced
an extraordinary tradition about the phoenix,[57] which has as much
in common with *Herodotus-at-the-Zoo* as it has with the standard
accounts. Achilles' version takes its starting-point from Herodotus, and the young bird duly embalms its parent.[58] But where
the model compares it to an eagle, he compares it instead to a
peacock - the favourite bird for ecphrasis, so that it must be
made to display itself.[59] This is the point where decoration becomes sabotage. The beautiful Phoenix reveals itself - including
its genitalia front and rear, so that the priests can check every
detail of its identity with the sacred book; the successor-bird
emerges as an ἐπιτάφιος σοφιστής.[60] We are only spared an ora-
tion in hieroglyphics. One thinks of Lucian's amusement with the
funeral of Severianus,[61] but this is far more facetious: Achilles
is learned and lascivious, as always.

The position of such episodes is no less important. The
author is usually taken to task for his tasteless digressions; but
nothing has been said about where he chooses to be tasteless; very
often irreverence has been mistaken for irrelevance.[62] When
Clitophon falls in love with Leucippe he goes to tell all to his
cousin Cleinias - only to have to listen to the latter's eloquent
attack on marriage.[63] Immediately Cleinias' own homosexual lover
is torn to pieces in a riding accident, by a sort of erotic rough
justice; his tirade has been undercut and his rhetoric in vain.
Again, it is when Clitophon has secured his elopement with Leucippe that he is plunged into the academic debate on the merits
of homosexuality.[64] Achilles carefully reminds us of its incongruity by pointing out that Leucippe was fast asleep and out of
earshot.[65] No less incongruous is the digression on the *militia*
of love.[66] It is all very suitable in the mouth of his general
Charmides, who puts his whole panoply of professional metaphor at
the reader's disposal: ἐπὶ πόλεμον νῦν ἐξελεύσομαι βουκόλων·
ἔνδον μου τῆς ψυχῆς ἄλλος πόλεμος κάθηται... But he is fobbed off

in the end by a middleman who pretends that Leucippe is having a
period.[67] Achilles contrives a situation where his general will
be taken aback at the prospect of a little blood - and settle
bathetically for a kiss instead. Charmides' other tour-de-force
is just as cynically timed. He engages Leucippe's undivided
attention with what purports to be an account of the hippopotamus,
which has to be kept going to enable him to keep his eyes on her:
but halfway through he digresses to the elephant, thence to its
aromatic breath, perfumed by the black rose of the Indians![68]
In isolation this might well be cited as a case of sheer taste-
lessness. But it is significant that Ovid counsels potential
seducers to spend time expatiating on the barbarian exotica at
Caesar's spectacles - with the same end in view.[69] And it says
something about Achilles that his most prominent irrelevance is
to follow the rescue of the reassembled Leucippe with a detailed
account of the crocodile's teeth.[70] This author is not above
spicing his version of *Love Story* with a hint of *Jaws*.

The structure of many such excursuses has to be noticed:
Achilles tends to allow a digression, or a whole series of digressions, to begin as if convincingly integrated into the narrative, but to deteriorate rapidly into some absurdly irrelevant
development. A still more obvious example is at I.15-18, where
the topos that nature is sympathetic to love is maliciously twisted: after an extravagant ecphrasis of the garden, Clitophon meets
Leucippe and takes his chance to perform a tour-de-force on the
subject of the peacock: so far school rhetoric neatly dovetailed
to the situation. But an account of the love of peacocks is
followed by the same for palm-trees, stones, and - poisonous
snakes! Leucippe is duly impressed by his recital.[71] Ovid
points out that lovers do not declaim at such moments;[72] Achilles
provides an absurd demonstration of the point.[73]

The more elaborate the irrelevance, the greater the anticlimax he will contrive for it. He enumerates Calligone's jewel-
lery at enormous length, not omitting a disquisition on purple
dye ... discovered by a fisherman, a shepherd and a dog.[74] But
the reader should have suspected that this glittering trousseau
belongs to the wrong bride, soon to be safely abducted.[75] The
whole accumulation of erotica in book II is also in vain,[76] from
the ecphrasis of the translucent cup[77] and the excursus on the
origins of wine (misinterpreted by the peasants as sweet blood and
purple water)[78] - to Panthea's intervention, just in time to
frustrate the lovers' fulfilment.[79] And Achilles provides

detailed description of the chastity tests, despite the fact that
both of them are of course bound to go wrong.[80]

Bold and convincing lies are themselves a frequent source of
fun throughout the novels. Achilles does not concoct any elaborate lying tales whose humour depends on corroborative details,
but he is given to commenting on skilful fictions as they are
being told. Clitophon admits that in order to allay his solli-
citous parents' suspicions he carefully selected such portions of
his affair with Melite as would give a favourable impression of
his own conduct; he had told no lies, and even slipped in an oath
by Artemis to his former continence,[81] before shifting his ground
to Leucippe's virginity.[82] But the main source of irony is the
affair between Melite and Clitophon. She is able to conceal her
own guilt (εἰ τι ἐψευσάμην, μεμοίχευμαι);[83] unknown to Thersander,
she has done both.[84] And it is with some panache that she insists
on her piety, having rescued Clitophon (from the shipwreck which
never took place), since whenever a plank was washed up she used
to wonder if it belonged to Thersander's ship.[85] This protest
is suspiciously similar to the argument Clitophon himself had been
using to dissuade her from sleeping with him at sea - their ship
was passing over the very part of it haunted by the shade of
Leucippe.[86] Again, when Thersander first assaults Clitophon, none
of his charges of adultery are true;[87] next time, the charges are
much the same, but he is not to know that they have been substan-
tiated in the interval.[88] No more does Leucippe, when she swears
to her father that neither she nor Clitophon has told any lies -
unaware that she is in no position to speak for her fiancé.[89]
But the virtuoso display of ironic lying is assigned to Melite,
who lectures Thersander on Rumour and Slander,[90] and so gives a
psogos of slander to a natural slanderer - to corroborate her own
lies.[91]

Achilles' main interest is not in characterisation, but he is
still able to use it incidentally for amusing ends. Leucippe's
mother and father are New Comic bourgeois parents, more concerned
with the family reputation than with their daughter's.[92] The
surly servants Conops and Sosthenes are stupidly malicious;[93]
Thersander is a pompous hypocrite, the general Charmides the most
inept of *milites gloriosi*.[94] But the problem is the evaluation
of Clitophon. This figure brought accusations of incompetence
from the nineteenth century: Rohde would still have liked love
stories to have had supermen for their heroes.[95] But he was
looking for the wrong thing. There is something of a subtle

anti-hero rather than an inept puppet here. Clitophon is always
being caught in the act - wrongly. He has to make the most elaborate amorous overtures to Leucippe, only to be found by Clio as
soon as he embraces her.[96] After close on two books of elaborate
preparations, he is caught in Leucippe's room by her mother,[97]
before anything can happen, and has to flee.[98] He is indignant
at being taken by Thersander as an adulterer in a 'husband's
return' scene, when he has not even exercised his legitimate con-
jugal rights with Melite (nor has he any intention of doing so at
this stage).[99] And it is no accident that when this hero chooses
to compare himself to Achilles, it is to the Achilles of the bou-
doir![100] The author's outlook and technique are already clear:
he is able to undermine the novel by the standard means at a
sophist's command. It is in the light of this that we have to
interpret his use of religious motifs, and not vice versa. We
already know the overall effect of the work, and there is no
prima facie reason to assume that its relatively minor religious
content will not be put to some wry but unexpected use. It would
take something like book XI of Apuleius' *Metamorphoses* to alter
the picture, but in fact there are no surprises: Achilles' religious machinery is consistent with his literary intentions.[101]

      Love is of course treated in a conventional Hellenistic
manner. Eros smiles at the sight of Zeus as a bull, and Achilles
acknowledges him as ruler of the universe,[102] while Clitophon
cheerfully announces his pious obsequies to Apollo: ...in breaking
off his engagement to Calligone.[103] *Impudicitia officium*, once
more. The gods must also be involved in the fiasco of the chastity tests: in effect they turn a blind eye to the duplicity of
both Clitophon and Melite.[104] And it is an irony not to be missed that Clitophon should complain of outrage in none other than
the temple of Artemis;[105] Thersander is perfectly entitled to
claim that his rival had no right to disgrace the threshold of the
goddess. Such a setting serves to heighten Clitophon's tirade
('You have turned Ionia into Scythia, Thersander, and Taurian
blood is flowing in Ephesus').[106] Achilles produces the sort of
sarcasm familiar from Seneca's Vestal *Controversiae*: the priest is
a tyrant and fellow-deity of Artemis, her temple a brothel, and
the like.[107] The irony of Pan as minister of a chastity test is
also fully exploited: Clitophon complains that he and Leucippe
have observed the conditions of the test, while Pan himself has
not; yet in the end he has beaten Pan at his own hypocritical
game.[108] In fact with the patronage of Artemis, Pan, Hermes god

of liars,[109] and the rapists Apollo and Zeus, Clitophon is indeed
in the safe hands of a guiding providence - which does not fail to
send very inconvenient dreams to future mothers-in-law.[110]

There is less fun with hocus-pocus than in Heliodorus or
Iamblichus, though Menelaus does pretend to raise Leucippe from
the dead, and is duly hailed as a minister of Hecate.[111] But it
is Achilles' use of the Mysteries which calls for the closest
attention: a cornerstone of Merkelbach's theory is that this
author's treatment should be no different from that accorded by
the other novelists.[112] But the metaphor is used in situations
as incongruous as can be imagined to any act of piety. Aphrodite
is to be the mystagogue for Clitophon and Leucippe - for their
clandestine extra-marital experiment;[113] Melite claims the same
role, in the knowledge that she is only preparing the way on one
single occasion for his permanent marriage to Leucippe, just as
the mystagogue initiates the novice prior to the latter's permanent union with the goddess.[114] This is an ingenious sanctifica-
tion of Melite's role as an adulteress. Moreover *not* to deceive
Leucippe by sleeping with Melite is to have no respect for love's
Mysteries[115] - or so Clitophon argues. We should also note the
context in which Achilles makes his most specific allusion to an
actual ceremony. It is when the outraged husband Thersander finds
Clitophon dining with his wife, and beats him up without explanation, that the victim compares the blows in a mystery.[116] Short
of applying the title *mystagogus* to a brothel-keeper, Achilles
could scarcely have handled the institution in a more sardonic
way.

In *Clitophon and Leucippe*, then, we are dealing with sophisticated and cynical savagery. This is carefully calculated sick
humour and the casualty list is impressive: a homosexual youth
torn limb from limb, a prostitute decapitated, a heroine disembowelled at regular intervals in dream, ecphrasis or *trompe l'oeil*,
and a fiancée and her proud parents permanently deceived. In the
midst of the carnage and deception Achilles flaunts all kinds of
sexuality while maintaining the appearance of utmost respectabili-
ty. Love and learning are at odds, and visual art is at the service of sadistic sex. Achilles is a virtuoso saboteur; and to
see him as such is halfway towards understanding the sabotage of
the *Satyricon*.[117]

CHAPTER FOUR

SACERDOTAL STRATEGY, VIRTUOSO VIRGINITY: HELIODORUS

Heliodorus is the most difficult case among the ideal novels.
It is generally assumed that he represents the genre at its most
serious,[1] and this assumption has been allowed to determine the
interpretation of individual passages. He is certainly committed
to the heroine's chastity, which in this case is positively scin-
tillating; his religiosity is not only pervasive but impressive
as well; and he is usually congratulated for his rhetorical com-
petence and a skilful and novel management of the plot. But we
must also take into account the role of wit and diversion, and
their effect on the author's ensemble. We might most helpfully
think in terms of a bizarre and sophisticated game, in which the
labels comic and serious are no longer relevant.

The opening of the *Aethiopica* has generally been admired for
its dramatic uniqueness: Heliodorus is the only novelist to open
with a *Marie Céleste*. But there is more to it than that. He has
arranged a series of sophistic paradoxes: 'the god had arranged
a varied spectacle in a small space, mingling wine with blood and
imposing a war on top of a banquet, joining together slaughter
and drinking, libations and slaying - and exhibiting such a theatrical spectacle to Egyptian pirates'.[2] Eventually they have to
overcome their bewilderment in order to get on with the robbery,
so that they appoint themselves victors. Only this last observation need betray perhaps humour rather than bizarre wit, and it
is difficult to find any neat way to characterise Heliodorus'
treatment. At this stage it is easier to say that he is the sort
of author who will bewilder even his own pirates with paradoxical
symposia.

Many of Heliodorus' most complex equivocations are concerned
with religion, and it is worthwhile to examine one of them in detail. The Athenian Cnemon asks the Egyptian priest Calasiris why
he keeps referring to Homer as an Egyptian:[3] surely a novel and
unique tradition, he argues - and Calasiris does not contradict
him. The reader can expect a stereotyped exercise in Homeric
epanorthosis, in the manner of Dio's *Troicus*, Dictys and Dares,

33

or Philostratus' *Heroicus*; but since not all these examples are
equally playful in intention or execution, Heliodorus must be
judged on his own terms. Calasiris reveals that Homer was an
Egyptian from Thebes, whose father was supposedly a priest of
Hermes, but was really the god himself. The poet was banished as
illegitimate because of a strip of hair on his thigh, hence
Ὅμηρος = ὁ μηρός.[4] Merkelbach notices that this explanation is
both bogus and deliberate: Heliodorus must be joking, a clear indication to the reader that a mystical and symbolic meaning is
intended![5] But the origin of the joke has now been demonstrated.[6]
It is a subtle variation on a celebrated enigma in the *Bacchae*:
instead of the Theban Tiresias' explaining that Dionysus did not
originate from a thigh but as a hostage, we are told by an informant from the Egyptian Thebes that Homer really did receive
his name from a thigh. Heliodorus has turned a classic mystery
upside down, even taking his authority from the wrong Thebes! The
episode can be explained largely in literary terms, and sets the
tone for erudite and playful mystification.

Once this is established, other features of the same passage
fall into place: Calasiris himself had started his exposition by
making himself more mystical;[7] Homer's father turns out to be
Hermes, the god of liars and trickery as well as eloquence; and
the somewhat neo-Pythagorean Calasiris neatly combines two famous
features of the Pythagoras legend. Instead of the golden thigh
or the golden hair of Euphorbus, Homer now has a hairy thigh,
hence his name. The passage has repercussions for a wider context. At this juncture Calasiris is 'proving' to Cnemon that divine intervention can be apprehended – on the authority of Homer,
son of a god![8] If the basis of this authority is false, we should
begin to suspect all that depends upon it.

Throughout his religious adventures Heliodorus is less concerned with establishing right belief than in smiling at wrong.
Not only do his pirate simpletons mistake the heroine Charicleia
for a goddess or her living statue;[9] he also specialises in contriving long chains of credulity. Hydaspes, the sanctimonious
priest-king of Ethiopia, points out to the Egyptians that if the
Nile is a god, then Ethiopia is the mother of gods; to his embarrassment and displeasure they proceed to worship him as well –
before he too falls victim to superstitious stupidity.[10] Again,
Heliodorus often sets up oracles and dreams only to be misinterpreted, especially when the error is the result of wishful

thinking. This thoroughly Herodotean procedure is all the more
amusing when applied to amorous situations. Thyamis dreams of a
patently equivocal oracle, which he interprets first according to
his hopes, then, when things go wrong, according to his fears;
neither interpretation turns out to be correct.[11] Or Theagenes
misinterprets an oracle of Calasiris as he shares the condemned
cell with Charicleia. He will go to the land of the Ethiopians =
the underworld; in company with the maiden = Persephone; delivered from his chains = separated from the body; pantarbe = all-
fearing.[12] Here the amusement lies in the fact that Calasiris'
oracle left no scope whatever for misinterpretation: it is the
only clear oracle in the book, and the hero insists on pretentious and over-subtle exegesis.

Heliodorus' interests in pseudo-religion extend naturally
into magic hocus-pocus of all kinds. He sets up an elaborate
situation in which Cnemon can imagine that he is over-hearing the
ghost of Thisbe[13] - and dwells in detail on how the Athenian
bangs his head against the pots and pans as he gropes his way
through a strange house in the dark - convinced that resurrection
from the dead is possible, and can happen in Egypt.[14] Calasiris
on the other hand goes to great lengths to discredit the disreputable side of Egyptian sorcery[15] - only to admit to doing exactly what *it* is used to do by helping in love affairs,[16] when he
sees that it is time to play the thaumaturge and 'divine' what he
already knows.[17] Such conduct belongs to an extensive tradition
of fun at the expense of the magicians, familiar from Apuleius[18]
or Lucian's *Philopseudes*.[19]

Heliodorus, then, might be said to revel in religion: he
specialises in misapplied piety,[20] priestly deception, pompous
processions, and ceremonies that will have to be abolished.[21]
Nor is Calasiris content merely to dupe Charicles and the lovers,
and abduct Charicleia to Ethiopia by a meticulous ruse.[22] He also
turns the religious capital of the world upside down,[23] by getting the whole population of Delphi up in the middle of the
night[24] and making them enact a piece of puritanical legislation
(the priestess must no longer be able to set eyes on the sacred
ambassador!)[25] - before sending them off on a wild goose chase
all over the countryside, while he himself embarks at leisure
with the 'abduction party' and sails off.[26]

As in the case of Achilles, Heliodorus' interests and pri-
orities affect his selection of rhetorical material and

techniques: these too are dominated by playful mystification.
When he uses pompous tirades or hopelessly discursive speeches,
he tells his reader that he is doing so; and by such admissions
he repeatedly calls into question the pathos of romantic rhetoric.
Charicleia launches into a virtuous and theatrical strain
(ἐπέτραγῴδει) against the pirates,[27] but when she has finished
the performance there is no reaction: they have not understood a
word, and so much rhetoric has therefore been wasted. So too in
the elaborate language game in book X: Sisimithres makes this most
complex of dénouements a bilingual affair, exploiting the language
barrier between Greek and Ethiopian as the last stage in the game
of mystification.[28] The most eccentric of these contrived impasses is the conversation with the fisherman: Heliodorus keeps
the exchange at cross purposes until Calasiris realises that his
addressee is in fact deaf.[29] The string of non sequiturs still
comes as a whimsical surprise even in a work with so many diversions.[30]

In their long narratives the minor characters are frequently
interrupted - or interrupt themselves, in order to provide amusing effects to offset the length and complication of the proceedings. When Charicles is reported (already at second hand) as
telling the story of his life, he announces a digression which is
to form the main part of his tale;[31] Calasiris in turn checks his
nautical narrative when it has gone adrift;[32] and his convoluted
account to Cnemon is complicated by a series of playful diversions: his listener insists on more and more detail about an irrelevant procession at Delphi, which he interrupts with a mental
picture of Theagenes and Charicleia ...which in turn distracts
Calasiris.[33] Heliodorus not only treats his narrative as a game,
but allows his characters to do likewise.

He maintains the same kind of virtuoso mystification in his
paradoxography, excelling himself with a digression on the evil
eye.[34] Charicleia is suffering from a mystery disease; her step-
father Charicles thinks it high time she showed signs of falling
in love. Calasiris knows she has already done so, and pretends
the disease is the evil eye, which his dupe had dismissed as mere
superstition.[35] He can now take the opportunity to explain the
physiology of the false disease by analogy to the real one - of
love: the genesis of the latter is thus used to establish the
existence of the evil eye, which in turn is used to imply that she
is not in love at all! Not content with the multiple irony
involved, Heliodorus delights like Achilles in blinding his victim

with the most obviously incongruous pseudo-science: to prove the
girl's susceptibility to contagion he cites the case of the thick-
kneed bustard and the basilisk.[36]

Other traditional rhetorical tours-de-force turn out equally
ridiculous. The pirates look foolish when they try to handle the
merchantman, and so provide a variation on Plato's celebrated
ship of fools.[37] In the final battle which decides the war between Persians and Ethiopians, the latter signal not with trum-
pets, but with timbrels and kettle-drums.[38] The much-vaunted
Persian *cataphractarii* are so well-armoured that the Ethiopians
kill them by piercing their only exposed parts - their bottoms;
while the victims of Ethiopian arrows run in confusion through the
host with arrows sticking out of both eyes - like a pair of
flutes.[39] And the Persians are embarrassed by the insolent satyr-
like leaps of the men from the cinnamon country, more like a game
than a serious manoeuvre.[40]

Heliodorus also finds room for a number of miniature scenes
which reflect the sophistic interest in amusing naivety. There
are two passages where he has time for the kind of interest in
children which one tends to expect only of Longus. Pirate babies
cannot toddle out of the boat because they have a thong tied to
their ankle to serve as a καινὸς χειραγωγός, 'a new kind of tutor
to take them in hand'.[41] And the children of Syene are so terrified by the miserable pleadings of their parents that they turn
in terror towards the enemy 'as if fortune had improvised a new
way of arousing pity'.[42] And in the midst of his pompous machinations, Heliodorus finds room for a delicate pastoral miniature
incised on the pantarbe:[43] a tiny roccoco detail amid the baroque,
and a sympathetic smile among all the surprises. The most reveal-
ing touch is perhaps the handling of exotic animals. Instead of
a risqué phoenix or a gaping crocodile like those of Achilles, we
have short whimsical surprises as animals keep popping up without
warning. Cnemon is surprised even by the shadow of a crocodile,[44]
while Nausicles smiles at a foolish bird-catcher sent to catch the
phoenicopter;[45] or the giraffe terrifies the Ethiopians at a point
in the plot when surprise is least expected - before Theagenes
improvises a hippotaur to deal with it.[46] This is again the world
of *Herodotus-at-the-Zoo*.

There is little room for the conventional topoi of love as
used by Chariton or Achilles; Heliodorus has too many other preoccupations, and the emphasis on chastity does not leave much

opportunity for *artes amatoriae*. But he can still take a wry look
at lovers' pangs: Calasiris meets Theagenes watching his beloved's
house - as if he derived satisfaction even from that;[47] or he is
the general of an amatory band, - all of it arranged carefully in
advance.[48] Nor of course can Heliodorus undermine the motif of
chastity itself by the same methods as Achilles. This time neither lover is allowed to 'cheat' the conventions of the plot. But
he can still smile at the lovers' prudery from time to time.[49] It
is ironic, for example, that the ghost of Odysseus of all people
should commend Charicleia's chastity - as it was ironic for
Achilles' Pan to be put in charge of a chastity test.[50] Moreover
that chastity is maintained by subterfuges which win the admira-
tion even of the devious Calasiris.[51] Having committed himself
to his heroine's decorum, this author is not however above em-
barrassing it. Theagenes is made to guarantee her virtue by an
oath taken under protest;[52] while Charicleia herself, in a unique
moment of frustration, still remembers to pray for a *chaste* dream
about her fiancé.[53] Such sanctimoniousness calls for some gratuit-
ous mischief: Heliodorus not only arranges for Cnemon to surprise them in a compromising posture,[54] but gives Charicleia a
full frontal encounter with a naked pirate for good measure.[55]

Chastity apart, he is also able to use wry glimpses of normal
human character and motivation. If he does not specialise in them
to the same extent as Chariton, he does tend to smile at the same
things.[56] There are more sarcastic asides against human self-
interest, this time of merchants as well as crowds;[57] while the
pirates are indignant at being deprived of what is not theirs,
and the limits of friendship and kinship are defined by profit.[58]
Above all Heliodorus smiles at stupid pretensions: of the pompous
Persian Oroondates, dictating the terms of his own surrender to
Hydaspes;[59] the Syenites boasting of wonders seen just as readily
at Meroe;[60] or the unbeaten athlete unable to lift the elephant
Hydaspes has given him as a prize.[61] Again Heliodorus' playfulness stretches to the most minute asides: people dismiss the genuine skills of the poor fisherman as due to luck.[62]

The convolutions of the plot itself are consistent with the
interpretations so far offered. Its mainspring depends on an out-
landish piece of medical paradoxography (Charicleia's conception
as the white child of a black queen, by maternal impression).[63]
To this the fictions about the birth of Homer are made to correspond:[64] Heliodorus' interest in eccentric interlocking puzzles
extends even to the structure of his work. We can see the same

outlook in his approach to dramatic irony: instead of sustaining
it throughout in the manner of Chariton, he sets up a conspicuously bizarre and complex display of it - of course in a context
of superstition, when Cnemon misattributes a soliloquy of Charicleia's to the ghost of Thisbe.[65] And he is more interested in
contriving his equivocations than in resolving them. Even at the
last it is unclear what religious stance, if any, he will choose
to take. Ethiopian religion seems almost as much discredited and
circumvented as that of Delphi (the great Ethiopian priest-king
included).[66] Only at the very last does he finally commit himself to further mystic ceremonies.

   We can now attempt to find the measure of Heliodorus, a task
he himself has done much to frustrate. The whole ensemble reads
like an improbable collaboration between Aelius Aristides and
Lucian: an *Aida* verging all too often on *The Magic Flute*.[67] Does
Heliodorus merely introduce a few bizarre jokes from time to time,
to relieve his high and sentimental drama? There seem to be too
many of them, and the sophisticated equivocation is an essential
part of his literary texture.[68] Does he try to strike a balance,
perhaps unsuccessful, between comedy and tragedy, concerned more
with novelty on the most ambitious scale than on the overall
effect? This is certainly possible: apart from his explicit and
persistent allusions to blends of tragedy and comedy,[69] it would
be difficult even for the author of so large a work to keep control of the tone at every point, let alone assess the final impact on the reader. But in the end it is perhaps easiest to
approach the problem through his techniques of mimesis and choice
of sources. We can appreciate the ethos of the *Aethiopica* in
terms of Aeschylus' *Eumenides*, Euripides' *Helen*, and of course
Herodotus. Both the *Eumenides* and the *Aethiopica* move from the
experience of a distraught priestess at Delphi to absolution from
a death sentence by the new dispensation of a court of elders:
Heliodorus has ingeniously substituted the sight of a lover for
the spectacle of the Erinyes, and Ethiopian gymnosophists for the
assembly of the Areopagus.[70] In his bizarre game of mistaken
identity between the unchaste Thisbe and the pure Charicleia we
might be in the Egypt of the two Helens; there is a very specific
allusion to Euripides' version at the height of the combat aboard
ship.[71] The ambiguity of the *Helen* easily merges with imitation
of the tone of Herodotus - curiosity about religion and scepti-
cism about one religious practice after another, combined with a
reserve about the most sacred mysteries.[72] In the resulting

ensemble imitations of Tragedy go side by side with a variety of
slapstick and *trompe l'oeil* for its own sake or for the duping of
those who are easily led; and all of it is presented in a pose of
scholarly detachment and superiority.[73] This author's *pseudos* is
as elusive as it is grandiose.[74] Korais once compared Heliodorus
and Achilles to a man and a monkey: I would prefer to think in
terms of two different species of pithecanthropoid - a
πιθηκαρχιερεύς and a πιθηκάνθρωπος.[75]

CHAPTER FIVE

SYMPATHY AND *SOPHROSYNE*: LONGUS

It is in *Daphnis and Chloe* that a novelist's sense of humour
is most delicately balanced and controlled. Many scholars have
decided that the balance here amounts to ambiguity; but recent
emphasis has been on serious and spiritual interpretations.[1] I
wish to qualify such views, or at least to try to rephrase them;
and to point out that within the framework of a delicate miniature Longus still shares some techniques with Achilles Tatius as
well as Heliodorus. Of all the novelists Longus alone makes it
clear in his prologue that his purpose is ἡμῖν σωφρονοῦσι τά τῶν
ἄλλων γράφειν,[2] and this will be important in defining the relationship between art and play in so elusive a work.

The most significant innovation here is the pastoral setting:[3] Longus has produced a *Gattungskreuze* between idyll and
novel, and made much of the incongruities which result. In the
first place everything is cut down to size. The absence of the
conventional voyage for hero and heroine is no obstacle: all the
statutory threats are in fact there, each as stupid as the last.
There must be pirates - thwarted by a musical herd of amphibious
cows;[4] there must be trials - Chloe judging between herdsmen, or
the herdsman Philetas between the Methymnaean invaders and Daphnis.[5] There is even the statutory shipwreck - a Methymnaean
yacht only suitable for an afternoon's outing;[6] and two military
exploits - its gallant crew of *jeunesse dorée* beaten off by a
bunch of villagers,[7] and a fleet of ten ships which succeeds in
capturing the heroine and her sheep - only to be immobilised by
Pan and the satyrs.[8]

Compared to all this, villainous rivals pose a threat that
is positively minute; Dorcon has an escapade with a wolfskin which
leaves him savaged by Chloe's dogs;[9] and the worst that anyone can
do to Daphnis is to stamp on his flower-beds.[10] In place of kings
and eunuchs lusting after the untouchable pair, there is no-one
more serious than the young bourgeois and his lascivious parasite;[11] Daphnis' rival Lampis is too much of a coward to cut down
the trees that will spoil the hero's chances.[12] And in place of

41

the lascivious queen or the highly sexed noblewoman, we have a
neighbour's sex-starved wife ready to take advantage of him.[13]
Everything, then, is in miniature, right down to the vines themselves: a toddler with its hands out of its cradle could reach
out and pick a bunch of grapes.[14]

It is easy to contrast Longus' rustic simplicity with the
elaborate and learned paradoxography of Achilles or Heliodorus.
But in fact he has succeeded in scaling down even this to the
level of pastoral. Daphnis explains to Chloe the reasons for an
echo, or for the singing limbs of Syrinx[15] - and simplistic myth
takes the place of pseudo-science. Like Achilles he provides a
description of Pan-pipes (the reeds are of unequal length - since
the love of Pan and Syrinx was unequal!);[16] or a full-scale ecphrasis of Dionysophanes' formal garden, with its own range of
conceits - competition between vines apples and pears, ivy-
berries imitating grapes, nature giving the impression of artifice.[17] Longus has no need of amorous palm-trees. He has also
scaled down the processions and festivals of the larger novels to
improvised rustic spectacles: Daphnis runs on tiptoe to imitate
hooves, with the woods as a marsh;[18] or trains a flock of musical
goats, like Lucian's musical dolphins.[19] And if there are no
exotic species on Lesbos, we can still be informed that cows swim
better than anything else except fish, unless their hooves are
sodden and drop off; Longus confirms the point with an etymology
of Bospori to 'prove' that cows can swim.[20] His setting also
offers the chance of sophisticated paradoxical encomium: one
might look far in the more conventional novels for a syncrisis
between a cowherd and a goatherd,[21] easily accommodated in a
pastoral contest.

In this miniature and good-humoured world Longus has placed
a pair of innocent lovers. Sophistic writers were particularly
well practised at exploiting the novelties which naivety gives
rise to, whether through the eyes of children, barbarians or
rustics.[22] In the other novels the lovers may begin impervious
to Love, and ignorant or innocent as regards intrigue; but Longus
opens up a new range of possibilities when he makes them innocent
of even the name of love itself, not to mention the basic facts
of human reproduction. This time there are no rules or oaths of
chastity to interfere; and no lack of opportunity, since they are
out in the country all day long. This makes their helplessness
all the more amusing and pathetic.[23] Even the ineptitude of

Dorcon's attempts to seduce Chloe is not as amusing as the fact
that both Daphnis and Chloe misunderstand them, and think that he
has simply invented a new game.[24] But their ignorance goes much
further: they do not know whether Love is a boy or a bird,[25]
while they misconstrue the first symptoms and the first kiss,[26]
or the effects of washing or swimming on each other's bodies.[27]
Of course they are spared the fear of outrage which so obsesses
the conventional romantic heroines; but Longus makes fun of even
this: when Chloe is abducted by the Methymnaeans, the worst Daphnis thinks will happen to her is that she will have to live in a
town![28] Daphnis even promises to give Lycaenion a kid, a cheese
and even the goat itself if she initiates him - not realising
that the 'lesson' itself will be adequate reward for her 'instruction'.[29] He is deterred from applying his new-found carnal knowledge to Chloe right away by a mysterious warning about defloration, which again he misunderstands;[30] she in her turn is too shy
to ask why he now exposes himself less to the temptation of seeing her naked.[31] Even her stepmother is afraid of her innocence:
there is nothing to stop this heroine exchanging her virginity
for apples or roses.[32]

Against such a background, Longus is able to play with the
chastity motif in a new way. Daphnis is initiated by a woman of
the world halfway through the action, and no detail is spared.[33]
This is not in itself an act of faithlessness against Chloe: his
innocence allows him to be deceived. But Longus still gives him
a convenient degree of complicity: he does not tell Chloe, but
embroiders the yarn Lycaenion had told him in a manner falsely
creditable to himself. The far from heroic Daphnis makes out that
he was protecting a goose from an eagle, when in fact he was making love with Lycaenion.[34] Nor is Chloe absolutely innocent,
wilfully expurgating even the story of Dorcon's death by cutting
out his dying kiss.[35] Moreover Longus is able to perform a
little sleight of hand with the standards of chastity. That of
pastoral has no rules but those of nature; but birth-tokens and
recognition mean a change to the rules of New Comedy, and there
will be bourgeois parents with awkward questions to ask. There
is no chastity test as such, but Dionysophanes does want to know
if Chloe is still a virgin.[36] Of course Daphnis gives him the
answer he wants, and it is true; but Chloe had been trying a good
deal harder and oftener than Leucippe to change the situation.[37]

The pastoral guise, then, is charmingly maintained, and with

it an ambivalent innocence: Love is a shepherd, and we are actually told that the pair are given suitable pastoral names.[38]   But
the conventions do not escape unscathed: Longus knows how to
create his ideal people, then qualify the illusion by reminding
us that they are clodhoppers after all.[39]   Not being aristocrats,
the peasants must be ugly: Daphnis has a snub-nosed father and a
bald mother.[40]   The shepherds are often inept: their wolf-trap
succeeds only in catching sheep and goats;[41] Dorcon's rustic
gifts provide the same kind of amusement as their counterparts in
Theocritus;[42] and the rustics make a dreadful din outside the
door on Daphnis' wedding night.[43]   But the main characteristic
of the country folk is avarice (while of course Daphnis and Chloe
themselves are generous, being of aristocratic birth).   The pea-
sant community swindles the young aristocrats from Methymna over
the price of bread and wine;[44] Lamon's first impulse is to ignore
the baby Daphnis and help himself to the birth-tokens,[45] while
Dryas wastes no time in paying his respects once he sees Daphnis'
change of fortune.[46]   Minor characters from the town come off
equally badly.   The parasite Gnathon combines the worst of Alci-
phron's parasites and courtesans, resolving to kill himself at
Daphnis' door[47] - but not till he has filled himself with a good
meal;[48] while bourgeois guests are somewhat embarrassed by the
rustic wedding with its farmyard intrusions.[49]   The political
framework is as trivial as Chariton's, with the Mytileneans simply
calling off the war because it's cheaper that way.[50]   Even Gnathon's triumphant capture of Lampis is not complete, since his
prisoner of war escapes.[51]   Daphnis himself for that matter is as
melodramatic and unheroic as any other romantic hero: his lone
soliloquies on the loss of Chloe are totally inept, all the more
so when he was up a tree when she was captured by the Methymnaeans; and a homosexual parasite has to retrieve her from kidnap
by the most cowardly of rivals.[52]

Longus breaks the illusion of pastoral with his mixture of
realism and sentimentality.   The other side of pastoral life
occasionally makes its appearance amid the rustic piping and fum-
bling attempts at love-making.   Yet the texture is lighter than
Virgil's blend of pastoral fantasy and social and economic realism: there is just a hint of *antibucolica* in the manner of Numi-
torius, playing with the trifling inconveniences of the countryside.[53]   After Dorcon's ludicrous attempt to seduce Chloe, the
sheep are scattered, so that Daphnis and she have to go to the
trouble of rounding them up again.[54]   There is room for a stinking

dolphin in addition to the farmyard smells;[55] and sometimes the
animals are a little too close for comfort, as when Daphnis kisses
the goats at the wedding,[56] or gets the leftovers when Lamon's
dog has finished with the meat.[57]   There are glimpses too of a
much crueller reality: Daphnis kills birds and pulls off their
wings,[58] or tells Chloe how Pan's maddened herdsman tore Echo to
pieces.[59]   Several such details suggest comparison with incidents
in Achilles: Dorcon's death at the hands of the pirates is no less
cruel than the fate lavished on Clitophon's friend Charicles;[60] or
Lycaenion preserves Chloe's virginity by telling Daphnis about the
blood-letting involved in defloration. We are not so far from the
period Cleinias had to invent for Leucippe.[61]

The most difficult feature to isolate or characterise in
Longus is the role of religion or spirituality. We do not necessarily have to pronounce in favour of either piety or mock-piety:
it is perhaps better to say that we see the techniques of adoxography in the hands of a writer with genuine insight into both the
real world and the dream-world of children and adolescents - with
which the other novelists scarcely begin to come to terms. The
result is a religious ethos far removed from that of the *Aethiopica*, for example. In *Daphnis and Chloe* even the animals are
initiates and initiators of the action: we are close to the world
of Plutarch's *Gryllos*, where animals are wise and men are simple.[62]   It is a goat and a sheep which suckle the foundlings,
finally shaming their human masters into taking care of them;[63]
it is thanks to the good offices of the swallow and the grasshopper (ὁ βέλτιστος) that Daphnis first explores Chloe's breasts;[64]
while his goats are not only legitimate wedding guests but will
nurse the next generation of Daphnis' family.[65]

Animals accordingly set the norms for moral behaviour: they
are not homosexual, argues Daphnis, and so neither is he;[66] and
he is as worried about *their* loss of Chloe as about his own.[67]
They are carefully integrated into playful comparisons: Chloe is
driven off like one of her own flock, while Daphnis runs from
Gnathon like a puppy.[68]   Nor is it surprising that animals have a
superior understanding: the sheep know better than Daphnis and
Chloe how to copulate.[69]   Indeed Daphnis himself cuts a ridiculous
figure when he boasts that he has increased his herd: they knew
how and he did not.[70]   Longus' attitude can be compared to Virgil's treatment of the bees: *esse apibus partem divinae mentis et
haustus/aetherios dixere*... but neither author finally commits

himself.[71] The hero's oath to Chloe by her own sheep does not
save him from the wiles of Lycaenion.

Formal religion as such is constantly present in Longus, but
its role has to be carefully defined. Opinions are sharply divi-
ded between seeing an overriding providence at work and and denying its operations altogether. Longus does explicitly relate the
growth of love to the return of spring, and thus provides the
chance to transmute ecphrasis into allegory.[72] But his σωφροσύνη
contrives that providence move in a way that is both subtly mysterious and amusing.

Time and again he is able to qualify suggestions of spirituality in a playfully ambiguous way. The picture representing
Daphnis and Chloe calls for an ἐξηγητής:[73] this suggests the
function of the mystagogue, since we are told it is in a temple.
But Longus does remind us that worshipping at the shrine of Pan
was only an excuse to look at the picture. Other instances are
similarly balanced. It is true that the work is an offering to
Love, but that in itself is scarcely a devotional dedication.[74]
Or again, for Daphnis and Chloe springtime is to be like a resurrection from death. But even the phrase ἐκ θανάτου
παλιγγενεσίαν[75] need not be a mystic allusion when read in context: what for others is sitting in front of the fire indoors in
a country winter is death to young lovers - and yet another smile
at their naivety and lack of σωφροσύνη. Moreover too much is
sometimes made of the name Dionysophanes. Of course Daphnis'
true father is indeed the 'manifestation of Dionysus', but his
allegorical title works both ways.[76] This agent of divine providence turns out to be no more than a typically bourgeois New
Comic father who owns the vineyards.

Two further passages seem to me to be crucial, and both are
ambiguous. Chalk quotes part of Philetas' monologue, offered to
help the lovers on their way: 'Eros is a god greater than Zeus
himself. He has power over the elements, he has power over the
stars, he has power over his fellow gods - far more than you have
over your goats and sheep (!). The flowers are the handywork of
Eros. These trees are his creations...' Is this Hellenistic conceit, or an expression of piety and belief?[77] Not only is the
material a well-worn cliché of Plato's *Symposium*, New Comedy and
the Second Sophistic itself: but the context and the speaker himself are against any kind of serious religious programme here.
Philetas is trying to tell the two would-be lovers the facts of

life in a beautiful story: one does not begin a sermon on the mystery of the Trinity with 'there are fairies at the bottom of our garden'. Although he embellishes his little *mythos* in terms of what is familiar to Daphnis and Chloe, they are too innocent to see the point of even his Sunday-school account. Longus smiles at the story, the teller, and his tiny audience alike, in a portrait of delightful innocence.[78]

It is the episode with Lycaenion, however, which seems to put the gods most clearly in their place. Daphnis' real initiation has nothing to do with Pan and the Nymphs, nor indeed do they do anything to bring it about.[79] Lycaenion persuades him to sleep with her because, as she claims, she has had a dream in which the nymphs instructed her to do just that.[80] But Longus leaves us in no doubt that she has had nothing of the sort. She found out about it by hiding in the bushes the day before! To keep traditional forces in charge, Longus had only to tell us that the nymphs *did* send Lycaenion such a dream, or put the whole idea into her head. In the meantime the reader has to accept that her initiative is a human one, combining sympathy and selfishness; and that the beneficence of the nymphs on this occasion is in the very naive mind of Daphnis. We could always argue of course that she is the embodiment of the providence of love; but that is to make her the ambiguous agent of an ambiguous god.

If Longus is not fully committed to his gods, we can look instead for his attitude to the two standard spiritual forces in the Hellenistic world, Providence and Chance. Here too *sophrosyne* prevails, again in a neatly ambiguous way. Nature, the countryside and adolescence all play their part in the increase of love; but they are still frustrated at strategic points by the most comically contrived intrusions.[81] If Longus portrays the course of nature with sympathy and sensitivity, he equally readily dislocates its mechanisms and upsets its rythms, making sure that social convention, ignorance, chance, and any other obstacle retards the course of love. It is special pleading to give Nature the final credit for the climax of Daphnis' *initiamentum amoris*, considering all that Lycaenion had to do to arrange it;[82] nor is it nature that stops him from going off to try out his new-found carnal knowledge on Chloe either. In the end the couple who had every opportunity, and two fertile herds to show them how, have still to wait until the usual happy marriage and birth-tokens can be arranged.[83]

Several other sophistic miniatures suggest the range of experience readily available: Lucian's Ganymede shows a naivety towards Zeus similar to that of Daphnis towards Eros: neither knows
love, and both are too ready to translate worship into terms of
milk and she-goats and Pan.[84]   But sophists could also use such a
charming framework to explore the transition from beautiful innocence to experience. The same Lucian can present - with the complete absence of comment - Europa's realisation that she is about
to be a bride, after describing her pretty procession of dolphins
and Nereids.[85]   Longus' lovers embody both kinds of Hellenistic
vignette within a single fantasy. At first they cannot relate
love to their familiar pastoral world either; but finally they
too have their sexual realisation, and all nature turns up to the
wedding.

If we choose to construct a miniature theology for *Daphnis
and Chloe*, we can make out several distinct levels of divine operation: Pan and the Nymphs work in a mechanical way, to get the
pair out of any immediate difficulties; Love is really in charge
of nature and the garden. But Love itself is presented in more
than one way: as the mischievous little boy - through the eyes of
Philetas; through the human experience of Daphnis, initiated by
Lycaenion; and of Chloe, finally married to Daphnis.[86] We can if
we wish see a progress from one presentation of love to the next:
from an old wives' tale delightfully told by a mealy-mouthed old
man; to an erotic deceit, pretended to be a gift of the gods; and
thence to the real experience of love. One might choose to say
that Longus achieves depth when the childish play is laid aside
and Chloe finds fulfilment as a woman.

But even the final wedding scene and its aftermath are not
free of playful equivocation. Longus' list of guests recapitu-
lates those who have contributed to the love-affair, including
Philetas, Lycaenion and the animals.[87] But as yet no reminder of
Eros: only afterwards, and quite inobtrusively, we are told that
he has been added to their tiny rustic pantheon.[88] By now of
course Chloe has at last lost her innocence and discovered what
love is really about, but that love is still seen, at least by the
couple themselves - in the same sort of terms as it was first presented by Philetas; and Eros is simply put on the same level as
Pan and the Nymphs - for all his domination of the universe.
In a sense there is a progression from illusion to reality, from
innocence to experience;[89] but in the end Longus keeps them both.

Even at the last moment he reminds us of Lycaenion and her part in
the affair, and Chloe discovers that the love-play was merely
ποιμένων παίγνια; and yet we know that in the fulness of experience Daphnis and she will still bring their children up in the
countryside.[90] In the altar to Eros there is a touch of 'Christopher Robin is saying his prayers';[91] but there is the intangible
beauty of Pooh's enchanted place as well; moreover we know that
Daphnis and Chloe are never really going to grow up, any more
than Christopher Robin. In Longus, then, the gods can sometimes
be very clearly left in the minds of the characters: *expedit esse
deos*. But their author has seen to it that all things still work
together for good, and all the world loves a lover.[92] If there
is any key required, he provides it at II.27.2: Love wrote the
story, as Pan points out to the Methymnaean general ... before
sending him home with the most gentlemanly force majeure - and a
guiding dolphin.

How, then, are we to relate this most delightful and elusive
of all ancient novels to the rest? Longus has produced a sympathetic, self-consistent, and as he would have it sober portrait
of naivety seen through the most sophisticated eyes; his gods are
as trivial as Heliodorus' are pretentious; and within a much
smaller compass he has been able to incorporate the same religious pretence, as well as the good-humoured delight of Chariton.
It is comparison with Achilles, however, that is perhaps most re-
vealing, for the differences as well as the similarities. Here
too we have initiation with another woman, surprising realism,
and bizarre contrivance: the treasure and stinking dolphin are
not so far from the retractable dagger washed up on the shore.
But Longus shows that the Second Sophistic also has the tools,
and the sensibilities, to produce delicate and poetic pathos.
The she-goat which suckles Daphnis is buried just outside the garden; and love the naughty boy points out that he has not done any
damage to the plants.[93] Longus has struck the ideal balance between burlesque mock-pastoral and poetic fantasy in prose.

CHAPTER SIX

POSSIBILITIES: THE SUMMARIES AND FRAGMENTS

The role of summaries and fragments in the scholarship of
the novel has always been a crucial one. But at first sight they
seem to promise much more for dating than for the assessment of
playfulness or humour, which relies so heavily on context and
cumulative arguments. Two major texts have however emerged since
the collections published by Lavagnini and Zimmermann,[1] both long
enough to show that their contents are not wholly serious: this
in itself makes it worthwhile to ask questions about more familiar material.

Iamblichus:

Achilles demonstrates the most clearly humorous combination
of bizarre incident and not-so-sentimental love among the extant
novels. The nearest among lost works is Iamblichus' *Babyloniaca*,
of which we have an extensive summary by Photius and a number of
fragments.[2] The patriarch's sense of humour is perhaps not always to be trusted, as readers of the *Onos* know to their cost.[3]
In this case he treats the novel as serious, but recounts the
plot in sufficient detail to cast doubt on such an assumption.
Iamblichus has undermined the heroine's chastity and fidelity
just as clearly as Achilles; but he has gone further. After her
initial escapade with Clitophon, Leucippe has only to be dis-
membered from time to time, while forestalling any further as-
sault on her somewhat tarnished virtue. But in the person of
Sinonis Iamblichus offers a more unusual heroine. Not only does
she move up ladders with more assurance than one expects of the
prima donnas of the novel;[4] when she has butchered the drunken
seducer Setapus, she prepares not without relish to do the same
for her innocent rival: ὁ μὲν πρῶτος ἀγών, ἔφη, διηγώνισται·
ἐχώμεθα τοῦ δευτέρου· καὶ γὰρ ἐν καιρῷ γεγυμνάσμεθα...;[5] disappointed in her designs, she volunteers for bigamy with Garmus,
and actually marries the (infant) king of Syria![6]

This behaviour might have belonged to a melodrama intended
only to be violent and 'exciting'; but two episodes in particular
suggest that a certain level of slapstick was maintained at least

in some of the details. In one short fragment the Babylonians
are forced to improvise new materials for their archers:[7] they
use eggs, boiled and raw, with results that may be imagined.[8]
Again, the camel carrying the wicked doctor over the river ducks
in mid-stream to eat her underwater forage; she sits down on the
bottom, while he is presumably thrown into the river, to experience a bout of βορβορυγμός.[9] This is a variant on the motif of
'the highly trained animal which lets its master down at the
wrong moment'.[10] Neither incident falls short of farce, and puts
similar material under suspicion.

Like Achilles, Iamblichus contrives carefully complex absurdities in his *Scheintod* scenes. There is a particularly bizarre and bloodthirsty adaptation of the Pyramus and Thisbe legend, in which Rhodanes has to stop two potential suicides at
once.[11] Even if this had been intended to provide mere tasteless
suspense, there is again something suspicious about the couple's
capacity to move with such facility from one *Scheintod* to another. They are not only mistaken for dead but provided with food
and clothing as funeral offerings by their pious pursuers;[12] mistaken for ghosts of a robber's victims;[13] and even supplied with
a well-appointed cenotaph prepared for someone else's *Scheintod*.[14]

In spite of the limitations imposed by Photius, it is clear
that Iamblichus has concentrated to the same degree as Heliodorus
on complex and ridiculous religious deception. Rhodanes and
Sinonis arrive at the temple of Aphrodite just after Tigris has
been killed by a beetle in a rose (!); his mother believes he is
now a hero. When Rhodanes and Sinonis are inevitably mistaken
for Tigris and Persephone, the hero plays up to such credulity
(συνυποκρίνεται 'Ροδάνης ταῦτα τῆς τῶν νησιωτῶν κατεντρυφῶν
εὐηθείας);[15] while Soraichus is able to persuade the Alans that
he has discovered buried treasure by divine instruction, when he
already knows it is there.[16] The most ludicrous situation arises
when Iamblichus combines the motif of religious deception with
other potentially comic motifs, unfeminine behaviour and comedy
of errors: the priest (of Aphrodite) becomes executioner, to be
impersonated in turn by his son and even his daughter-in-law.[17]

In the light of such manoeuvres we should know what to think
of Iamblichus' claims to be a magus in his own right, with a
range of impressive skills in divination. Having demonstrated
religious trickery in the plot, he goes on to practise it in his
own person. And he goes one better than Calasiris' Homeric

etymologies: this time we are asked to believe that μυστήριον
comes from μῦς![18] By such infallible means Iamblichus even claims
to have anticipated the end of the Parthian War. Lucian revel-
led in the hoaxes of prophetic historians who did just that; his
fellow Syrian practises them in the first person.

Two of the three long fragments complement the impression
given by Photius' summary. One describes Garmus' royal procession, with the usual profusion of detail on the king's chariot
and extravagantly accoutred retinue.[19] But then the author changes direction: we are told that horses' tails are got up like
women's hair and tightly bound with purple and many-coloured
bands; and there is even a disquisition on the artifice of their
movements, right down to neighing. Iamblichus' choice of details
seems to point to the technique of Achilles rather than Heliodorus: a digression which 'goes wrong' and concentrates its learning on the trivia; it is not far from this to the aromatic breath
of Charmides' elephants.[20] Much however depends on the placing
of such a passage. It would not have had a great deal of playful
impact at the beginning, where Habricht places it:[21] if Rhodanes
and Sinonis fell in love during a procession, the horses' tails
would have nothing to do with the case. But the description
would have been highly incongruous, and all the more effective,
at the point where Garmus is making ready for his wedding to (the
false) Sinonis - all his trouble would then have been for nothing,
and the more elaborate the preparations, the greater the anticlimax when the wrong bride came to be discovered.[22]

The other long fragment is a court-scene, with its predictable array of surprises.[23] But it is set within a piece of absurd paradoxography: a master accuses his slave of adultery,[24]
when his own wife confesses that she merely *dreamt* she had slept
with him - in the course of a temple-incubation, whose participants can tell no lies. All this is very similar to some of the
erotic nonsense Lucian accuses Alexander of Abonoteichus of making up in his bogus oracles.[25] There may be a smile here at
temple-prostitution itself; and we are back in the world of un-
reliable chastity tests.[26] In Achilles Melite was wrongly ac-
quitted by such a means; here a woman is wrongly condemned when
the temple ritual makes her confess an adultery she committed
only in a dream. On the strength of the long fragments alone we
might prefer to wait and see what sort of novelist Iamblichus
turns out to be;[27] but when their author claims to be the

Archimagus of the Mouseteries...?

Antonius Diogenes:

    Photius also includes a summary of Antonius Diogenes' novel
τὰ ὑπὲρ Θούλην ἄπιστα.[28] At first sight one might assume that
this was indeed a serious work: Lucian may have parodied it,[29]
and Porphyry actually quotes it in good faith as an authority on
Pythagoreanism;[30] but neither circumstance guarantees the tone of
the work itself.[31] It is not easy to find situations here which
can only be comic:[32] Photius' summary is too short, and he men-
tions matters for their value as mirabilia. We can however suspect two different motifs on which Antonius offers several variations: there are at least two varieties of dupable barbarians:
the Celts, cruel and stupid, from whom the party escapes by means
of horses which change colour;[33] and Throuskanos, who mistakes
Paapis' magic spittle for an insult.[34] Such types offer the
possibilities of magical or pseudo-magical slapstick, in the
tradition of the *Charition* mime, or the various stratagems used
to fool Heliodorus' or Longus' pirates. Antonius also has a
taste for paradoxography which involves the alternation of night
and day: kings who succeed each other according to the phases of
the moon, Iberians who see by night and are blind by day; and
even the hero and heroine themselves, forced to live during the
night and die during the day.[35] We can suspect the sort of expostulations Antonius could have given his *Liebespaar* after that
sort of inconvenience.

    Photius also stresses Antonius' interest in *pseudos*, charg-
ing him with the use of forged authorities and other tricks to
establish plausibility.[36] These again would not settle the 'tone'
of the work, even if we did have most of the text; but in conjunction with playful paradoxography this feature may also have
been a playful touch. It seems reasonable to suspect that Antonius
was guilty of the same sort of games with religious lore as Heliodorus plays, even if he maintains or affects religious commitment
to the same degree; but that is as far as we can go.[37]

Metiochus and Parthenope:

    Fragments of historical novels may also have something to
offer. The missing link between two short fragments of *Metiochus
and Parthenope* has now been discovered,[38] and we can form a reasonably clear idea from the resulting ensemble about what is hap-
pening. Like Chariton, the author has taken considerable liber-
ties with authentic historical personages,[39] in this case

manipulating Herodotean names, including Polycrates of Samos, to
his own amorous ends. Metiochus and Parthenope would seem to
have been invited by Polycrates, after some kind of diplomatic
discussion, to a symposium at which the philosopher Anaximenes is
present.[40] Love itself is proposed as the theme for discussion,
to the apparent dismay of the lovers, after all their suffering
hitherto.[41] Metiochus holds forth in an elaborate speech on the
nature of love, ridiculing the popular conception of Eros as a
little boy ('Why doesn't he grow up, and how does he traverse the
whole world?');[42] of course the hero himself has never experienced it, or so he claims.[43] He is ready instead with a coolly
rational explanation of love for the benefit of Anaximenes: it is
a κεινημα διανοιας ὑπο [κ]αλλους γινομε|[νον].[44] This suggestion
naturally starts a lovers' quarrel with Parthenope,[45] at which
point the fragment ends. Of course this is similar to Achilles'
Tatius' travesties of Platonic love:[46] the lover discourses in
wholly metaphysical terms about Eros, all the time dissembling
the love-affair itself. As in Achilles, the whole business is
elevated to a pseudo-science, appropriate to the presence of a
Presocratic philosopher.[47] There is enough evidence here to suggest that playful erotic historiography was not confined to *Chaereas and Callirhoe*.

Ninus:

The publication of the first two fragments of *Ninus*[48] did
much to upset established theories of the development of the
novel; they ought perhaps to have changed rather more than they
did. Ninus and Semiramis appear in a new light when cast as a
Liebespaar. The hero's extraordinary courting speech could have
found a place in Achilles or even Longus: this Assyrian potentate
boasts about his chastity and military prowess in the manner of a
Miles gloriosus (fr. A.2 lines 8-17: διελ/θὼν γὰρ τοσαύτην γῆν
καὶ/τοσούτων δεσπόσας ἐθνῶν ἢ δορικτήτων ἢ π[α]τρώιωι κράτει
θεραπευόντων με καὶ προσκυνούντων ἐδυνά/μην εἰς κόρον ἐκπλῆσαι
πᾶ/σαν ἀπόλαυσιν· ἤν τε ἂν μοι/τοῦτο ποιήσαντι δί ἐλάττονος ἴσως
ἢ ἀνεψιὰ πόθου).[49] The coy and sentimental portrait of Semiramis
also flies in the face of her traditional reputation.[50] Is this
modest and speechless young girl a deliberate contradiction of
Ctesias' bloodthirsty and unscrupulous queen?[51] Perry offers an
interpretation which is false even on the meagre evidence available: 'only an obscure Greek romancer addressing himself to juve-
nile readers would write in that fashion about the national
heroes of any country'.[52] This is typical of the condescending

presuppositions which underlie the study of the novels. In fact
the Ninus-author engages in one of the standard sophisticated procedures of Hellenistic literature, by investing a pretentious
historical tradition with delicate preciosity. The conqueror
Ninus pleads with propriety for what is his to take: we can compare Propertius' picture of Heracles cringing before a priestess
for a drink of water - boasting of his amazing exploits, and being refused the most trivial request.[53] It is true that the
lovers in Ninus are the soppiest outside Xenophon of Ephesus; but
the phenomenon can still be explained in more than one way.

P.Oxy.3010 ('*Iolaus*'):

This recently-published papyrus[54] offers exciting possibilities, either as a comic or an ideal novel. On the strength of
what has been said so far about the latter I wish to defend the
view that it could be a comic situation from either. It is clear
that the passage deals with a mock-ritual in the course of a complex plot involving amorous adventures. Such an event would of
course immediately fit into a comic novel in the same way as the
Quartilla or Oenothea episodes in Petronius. But it has to be
borne in mind that there are three very similar episodes in the
extant ideal novels. In Achilles Tatius the hero's two friends
become priests in the service of the pirates, and perform a mock-
sacrifice of the heroine;[55] in Heliodorus the plot is never out
of the hands of crafty priests for long;[56] while in Antonius the
magician Paapis has sexual motives for staying with Dercyllis'
parents.[57]

The nameless speaker in our fragment is a gallus. That
might be taken to suggest a less elevated genre, but such persons
did not always move in a world of low life. The author of *de Dea
Syria* presents an elaborate mock-Herodotean picture of the cult
of Atargatis *in situ*,[58] and Lollianus' *Phoenicica* has some material in common with it.[59] Two different kinds of context seem
possible: either the hero and his friends are trying to gain access to the heroine,[60] like Achilles' pirate-priests Menelaus and
Satyrus;[61] or some contemptible rivals, nauseating desperadoes,
might be trying to force similar attentions on her under a cloak
of religion.[62] Even the latter scenario would still fit the ideal
novel equally well: intrigues involving eunuchs are commonplace in
the genre,[63] and it must have been only a matter of time before
they were combined with conventional humour at the expense of
priests.

Lollianus' Phoenicica:

The same kind of interpretations have not been slow to impose themselves on the other new major fragments, from Lollianus' *Phoenicica*.[64] But here again the implications of humorous detail have not been adequately explored.[65] One fragment describes an orgy which includes some kind of διακόρησις between Androtimus and a girl named Persis. Henrichs seems right to assume that she ought not to be the heroine, and that we are dealing with another *initiamentum* scene like Longus III.18.[66] We have of course no way of telling whether or not it played a comparably cynical role in the plot. In view of the outrages which follow, however, we might have to accept that a deflowering of the heroine herself, acceptable in New Comic plots, did find its way into the novels, if only as a comic and outrageous exception.

The next fragment is a *Scheintod*, or at any rate a gruesome meal which might well turn out to be such. Henrichs dismisses this as a tasteless piece of hack work: Achilles and other extant novelists knew what they were doing, but Lollianus does not. He has described the sacrificial cup containing the blood of the child-sacrifice, complete with its decoration of lapiths and centaurs.[67] Henrichs evidently objects to the very idea that an *ecphrasis* should appear at such a point. But nothing could be more humorously appropriate than to provide an artistic *objet d'art* with a scene of mythological blood-letting to match the event in question, and it is to no less a literary artist than Petronius that we can look for a parallel: Trimalchio boasts of *scyphos urnales... quibus effictum quemadmodum Cassandra occidit filios suos, et pueri iacent sic ut vivere putes* (*Sat.* 52.1). It is certainly misguided to contrast this apparatus with anything in Achilles: this is precisely the sort of detail he delights in, and we have what amounts to a painting of Prometheus' liver to prove it. But there is worse: during the meal Androtimus, evidently the hero, objects to the ill odour caused by the vomitings and farts of the Phoenicians as they eat:[68] παύσασθε βρωμόν] τινα διὰ τοῦ στόματος, τὸ(ν) δὲ κἀκ τοῦ ὄπισθεν ἐπιπέ[μποντες· συχνὸν γὰρ χρόνον] πρὸς τὴν ἀηδίαν τῆς ὀσμῆς [ἀντέσχον. But at the same time he complains that his own meat is raw:[69] ὁ δὲ Ἀν[δρότιμος μέγα ἀναβοήσας ˙ κακ]όν τι ἔφη ἔπαθον ἀπέπτου μ[ο]ι τῆς τροφῆς ἔτι οὔση[ς·. This is perhaps even more outrageous than anything in Achilles; though the mention of Leucippe's period has to be borne in mind.[70] The real affinities of this scene are with cannibal, missionary and cooking-pot jokes. But I should find it hard to

believe that this is inevitably the work of an unsophisticated
author who is merely cheap and sensational; there is room here
for the calculated outrages of a sophisticated writer concerned
to break conventions, rather than the blundering of a Xenophon of
Ephesus.[71] On the strength of the fragments we are in no position to be certain; but there is nothing in the *Tendenz* of what
remains that is inconsistent with an Achilles or Iamblichus.[72]

When all the reservations which must attach to fragments
have been made, there is substantial corroboration here for the
arguments already applied to the complete novels.[73] It would not
have been either disconcerting or surprising had all the fragments been wholly sentimental and serious; we could amass a collection of passages from Achilles which would produce a totally
misleading impression of the complete product. It is all the
more important, then, that a considerable proportion of the material listed in Pack, as well as the new finds, is either clearly
humorous as it stands, or invites strong suspicion of playfulness or ambiguity. The two new fragments do not necessarily con-
fuse the picture: they break the carefully-drawn lines dividing
comic and ideal novels; but such lines may well have been wrongly
drawn in the first place.[74] The spectrum of humour in the novels
may extend from the cynical wit of Achilles to crude juxtaposi-
tion of shock-horror romanticism and slapstick worthy of the
Chariton mime. In some cases only the context will show clearly
whether we are dealing with sophists practising *pseudos*, or a
Tarzan-story complete with performing apes. If there is not
enough evidence to show that these works correspond exactly in
nuance to extant ones, it is clear that they exhibit the same
wide range of *jeux d'esprit*.

CHAPTER SEVEN

MISSED OPPORTUNITIES:

THE DEVOTIONAL FRINGE AND XENOPHON OF EPHESUS

Besides the 'ideal' and 'comic' novels there are a number of
works which make use of novelistic elements without the main
love-plot, or subordinate their use of erotic themes to some
clearly different and often non-literary end. Some of these products are subliterary crudities - the Alexander-romance in the
forms we have can scarcely be called more than a compilation -
and in almost every case it is right to suspect that an author of
mediocre ability and questionable motivation is taking over, but
scarcely digesting, more literary material. Playful elements
are conspicuous for their rarity, and for the author's failure to
integrate them convincingly with the purpose of his text. For
this reason one might rightly disregard this evidence as an exhi-
bition of irrelevant curiosities. But it is important precisely
because it shows what romantic elements can be like when *not*
manipulated with lighthearted intent; and it also reminds us that
a serious religious purpose tends to discourage any consistently
humorous treatment.

There is little humour (though plenty of diversion) in the
novels specifically intended for Christian propaganda or edifi-
cation.[1] But it is instructive to notice what sort of material
was admissible, and in what proportions. Christian romance shares
its themes of trickery, adventure and wonder-material with the
ideal novels, but the orientation is quite different. It is in
these works that the theme of chastity really comes into its own,
of course without the temptation of equivocal handling which the
ideal novelists so often allow themselves. In the *Acts of Paul
and Thecla*, the heroine actually strips her assailant's garment
from him in the street when he tries to embrace her, and so makes
a fool of him.[2] Of course this would be amusing in the sort of
contexts established by Iamblichus; but here it merely emphasises
her aggressive virtue. When she is forced naked into the arena,
a convenient miracle ensures that her nakedness is not exposed to
view:[3] again an amusing touch in the hands of Ovid, Apuleius, or
even Heliodorus;[4] but here only a sop to a prudish public. The

wild beasts are put to sleep by an abundance of perfumes from the
women in the audience;[5] not farce, but a suitably Christian use of
luxury. No doubt these pious works were intended to entertain as
well as instruct; but there are not enough comic touches to show
that the writer intended, or the reader expected, anything more
than cheap and wide-eyed wonder.

Other amusing material is conspicuously lacking: Aristophanes' jokes against the sophists make a surprising appearance in
the Ps.-Clementine corpus, but only because the redactor himself
wishes to attack sophists;[6] Peter for his part sees through an
elaborate web of *pseudos* put forward by a bogus astrologer, but
the author is no Heliodorus.[7] Often naively humorous material can
be related to Biblical rather than classical subject-matter.
Christ ingeniously dupes Thomas, reluctant to go to India, by posing as his slave-master and selling him to a dealer who will get
him there.[8] But pious readers nurtured on the stories of Jonah
and Jacob's birthright could still have been suitably edified.

The nearest religious work to a conventional novel, *Joseph
and Aseneth*, is not Christian but Jewish;[9] it seems clear that
this is a presentation of Biblical material which has been inves-
ted with the trappings of romantic narrative, but without rising
above a simple, unpretentious and didactic level. The result is
that a few standard jokes have found their way in here also; but
the author's overall emphasis lies elsewhere, in the conversion
of Aseneth to Judaism, and many other opportunities are missed.
We are told, for example, that the suitors were preparing to fight
for Aseneth;[10] but the comic ineptitudes familiar from Chariton or
Longus in such a situation are not developed. There is just a
hint of the subordination of history to a love-affair as we know
it in Chariton (isn't Joseph the man who slept with Potiphar's
wife, argues Aseneth[11]). There are lovers' misunderstandings and
ironies: Joseph is assured that she hates all men, now that she
has fallen in love with *him*;[12] and there is even a touch of mira-
culous slapstick, when the soldiers detailed to threaten Aseneth
find their swords disintegrating;[13] but again the effect of each
detail is isolated and incidental to an edifying narrative.

In contrast to these simple sacred soap-operas, *Apollonius of
Tyre* is impossible to characterise adequately in its present
form.[14] There is the strong possibility that this is a much modi-
fied popular version in Latin of an original Greek ideal novel;
and parts of it have been subsequently Christianised. But it does

show how casually humorous effects are managed at some stage in a
dimly-discerned transmission. Only two episodes do emerge as
comic, and both are concerned with altercations between unsuccessful suitors - contradicting each other's claims to Archestratus'
daughter, or pretending to have deflowered Tarsia in a brothel.[15]
The brothel-keeper is himself a somewhat Plautine character,
whose professionalism is similar to Theron's.[16] But there the
humour ends. The author has not convincingly dovetailed his comic
episodes into the plot as a whole; and he betrays a rambling ineptitude similar to that of the ps.-Clementine author in his handling of an all too similar plot. The nature and history of this
complicated text should perhaps be settled in order to account for
its humour, rather than vice versa; but Klebs is probably right
to regard it as a folk-novel which simply annexes sophisticated
material and phraseology, be it derived from Roman Comedy or declamation.[17]

In contrast to the last two examples, the so-called *Alexander-Romance* offers an illustration of popular and exotic romantic
material without a trace of the *Liebespaar*.[18] As with *Apollonius
of Tyre*, our evidence comes from an intermediate stage in the
formation of the tradition; but the priority of any original redactor was storytelling and not artistry. There are certainly
sacerdotal strategies,[19] ironic deception,[20] and military slapstick;[21] but again both the central amorous plot and the overall
sophistication required to accommodate the material is lacking.
We need only ask what Heliodorus would have been able to make of
queen Candace's stratagem with Alexander's portrait,[22] or the
correspondence with Aristotle, to see how much is missing.

We are fortunate in having an equally eccentric text at the
other extreme - a work by an author capable of humorous sophistication, who has nevertheless resisted the temptation to write an
amusing ideal novel. Philostratus was a sophist of distinction,
and his command of the techniques favoured by the Second Sophistic
is not in doubt.[23] But the conditions under which he wrote the
Life of Apollonius of Tyana left only incidental scope for wit or
humour. This is a serious apology for his philosopher-saint. The
author explicitly offers mixtures of comic and serious,[24] as well
as a whole range of satirical *apomnemoneumata*, many of them concerned with the superstitions of others.[25] But he tends to go no
further than the obligatory wit appropriate to Socratic and dia-
tribe literature,[26] while the serious content is unequivocally
serious, and there are no attempts at ambiguity of mood. If the

cumulative effect of Philostratus' urbanities is considerable,
they usefully show just how far short of comic effect such orna-
mentation can fall. What above all is missing is the light-hearted treatment of love itself. Philostratus is determined to defend the purity of Apollonius' life, and is careful to avoid at-
taching any amorous deceptions to him. Even in erotic episodes,
the tone is puritanical, so that the sage neither acts as the
abettor in a love-affair, nor uses his sanctimonious panoply to
carry on one of his own (though Philostratus was capable of marrying off Achilles and Helen when he wished).[27] Here then we have
a genuinely serious, or at least didactic, sophistic work; and
advocates of a serious tone for Longus, Heliodorus and Apuleius
would do well to compare them with it. The overall impression is
similar to that of the *Cyropaedia*: can we really say the same for
the *Aethiopica*?

Such works are as consistent as the fragments in helping to
define the character of the ideal novels. There is probably more
humour and *jeu d'esprit* in a few pages of Longus or Chariton than
in all the Christian romances put together. Serious moral edifi-
cation and lively sophisticated humour do not easily coexist in
the same text. Amid so many literary curiosities and missed
opportunities it is useful to consider Xenophon of Ephesus. The
Ephesiaca offers the framework and situations familiar in the
standard ideal plot, but with next to no attempt at exploiting the
possibilities of playfulness. This may be because of the writer's
incompetence, or because the text as we have it is an epitome;[28]
either way Xenophon provides an excellent control, and three common situations will illustrate the opportunities which Chariton
and his kind consistently choose to take, and which the author or
epitomator of the *Ephesiaca* as consistently declines.

Xenophon's hero Habrocomes slights Eros, falls victim to Anthia at first sight at a festival, and is duly brought to heel for
his arrogance.[29] Other novelists automatically exploit such a
situation: Heliodorus' model couple are subjected to the elaborate
manoeuvres of Calasiris,[30] Chariton's to a little trick by Love
himself.[31] And whereas in Xenophon some of the crowd exclaim what
a fine match the couple would make, in Chariton the whole assembly
goes wild over them, with Love himself taking charge once more;[32]
Achilles for his part cannot resist a Platonic disquisition on the
arrow piercing the soul.[33] Not every novelist uses every witti-
cism every time;[34] but most have clearly made the effort, and one
has not.

A second instance: Hero and heroine are forever being mistaken for gods and goddesses, a situation which enables Hellenistic poets and Ovid alike to smile at innocent bystanders.[35] The
motif does appear in Xenophon, but as no more than a bald and pious statement: καὶ ἦσαν ποικίλαι παρὰ τῶν θεωμένων φωναί, τῶν μὲν
ὑπ᾽ ἐκπλήξεως τὴν θεὸν εἶναι λεγόντων, τῶν δὲ ἄλλην τινὰ ὑπὸ τῆς
θεοῦ περιποιημένην· προσηύχοντο δὲ πάντες καὶ προσεκύνουν· καὶ
τοὺς γονεῖς αὐτῆς ἐμακάριζον.[36] In Chariton however such error
provides a miniature comic drama of its own: Dionysius blames
Leonas whether he makes Callirhoe a goddess or a slave.[37] If
Heliodorus spares only a smile at the pirates who mistake Charicleia for a goddess,[38] it is because he has much greater misunderstandings in store; while Iamblichus' characters seem to thrive
on misapplied worship.[39]

It is in heroes' laments that Xenophon comes closest to the
others. If his expostulations are serious, why are theirs so often less so? In Heliodorus the author himself actually allows
his characters to dismiss mere rhetoric as such; Chariton offsets
his heroes' frequent suicide outbursts with the ironies they create, and too often his heroes are made to lament in the wrong
places;[40] while in Achilles elaborate erudition too often turns
out to be in vain.[41] Moreover Xenophon's pirates are simply *subjected* to heroine's laments: Heliodorus and Achilles' pirates are
regaled with much better ones - but cannot understand them.[42]

Xenophon's omissions are equally striking: no treachery by
the gods, no duplicity by one of the lovers against the other; not
a trace of fun with the pirates, or amusing evil in the robbers'
debates. Is it coincidence that the one ideal novel which insists
on the integrity of hero, heroine and gods is the only one which
shows no consistently light touch? Either way Xenophon, not
Chariton, is the real odd man out among the five, and it is he,
not Chariton, who should be accused of not being able to exploit
his medium.[43] We are entitled to suspect that he represents an
extreme point - close to the border-line between religiously-
orientated romance and genuine but inept religious propaganda, so
evident in *Joseph and Aseneth* or the Apocryphal *Acts*. The other
ideal novels embody art and (relative) lack of piety; Xenophon
genuine piety and lack of art. In the end we are left asking:
how ideal is the ideal novel?

CHAPTER EIGHT

PRIAPUS PRAECEPTOR? PETRONIUS

The problem of playfulness in the comic novel is more familiar; and the fact that it can still be raised at all might call
such a title into question. Petronius[1] and Apuleius have each
received generous attention in comparison with the ideal novel;
in the present state of scholarship it would be superfluous to
enumerate examples of verbal humour[2] or catalogue comic effects.
I wish instead to deal once more with the familiar impasses that
have plagued the last two decades: relations with the ideal novel,
and the internal balance between comic and serious in both Petronius and Apuleius.[3] There is some new evidence available in
the new papyri of *Iolaus* and the *Phoenicica*; I have also tried to
bring the evidence of the ideal novels and sophistic literature[4]
more closely to bear on the problems.

Does Petronius parody the ideal novel? The question has
been fought out repeatedly since Heinze's claim of 1899,[5] and
there is now little to add by way of detailed evidence. Apart
from any question of establishing echoes, however, there are a number of reasons *a priori*. The *Satyricon* as we have it is far from
being an equal partnership of prose and verse: it is an extended
narrative in prose, and the most obvious target for such a form,
apart from historiography, is the ideal novel. Also, what we
know of Tacitus' Petronius himself[6] fits the kind of temperament
which would have enjoyed sabotage of this particularly vulnerable
genre. But more important: like the mime,[7] the novel could claim
to be a popular form (with considerable pretentions). If Petronius made a point of using familiar popular material, as in the
case of mime, then the novel was an equally obvious ingredient.
Moreover contamination of genres in itself may have the effect of
parody. If a writer dresses up his novel as Epic, he may demean
the latter; and if he contaminates both of them with mime, he can
pull both of them down together.

In recent years the case against parody of the ideal novel
has been vigorously restated on a number of grounds,[8] none of them
completely convincing. It is difficult to deny the existence of

such a form for Petronius to parody. If Chariton can fall chrono-
logically on either side of him, *Ninus* can scarcely be anything
but a predecessor.[9] Nor can the plot of the *Satyricon* be presented as essentially different from that of the ideal novels. It is
true that the lovers in Petronius are together for most of the
time; but this is also the case to a greater or lesser degree in
Heliodorus, Achilles and Iamblichus, whose lovers are prevented
from consummation by some other circumstance altogether.[10] Nor
should it be objected that Petronius does not include sufficient
travel;[11] again the same might apply to Iamblichus or Longus; and
Encolpius offers plenty of comings and goings in our very limited
sample.

The central target for parody of the ideal novels would of
course be the *Liebespaar*, for which Petronius has substituted a
homosexual couple. It has been objected however that homosexual
themes are not treated with repugnance in the Greek novels, so
that the effect of any such parody would be lost.[12] But Petronius
is writing in a *Roman* context, where attitudes to homosexual relationships could be more puritanical;[13] and in the ideal novels
homosexuals are often subjected to the same disdain or misfortune
as adulterers and other disreputable characters: Gnathon's advances in Longus are an illustration of his loathsome appetite;[14] in
Achilles one apparently acceptable relationship is sabotaged,
while another is used as a cynical thrust at the plot itself.[15]
Xenophon of Ephesus also uses such a liaison as one of the contemptible threats to the lovers, or as an episode in the life of
a pirate.[16] Only in such contexts is homosexuality used with any
semblance of neutrality; but no extant author of an ideal novel
glorifies it. We might reasonably assume that for Petronius it
was sufficiently disreputable to indicate a turn for the worse.

The main argument against parody of the novel is that the
pattern of parodies would soon be blurred. But where popular models overlap, any parodist will be faced with an occupational
hazard - and fresh opportunities. If Eumolpus, for example, can
be related to characters in satire and comedy (which already overlap), this does not prevent him from embodying a stock character
of the novel as well, since it finds room for a wide range of lascivious villains, confidence tricksters and diversionary idiots.[17]
It might of course be argued that the ideal novel and the *Satyricon* use Epic independently.[18] This would be reasonable in respect
of an author whose literary outlook was narrow; but given the

demonstrable variety of Petronius' sources for parody as it is,
would he be likely to draw the line at the novel, when he has already contrived a *Gattungskreuze* between Epic and Satire, and
finds room for Paratragedy as well? When the outline of novel,
Odyssey, and *Chariton* mime, for example, are so similar anyway,
Petronius could have kept at least three basic levels of love-and-
travel plot going indefinitely.

This convergence can be readily illustrated. Encolpius finds
himself in a picture-gallery, reflecting on the loves of the gods
and the infidelities of Giton: can we accept that the episode is
wholly accountable in the shield of Achilles and the scenes in
Dido's temple?[19] Even if we discount the closeness of Encolpius'
meditation to the opening of Achilles Tatius, it is hard to ignore
the fact that Eumolpus' unwelcome competition is prefigured in a
picture of the rape of Ganymede. If the gallery in itself does
not point specifically to the novel, the conjunction of picture-
gallery and erotic experience certainly does. Nor must we be content to compare Petronius' Circe to the sexually insatiable women
of Roman Satire or the *Odyssey*:[20] such women are well established
in Hellenistic literature, as in the persons of Stratonice or
Semiramis; and Circe is scarcely more demanding than Arsake or
Melite. The novel should not be left out of account either in the
scene of Encolpius' impotence with Circe in the garden. Of course
this calls to mind Odysseus' address to his heart, Ovid's Elegy
on his own impotence, and the rhetorical *locus amoenus*; but in
Longus there are also repeated scenes of sexual failure, and they
are not likely to have been unique in the tradition of prose fiction.[21]

The novel, then, must be considered in conjunction with other
sources for parody, not in competition with them;[22] and Petronius
could only have used it in a wry manner. Sentimentality is morally pretentious, and he knew how to deal with a genre which had
room for so much of it. We can now deal with the question of
comic and serious as such. Scholars have vigorously defended and
reformulated extreme positions over the last two decades; we can
still choose between a Petronius who is reacting in some way a-
gainst the vision of society he is portraying, and who wishes to
convey this reaction to his readers; and a Petronius engaged in
writing a work of literature, whose aim is neither higher nor lower than to produce literary entertainment.

Moralist interpretations of the *Satyricon* have proliferated

in recent years:[23]   the problem is to evaluate the extent and purpose of themes from Roman Satire in the work as a whole.   By opt-
ing for Menippean Satire as one of his forms, Petronius could of
course have claimed the right to mix comic and serious:[24] but this
does not help us to define the relationship between the two: do we
have a burlesque frame with serious insets, or do moral sermons
and attacks on luxury invalidate their setting?   Much moralist
argument has proceeded on the assumption that Petronius is somehow a self-evident moralist, and it is worth looking in some detail at the broad questions of principle so persistently invoked.

Petronius' sheer lack of inhibition has been used to support
the moralist case: Highet once conceded that 'the author never
says that (the characters) are wicked men, and they seldom if
ever behave as if they felt they were wicked'.[25]   But wicked they
must be in moralist eyes, because 'no audience, ancient or modern,
could approve of theft, murder, and outlawry; no audience could
do anything but disapprove of them... To show their repulsiveness,
to describe their constant danger and guilt, without ceasing to
be interesting, is to be a moralist and a satirist'.   But the
ideal novelists are neither moralists nor satirists, yet they are
capable of creating lovable, memorable and amusing pirates without preaching against tomb-robbery or abduction: if such crimes
can be presented for amusement only, they can be multiplied and
intensified for the same reason.   So can such social abuses as
sponging, so prominent in the *Cena*.   It is clear from the treatment of the parasite in Comedy, Lucian, and Longus that moral indignation is not a necessary product of every portrait of the
parasite.[26]   Fluent and assured shamelessness appears in ancient
literature for the purpose of pure entertainment, and a writer
can admire virtuoso vice without moral commitment.   Disgusting
realism can also be made subservient to artistic purposes: before
we assume that constipation or illicit sex belong to the domain of
the satirist we must weigh their effect in Catullus[27] for example,
where humorous invective so often outweighs moral statements.[28]

Moreover we have to bear in mind that not all *Satura* was satirical in any case.[29]   Two examples in Horace are particularly
relevant to discussion of the *Satyricon*.   In *Satire* I.8 we have a
case which clearly pokes fun at a witches' sabbath: but is it
satire in the sense of moral indignation at all?   It is an absurd
Ich-Erzählung by Priapus himself: his own untimely fart, rather
than any show of courage on his part, has put the witches to

flight. Is Horace really satirising Priapus[30] or the witches, or
is he simply having fun? Here we have a particularly useful approach to the nuance of the *Satyricon* itself, with a smile at
popular superstition, and fun at the expense of the sexually over-
endowed hero: it is not his usual weapon that Priapus brings into
play. The scene has a similar tone and similar ingredients to
those of impotence and mock-ritual in the *Satyricon*. At most it
can only be mock-moral (a 'cautionary tale'), and offers clear
proof that death, defecation and sex can be easily manipulated
into a comic ensemble.

This brings us to Priapus himself. *Priapeia* are amoral almost by nature; and Priapus is an excellent vehicle for mock-
morality, all the more so when he pretends to be serious with such
announcements as *omnia, quae loquor, putare / per lusum mihi per
iocumque dici*.[31] He is a moral god in the same equivocal way as
Pan in Longus or Achilles, only still more obviously so. The
gravis ira Priapi conveniently recalls the divine machinery of
both Epic and prose fiction:[32] that of Poseidon against Odysseus
and the revenge of the slighted Eros in the ideal novels.   It
should also be said that almost any entry of Priapus into literature is likely to be funny.[33] A little of his memorable attributes and powers goes a long way; and his anger should not be
constricted, or forcibly separated from the influence of the novel. It would not take very many allusions to sustain this ludicrous god and his ludicrous embargo throughout the plot.

The two new papyri also have important implications for Petronius. Both *Iolaus* and the *Phoenicica* leave no doubt that their
authors are using topics which are normally shocking or disgusting for humorous effect, and it would be very difficult to extra-
polate moral indignation out of either.[34] Androtimus' disgust at
the table-manners of the Phoenicians is equalled by that of Encolpius throughout the *Cena*; the effect in their case is not moral
protest, but the reader's amusement at Androtimus' expense. And
like Encolpius he has other discomforts to put up with: the meat
is raw![35] The scene in *Iolaus* has also something in common with
the bogus rituals of the *Satyricon*;[36] given the unsavoury reputation of the galli, there would be the same scope for disgust in
the service of amorous escapade as there is in Petronius.

The extant ideal novels are much more of a help than we
should expect: they show what can be done, and what standpoint is
available to an author, within complete novels. Each of the four

considered has some moral or philosophical pretentions, in every
case effortlessly turned into part of the fun. The lying hypocrite Theron dies a cruel death at the hands of providence;[37] but
Chariton is surely not wishing to tell his reader that it always
pays to tell the truth; nor is Dorcon's discomfiture a warning
that one ought not to disguise in wolfskins in order to seduce
innocent shepherdesses.[38] In Heliodorus no amount of piety can
conceal the trickery used to uphold it, and the very lourdeur
of the pious effusions themselves makes their effect all the more
amusing.[39] In both Achilles and Longus sexual and philosophical
themes are put to work side by side; and in both cases the former
undermine the latter. Achilles' long Platonic tirades are undercut by the cynical deception he plays on Leucippe;[40] in Longus the
idyllic countryside is offset by the inconveniences of puberty and
the trick with Lycaenion. The fact that Achilles makes Clitophon
suffer numerous sexual humiliations does not mean that he is dis-
gusted by his hero's attempts at premarital sex.[41] An anti-hero
is more amusing than a hero, and that is the end of the matter.[42]

     The real test for Petronius' seriousness lies in individual
passages and their cumulative force.[43] It is difficult to find a
single episode in which he does not neutralise his satirical
material or pervert its satirical effect.[44] The Quartilla episode
describes a prolonged orgy, presented as the priestess' revenge
for the trio's having seen an unholy sight.[45] Sham ritual, as we
have seen, is a persistent source of diversion in the ideal novels.[46] The episode is also a topos conveniently shared between
satire and the novel, and it is pointless to deny it to either.[47]
At first sight another moralist argument seems to work: that such
a scene contains more perversion and sexual gluttony than the hero
and his friends can physically accommodate;[48] even Ascyltus is ex-
hausted by the attentions he has undergone.[49] But satiety as a
theme can also be used in the service of fun, as shown by Eumolpus' story about the Pergamene boy: the homosexual seducer soon
finds himself outdone both in appetite and deceit by the victim he
set out to seduce.[50] A cautionary tale, perhaps, but is there
anything more than a mock-moral in such a case? The point is
surely Eumolpus' embarrassment and discomfiture when he discovers
that things are getting out of hand. So at Quartilla's: there is
always one more sexual diversion to be endured. In addition, the
reader has to bear in mind that this is a ridiculous revenge in-
flicted on behalf of Priapus.[51]

     The same argument applies to the *Cena*: of course Trimalchio's

nouveau-riche manners are ridiculed, in a well-established tradition of Roman Satire; but one of the effects of this is once more
to discomfit Encolpius and his friends, who realise only gradually
that this vulgarity is going to go on and that there is no escape.
Much emphasis has been laid on the tasteless mock-funeral as being
the culmination of emetic horror, brutality, lack of culture and
death.[52] But it has also to be seen in literary terms. Trimalchio actually wants to watch his own funeral - as Claudius had
done in the last piece of Menippean Satire we know of before the
Satyricon.[53] And if we accept an awareness of Plato's *Symposium*
in the *Cena*,[54] Trimalchio's final monologue will be an absurd
negation of Socrates' speech of Diotima, advocating values indif-
ferent to death, wealth, and physical gratification; it will also
be an antithesis to Alcibiades' confession. The grimness of the
scene (as opposed to its disconcerting effect on Eumolpus), is
easily exaggerated. Trimalchio's most distasteful antics scarcely
compete with the emetic horror, cannibalism, drunkenness and boor-
ishness of the Homeric Cyclops, for example; nor can Eumolpus'
helplessness be compared with that of Odysseus, except in a playfully mock-heroic way.

The presentation of Lichas and Tryphaena is more than a
standard portrait of superstition and hypocrisy:[55] when Encolpius
and Giton are betrayed into their hands by a double dream, a standard motif in the novel, the irony is that for all Eumolpus'
attempts to dissuade them from believing such rubbish, the revela-
tion turns out to be correct:[56] Priapus, like Longus' Pan, knows
how to handle divine machinery.[57] And Lichas' reaction to the
widow of Ephesus is not to be missed: any satire of his hypocrisy
must at least be offset by the amusement at his discomfiture. He
has, after all, to remember that his own wife has been very ac-
commodating to Encolpius.

Satirical interpretations are most vulnerable in the lament
for Lichas: Encolpius pronounces his idyllic meditation, so admired by moralists, *before* he sees whose corpse he is lamenting:[58]
he then promptly changes to prose, and his rantings are not without a suspicion of *Schadenfreude* - especially if we bear in mind
the celebrated curse of Hipponax.[59] There are comparable mock-
laments in the ideal novel. Modern parallels to Death by Water -
itself an emotive phrase[60] - are no substitute for the *locus clas-
sicus* in Achilles Tatius, which contains more than a suspicion of
parody: ὁ γὰρ ὀφθαλμὸς πελάγους γεμισθεὶς ἀόριστον ἐκτείνει τὸν
φόβον, ὡς καὶ διὰ τούτων θάνατον δυστυχεῖν πλείονα· ὅσον γὰρ τῆς

θαλάσσης τὸ μέγεθος, τοσοῦτος καὶ ὁ τοῦ θανάτου φόβος.[61] So too
does Melite's pretence that she used to mourn her husband in every
shipwrecked sailor she found - as a cover for her love-affair with
Clitophon.[62] Mock-mournings by the shore can claim to be an established topos in mock-rhetoric. It is true that Encolpius does
decide to burn the corpse, with conceits about the manner of
death: this is also a 'Cynic' topos against mourning,[63] similar at the same time to the tasteless lament for the homosexual
favourite in Achilles Tatius.[64] But in the end Encolpius' last
words on the matter do not betray sympathy for Lichas: they have
the same kind of cynical black humour as the final gesture of the
widow of Ephesus - disposing of one's former lover. The final
insult to Lichas' corpse is an epigram from Eumolpus.

The entry into Croton has also invited satirical readings:
this is a march on a dead city professionally and obscenely devoted to *captatio*.[65] But this satirists' standby has to be considered in the light of the fun it gives rise to: the informant
stresses that this is no place for literary men: Eumolpus, of all
people, is undeterred.[66] And his imaginative scheme is developed
for its own sake: we should compare the delight that Calasiris
and even Charicleia take in their disguises.[67] An obvious target
for moralists is the story of the mother who pimps for her daughter in the hope of obtaining a legacy from Eumolpus.[68] For
Highet the latter 'treats the girl in a particularly disgusting
and slavish way, although his acts are described as if they were
uproariously funny'. But the humour here is concerned with the
ingenious ruse which Eumolpus needs to invent in order to seduce
his pupil, while still concealing the fact that he is not a crip-
ple. Is all this less funny for being morally neutral? It is
simply a case of one villain against another, while the physical
arrangements are similar to those of the lovers on top of the tub
in Apuleius[69] - with the same element of amused voyeurism as in
the episode of the woman and the ass in the *Onos*.[70] Both of the
latter cases are morally neutral, and it is difficult to see what
is different about this one. Nor are we told that the captator's
daughter objected to being sexually exploited in this bizarre
way.[71]

The last extant episode need be no more serious. Eumolpus
invites his *captatores* to eat him,[72] but Petronius is not obliged
to treat the subject of cannibalism in the manner of Juvenal's
fifteenth *Satire*; it was as open to him to deal with it, if he
pleased, as playfully as Ovid had done with Erysichthon.[73] The

point of this handling is in the cynical brilliance of Eumolpus'
trick to outdo the *captatores*, and the panache with which he fur-
nishes literary precedents for cannibalism. In their narrative
context, Eumolpus' deathbed antics are no more disgusting or emetic than the robbers' plans for Charite in the *Onos*,[74] or the
cannibal rituals in Achilles or Lollianus.[75] There is of course
an ironic contrast between Pythagorean vegetarianism and latter-
day cannibalism in Croton:[76] but refined cannibalism (with a
veneer of learning) is still a proper subject for sick jokes:
among the anthropophagi one's friends are one's sarcophagi. There
is such a thing as vicious virtuosity, and Petronius knew it as
well as Achilles Tatius.

These examples are sufficient to show the difficulties which
moralist positions have still to overcome. The onus is on their
advocates to prove that any single instance of moralising or moral
satire is not being undermined by its delivery, so diluted by its
literary presentation, or so ludicrously exaggerated, that it can
safely be taken as sincere conviction on the part of its author.
Till then we must be content to acknowledge that Petronius is as
adept as any ideal novelist in the ambiguous and ironic manipula-
tion of literature and lovers.

CHAPTER NINE

PHAEDRUS FABULATOR? THE *ONOS* AND APULEIUS

The problems in Petronius are at least in sight of solution. We might reasonably hope that if we knew some more about the 'Greek *Satyricon*', and had the rest of Petronius himself, we should know what it was all about. But in the case of Apuleius we do have the whole novel, and yet we are still none the wiser as to why he should have written the *Metamorphoses* as he did. Once again the main problem is the relationship between comic and serious.

There are relatively few problems in interpreting Λούκιος ἢ Ὄνος, the surviving Greek version whose original was used by Apuleius as the framework of his own;[1] and it is not difficult to see here too a parody of the Greek ideal novel rather than a simple tale told for its own sake.[2] The fun lies in mishandling the conventions of the ideal novel in an extreme and perverse way. In place of the conventional hero, we have a man-turned-ass, so that the author can translate the novel into the milieu of Aesopic fable. The circular construction of the ideal novel plot is well provided by the metamorphosis itself: Lucius cannot resume his amours until he has regained his human shape, and many of the standard diversions of the ideal novel intervene to prevent him: kidnap by robbers, which starts off the wanderings;[3] chance recapture,[4] followed by a robbers' debate on his fate;[5] episodes involving priests and a sorcerer's apprentice,[6] which supply the standard ingredients of religious and magical hocus-pocus respectively; and the affair with the rich voluptuary,[7] who offers enticements similar to those of Melite or Arsake. In several instances the author is able to turn the conventions upside down. The normal standards of the ideal novel call for chastity, however it may be circumvented. But Lucius begins with initiation by an experienced and physically demanding housemaid.[8] The ideal hero can expect to resist the advances of rich and demanding foreign woman: Lucius gratifies his enthusiastic client, with only the slightest misgivings, in the most bestial way.[9] The ideal heroine can expect a public chastity test: here the final spectacle is to

be an ass having intercourse in the theatre with a mass murder-
ess.[10] The ideal *Liebespaar* can look forward to reconciliation
and consummation; when Lucius resumes his human form, his bestial
lover refuses his ordinary human advances.[11]

     Apart from this perversion of the ideal romance, the most
sustained source of amusement - still more easily exploited than
in Petronius - is the protagonist's sexual and physical insecurity. Lucius is uneasy with the horses, who regard him as an intru-
der and an adulterer;[12] or indignant at the prospect of castra-
tion, resolving to commit suicide with his members intact.[13] He
is even afraid to have intercourse with the foreign voluptuary,
in case he does her a mischief,[14] and feels that wild animals will
be ready to attack him in the arena.[15] At the same time he re-
tains a certain puritanical attitude, hence his indignation at
the priests' homosexual exploits;[16] or is ashamed to show off his
sexual feats in front of the whole arena, while evidently enjoying them as such.[17] Like Achilles or Longus, the *Onos*-author
skilfully explores the balance between prudery and prurience.

     Although the fable calls for simple and straightforward nar-
ration, there are also a number of opportunities for incidental
humour en route. The bad boy tells whopping lies about Lucius'
amours, when he cannot even have normal access to the mares;[18]
but the kindly farmer gives friendly advice to have him knackered,
and obligingly offers to do the job for the benefit of Lucius himself.[19] The robbers for their part feign politesse towards the
young lady when they find her trying to escape;[20] and show uncon-
cealed relish at the sheer virtuosity of the fate they have contrived for her.[21] The handling of the rascally priests who use
the cult of Atargatis as a cloak for seduction has caused difficulty: if this is satire, why is there not more of it? But rascally priests and religious trickery are so frequent in the ideal
novels that this incident differs only in degree from the examples
in Heliodorus or Achilles. The author has only had to translate
his charlatans to a suitably low level.[22]

     Apuleius' Latin version of the original Ass-story is much
more difficult to characterise:[23] it is among the most eccentric
ensembles in ancient literature, both in its approach to detail
and in its overall arrangement. The author exploits a much greater variety of mood than the extant *Onos*, so that individual episodes often show an abrupt fluctuation between comic and serious,
and we have to decide whether he is attempting to produce a

genuine balance between moral commitment and entertainment, or
whether these abrupt alternations are themselves contrived as
jokes on the reader which can in turn be related to some more
whimsical purpose. One example will serve as a warning of the
kind of author to be interpreted: at X.2-12 Apuleius announces to
the reader *iam ergo, lector optime, scito te tragoediam, non fabulam legere, et a socco ad cothurnum ascendere*.[24] The tale in due
course ends happily. Devotees of an integrated interpretation of
the *Metamorphoses* have still to admit that Apuleius may not have
known when he began to write how the tale was going to end;[25] if
that is so, the most we can say is that he uses a serious tone for
purposes he has yet to determine, or that he may be striking a
pose which is intentionally ironic, by announcing as serious a
tale which the reader will only long afterwards find to be comic.
By neither explanation will he be wholly serious. The element of
whimsical surprise is also prominent in all three of the major
magic tales: Socrates suddenly dies the moment he is apparently
out of danger;[26] Thelyphron loses his nose and ears, a fact which
the reader could not have anticipated from any previous comments
on his appearance;[27] while Lucius' condemnation in court is
abruptly revealed as a star turn in the Risus-Festival[28] - to be
followed by the grim account of why the mistake over the wine-
skins occurred.[29] The most striking case is perhaps that of the
baker, in which the righteous and resourceful husband is in due
course poisoned by the magic contrivances of his wife.[30] Each of
these twists can be seen as dexterous perversions of the audience's expectations. One must not discount that the elevated tone
of the conversion itself may be a twist of the same order. Nor
is the avowedly tragic element in Apuleius consistently sustained.
Even the grim tale of Charite has its humorous touches. Tlepole-
mus and Thrasyllus are to hunt for wild beasts - if goats are
wild beasts, since Charite will not allow him to hunt anything
more dangerous.[31] And she ends her long and perhaps over-dramatic
suicide soliloquy over the sleeping murderer only at the thought
that seduction is already taking place in his dreams.[32]

It is difficult to characterise Apuleius' humorous diversions, given that variety is itself one of his obvious artistic
aims. But one comic motif is developed again and again in different
disguises. Apuleius enjoys laughter at the expense of the self-
confident braggart who faces sudden and total humiliation. Thelyphron treats the task of guarding the corpse with gay noncha-
lance, asking whether dead men run away in these parts;[33] or

tries to make his vigil a pleasant evening with too many home com-
forts, and commits a further faux pas by offering the widow his
services for any future bereavements.[34] Moreover he remains confident that his vigil has been a success - till the corpse gives
evidence that the witches took his nose and ears, so that he has
to slink shamefacedly away amid laughter.[35] Aristomenes comes off
little better. He has nonchalantly condemned Socrates' associa-
tions with the witch, so that he himself is a marked man when witches actually arrive. Having finally escaped through no virtue of
his own, he instantly dismisses the whole episode as a drunken
nightmare - only to hear an ominously similar account from Socrates himself.[36] The robbers fare likewise, providing the same kind
of humour as their counterparts in Longus or Chariton.[37] For all
their show of bravado they come to grief in ignominious ways, the
gallantry of their names at variance with their ludicrous exploits.[38] And all their heroics are in any case ironic: Lamachus'
'heroism' is concerned with mourning the loss of the arm he uses
to steal and slaughter.[39]

One of the established differences between Apuleius and the
Onos is the former's greater interest in moral tone: wickedness is
to be punished and virtue rewarded. But much of the time this is
in fact an extension of similar hints in the *Onos*, and these have
an ironic undertone which Apuleius has also taken care to exploit.
It is pointless to insist on Lucius' serious indignation against
unjust judges, when the ass pulls himself up for his excessive
asinine moralising: *sed ne quis indignationis meae reprehendat im-*
petum, secum sic reputans: Ecce nunc patiemur philosophantem nobis
asinum, rursus unde decessi revertar ad fabulam.[40] After all,
Lucius has had his fair share of sensual pleasures before his
metamorphosis, and does not take long to regain his appetite for
an attractive consort when the opportunity arises. His own exploits have to be borne in mind alongside his indignation at wicked and deceiving adulterers. It is useful to bear in mind the example of Lucian's *Gallus*, in which the cock fulminates against human dishonesty and luxury, but has to admit to being a sophist and
keeping a mistress himself.[41] Sophisticated animal superiority is
amusing enough; sophisticated animal hypocrisy even more so.

These examples, among many, are sufficient illustration of
Apuleius' whimsical alternation of comic and serious. They do not
encourage the reader to look for a sustained and logical intention
for the work as a whole. But we should examine the practice of
mixing comic and serious elements in comparable contemporary

literature. Scholars in the past have been misled by the assumption that the *Metamorphoses* must be unique;[42] yet it might usefully be considered not as an isolated experiment, but as an extreme and eccentric version of a common one. Those who have look-
ed elsewhere for a blend of comic and serious have tended to assume that Christian homiletic literature will somehow provide all
the answers. Pfister quotes the example of the obedient bugs in
the *Acts of John* to show the sort of comic incongruities which
came naturally in this religious writing.[43] But from chapter VII
it will be clear that such comic effects tend to be rather incidental, even in works without literary self-control; and they are
for the most part the privilege of the sub-literate. It is at
the *other* end of the literary spectrum that the second-century
sophist is likely to approach the problem, through the most urbane and literary works of Plato;[44] and it is here, I think, that
the best explanation we are likely to get for σπουδογέλοιον in
Apuleius is to be found. Platonist interpreters have tended time
and time again to assume that his use of the master must be 'professional' and serious, as befits the author of a *de deo Socra-
tis*;[45] and this path has led to extremes of allegorical exegesis
as surely as those that lead back from the Isis-book. But we
should ask what Platonic techniques can produce when used for
purely narrative ends. The most convenient example is to be
found in Apuleius' contemporary and fellow-countryman Fronto,
writing his own version of Platonic myth for the diversion of his
pupil Marcus Aurelius. He begins with a creation-myth similar to
that of Aristophanes in the *Symposium*:[46] Jupiter divides man into
two - this time by cutting his life into day and night. As in
Plato, division is not enough, and a celestial council is needed
to assign the responsibility for night and rest... but Venus and
Bacchus are already committed! Jupiter accordingly begets Sleep,
who is duly endowed with wings on his shoulder like Amor, and
congenial dreams for mankind.[47]

 I have quoted this delightful fantasy at length because it
shows that a mixture of Platonic technique and conventional Olym-
pian myth will produce the apparently distinctive texture of
Cupid and Psyche itself. One notes in particular the balance between pathos and humour: Sleep has a herb for death (*guttam unam
...quanta dissimulantis lacrima esse solet*), but is not to dash
into men's eyes *curruli strepitu et cum fremitu equestri*, doubt-
less a grimace at the *Phaedrus* charioteer.[48] Yet this ensemble
was put together by the most superficial of rhetors for no more

serious purpose than to persuade a philosophic emperor to have a
good night's sleep. When *Cupid and Psyche* is read alongside such
a text, the need to impose serious religious or philosophic allegory on the former should be called in question.

We should look, then, at the way Apuleius manages *his* Platonic *plasmata*. At the beginning of the *Symposium* Plato offers a
second-hand account of how Socrates did not reach the party in
time, because he was lost in meditation on the way - of course
waylaid by his *daimon*.[49] Is it coincidence that the *Metamorphoses* opens with a second-hand account of how *a* Socrates was waylaid - by a witch?[50] Again, the *Phaedrus* opens with the celebrated stroll beside the Ilissus and its plane-trees; in just such a
locus amoenus Apuleius' Socrates - drops dead.[51] It had struck
the Platonic Socrates as he was about to cross the Ilissus that
he had offended Aphrodite by his speech on love; is it coincidence that Apuleius' Socrates is struck by his lover the witch's
vengeance the moment *he* bends over the stream?[52] What sort of
game is going on here? The author has woven an eccentric pot-
pourri of magical slapstick from several easily recognisable Platonic features, twisted or turned upside-down at will: Apuleius
begins with a *divertissement* in Platonic black magic.

It is in the light of these procedures, and not of Book XI,
that the reader comes to *Cupid and Psyche*. The delightful nature
of this tale is self-evident, and so is the considerable range of
humorous effects. It is also so complex and literary that we
should at least suspect that it is just such another playful syn-
thesis, until such time as a papyrus provides us with evidence of
a fully-fledged predecessor.[53] The details are easily accountable in terms of the most familiar classical mythology. Psyche
is abandoned, like Andromeda; persuaded by a jealous rival to
want to see her lover as he really is, like Semele; punished by a
jealous goddess with perpetual wandering like Io; sent to recover
dangerous objects, like Jason, Orpheus, or Demeter; and allowed
to open a forbidden box, like Pandora. It is to this amalgam
that Apuleius has attached his Platonic credentials with the allegorical labels of Love and Soul. It need not be seen as much
different from Fronto's allegory of man and Sleep, or the fore-
going Platonic *jeux* in Apuleius himself. Here too he has allowed
himself a mythical and folkloresque projection of Plato, coloured
with sophisticated humour[54] and incorporating a large pot-pourri
of romantic elements. In the end too there is still at least an
ambiguity about any 'moral' of the allegory that pleasure is the

child of love's union with soul: that might be the moral of every
romantic tale that ends happily ever after, and Psyche has her
fair share of sexual fulfilment. Apuleius is able to practice
the same sort of brinkmanship between physical love and fairy-
tale sublimity as Longus.

So far, then, whimsical wit and Platonic *jeu d'esprit*. But
the real oddity of the *Metamorphoses* is its form. Apuleius has
used an anti-novel about a man changed into an ass, thickening
the texture and insetting a number of extra stories of a kind not
very different from the original. So far his technique is predictable. He is an accomplished if rather undisciplined rhetori-
cian,[55] but his procedures are at least intelligible. Yet the
two major developments we could never suspect on the strength of
the epitome alone: a large interpolated tale entirely different
in ethos from the Ass-tale, and finally an abrupt conversion-
scene in which the narrator appears to change his identity, and
appends a long account of his initiation to the cult of Isis.
What is it all supposed to mean, if anything? A mystery of this
magnitude has attracted an enormous amount of speculation.[56] Because Apuleius is demonstrably eccentric by nature and intention,
it is hard to feel one's way through the interpretations. Apuleius himself would have believed just about anything, and so
anything can be believed of him. Numerous analogies can be suggested, without needing to be pressed too far, because the author
himself would not discipline himself to carry them through. It
is tempting to turn him into another Fulgentius.

But that is a last resort. Before we begin the search for
hidden meanings, we must once more ask what the author's less
mannered contemporaries were doing with their common heritage.
That will give us a foundation on which Apuleius could impose his
own personal eccentricities. Rhetorical experiments with the
blending of comic and serious were current sophistic practice,
and not always received as the author intended: Lucian, intoxi-
cated with the literary side of Plato, wrote a bizarre dialogue
Nigrinus, which makes sense only in terms of Platonic pastiche.
The considerable controversy over this last piece shows how trea-
cherous and equivocal the literary re-assemblings of Plato can
be.[57] What Lucian did was to tie the preliminary banter of the
Phaedrus to the conversion-scene at the end of the *Symposium*, in-
serting between them his idea of an elevating philosophic discourse.[58] An equally bizarre *epideixis* can be found in Dio Chrysostom, whose *Borysthenicos* (*Or.* 36) is concerned with an incident

in the course of his wanderings: he had come across a receptive
audience in the wilds of Borysthenes, and ended his discourse on
the divine city with a quasi-Platonic myth.[59] In fact it is an
absurd tongue-in-cheek improvisation based on the charioteer myth
in the *Phaedrus*, but attributed, with a number of wry asides, to
the Persian magi. Dio makes a final apology εἰ δὲ ἀτεχνῶς ὑψηλόν
τε καὶ ἐξίτηλον ἀπέβη τὸ τοῦ λόγου σχῆμα ... οὐκ ἐμὲ ἄξιον
αἰτιᾶσθαι.[60] He knows how to conclude his performance with a
flourish of Plato at play in exotic surroundings.

Does Apuleius attempt to use a similar sophistic formula?
We have already seen that he draws on motifs from the beginning
of the *Phaedrus* and *Symposium* for his tale of Aristomenes; and he
has positioned his myth of Love and Soul in the centre, like the
myths of Soul in the *Phaedrus* and Love in the *Symposium*.[61] Does
he carry through the scheme and leave a whimsical Platonic *sphra-
gis* at the end? On Apuleius' performance so far we should have
expected him to combine some of the literary diversions at the
end of the *Phaedrus* and *Symposium*, and attach them to the end of
the *Metamorphoses*; we should also have expected some sort of surprising twist to this material. Now the major literary 'events'
at this point in the Platonic sources are a playful Egyptian myth
about Thoth, and Alcibiades' confession of his conversion by Socrates.[62] Apuleius has indeed come up with something which seems
to correspond to both: for the playful Egyptian myth we now have
a serious Egyptian cult; for a confession of Alcibiades we have
Lucius' own. It might be reasonably argued that if this was the
scheme Apuleius intended to execute, he has not done so as clearly here as he did in the tale of Socrates or *Cupid and Psyche*.
It is a counsel of despair to point out that Apuleius seldom executes any design with consistency, though that is also true. Instead it is worth noting that the elements suggested by the end-
ings of the *Phaedrus* and *Symposium* at this point are the very
ones most difficult to explain: why else does Apuleius opt for
Isis (out of his many initiations); and why the motif of conversion and autobiography as well as the simple salvation required
to end the story? We might suspect on the other hand that the
abandonment of direct reference to Plato and the advent of Isis
may reflect some change of plan en route. Yet these two strands
were surprisingly easily associated,[63] and there is a good case
for suggesting that Plato was a catalyst in this most un-Platonic
ending. Nor was he the only one. Apart from the rescuing deity
at the end of ideal novels, we should also bear in mind the

closing stages of the other great Latin *Metamorphoses*. After an
equally whimsical and convoluted series of episodes, and an equally bewildering alternation of moods, Ovid arrives at a high-flown
sermon on transmigration, delivered by Pythagoras himself, and
elevates a near-contemporary in the final apotheosis of Julius
Caesar.[64] Apuleius produces a corresponding range of surprises,
combined in a highly personal way. If any other sophist had set
himself the task of blending the standard ending of a novel with
that of the *Symposium*, the *Phaedrus*, and Ovid's *Metamorphoses* the
result would no doubt have been different. But like Petronius,
Apuleius has skilfully exploited the possibility of convergence;
what he has lost in clarity he has gained in suggestion and rich-
ness of texture. But that makes it all the harder to probe for
specific 'meaning' or 'significance' behind his techniques.

But is book XI entirely serious? One looks in vain for any
consistent comic undermining of the description of Lucius' con-
versions and initiations: Apuleius has not chosen to practise the
technique of λέξις ἐσχηματισμένη used in the sacred descriptions
of Lucian's *de Dea Syria*. But as in the tale of Charite, Apuleius does not seem to be able to remain unequivocally serious
for too long.[65] The procession of Isis is not without its carnival diversion, including an ass with wings stuck on, walking beside a frail old man, so that you would take him for Bellerophon
and it for Pegasus: Apuleius scarcely needs to add: *tamen rideres
utrumque*.[66] Yet the speech of the priest to Lucius has no suspicions of a Calasiris, or of Achilles' priest of Artemis.[67] But
how do we interpret his lecture to Lucius? To turn the hero's
asinine adventures into a cautionary tale at this stage ('Let
that be a lesson to you, Lucius'), is at least ambiguous.[68] The
initiation which follows is securely based on Isiac ritual, yet
even this is surrounded by the kind of flippant equivocation
familiar in Heliodorus: *Ecce tibi rettuli, quae, quamvis audita,
ignores tamen necesse est*.[69] And the following initiation to the
mysteries of Osiris is conducted by a lame priest Asinius, whose
name Apuleius explicitly connects to his own fate.[70] Again the
effect is at least ambiguous: does it really take an ass to ini-
tiate an ass? Moreover it is particularly striking that the two
final initiations of Apuleius are said to be profitable to his
career: inter alia the conversion carries a flippant aside ('so
now you know why I am such a successful orator, and it was well
worth the investment').[71] And just before the end we are con-
fronted with the surprise that Lucius is now *Madaurensis*,[72] and

so is identified with Apuleius, yet the ending swings back from
whimsical surprise to piety.

Once more the *Phaedrus* provides a commentary on the moods of
its devotees: just before the end Socrates shifts his allegiance
from the *Eroticus* of Lysias to the new career of Isocrates,[73] the
up-and-coming rhetor with a touch of philosophy, who can expect
to rise to higher things; at the corresponding point in the *Metamorphoses* we find a different sort of *eroticus* of Lucius giving
way before the new career of Apuleius, the philosopher who is
rising higher through Isis. Socrates ends with a prayer to Pan;
Apuleius we leave as a priest of Isis.[74] The author maintains
his ingenious and more or less perverse relationship with Platonic holy writ, and still remains unpredictable to the last.

It is almost irrelevant to ask whether such a writer is
comic or serious. As in the final book of Heliodorus, it is next
to impossible to predict on what note he will even bring himself
to finish. Again Aristides and Lucian provide useful co-ordina-
tes: the former attributes his success in deadly earnest ad nau-
seam to the grace of Asclepius; Lucian attributes *his* to a tongue-
in-cheek literary conversion to *Paideia*.[75] Apuleius, as ever,
seems to alternate whimsically between the two moods and attitudes.

Some will find this solution as speculative as so many
others; but to detect a whimsical and literary *clef* in the text
at least serves to break the arbitrary link between seriousness
and allegory which has prevailed for so long. The presence of
Allegory, symbol, Platonic allusion and Isiac initiation are obvious and undeniable: but they do not of themselves demand serious and didactic interpretation. If one kills off Socrates at
the beginning by black magic, gives the soul an affair with a
Hellenistic Cupid behind the back of her future mother-in-law,
then turns an asinine Alcibiades into an Isocrates Madaurensis,
one is playing games:[76] to substitute an aretalogy of Isis for
the *Phaedrus* myth of Thoth is perhaps the cleverest and most surprising of them.

Such interpretation does not preclude the verdict that book
XI exhibits 'an artful but sincere Evangelism'.[77] But this description raises another question, to which we are never likely
to find a satisfactory answer. The problem is that Apuleius'
brand of evangelism is a quite different commodity from that of
Aristides, for example, because his temperament itself is so

different. In the end the present author will find himself asking what sort of priest of Isis Apuleius would have made: a Calasiris before his time would be a reasonable guess. From the
mouth of such a figure, we have finally to ask what any moral
would actually have turned out to be. Apuleius seems to be saying something like 'So now you all know that I owe my present
priesthood to Isis; the man she rescued from an inglorious career
as an ass was none other than myself. And I would strongly ad-
vise the curious among you not to watch witches undressing...'.
If a key is to be found, one need not look much further back than
the last 'anticipation' before the transformation back to Lucius.
The hero sees an ass in the procession of Isis... with wings
stuck on for the carnival - as whimsically and incongruously as
Book XI is tagged to the rest of the work. The spirituality of
an ex-ass, however meticulous the details of his conversion, is
a little like that of Eliot's sanctified hippopotamus: both re-
quire a wider wing-span than either author is prepared to provide.

CHAPTER TEN

CONCLUSION

We have now to characterise the nuances of the novels in re-
lation to one another; and we might be tempted to re-write, or
even un-write, the history of the genre in the process. My con-
tention is that the extant novelists tend to use their sophistication with a light and mischievous touch; and that they are con-
sequently less committed in their attitudes to sentimental love
and religion than is usually assumed. The result of our small
sample is often deliberately contrived ambiguity, which in turn
may often be seen as the careful and artistic control of humorous
or playful elements. Only Apuleius seems exceptional, in that he
appears to embody religious conviction, or even propaganda, in a
comic novel. But in so doing, he may still be bound, in contrast
to the genuinely religious romancers, by eccentric but identifi-
able literary aims. How much comedy or wit is needed to make
such authors less than serious? Much less, it seems to me, than
the ideal novelists provide, and much more than is offered by
novels of genuinely popular character or religious conviction.
What Chariton, Heliodorus, Achilles and Longus have in common is
the consistency of whatever nuances they choose to develop; and
each of them has much more than the minimum rhetorical and dramatic skill required to manipulate his resources in an individual
way.

The most obvious vehicle for humour or wit is that very religion so often held to be the mainspring of the novel. Where
there are heroines there will be protecting gods and demons;
where there are gods and demons, there will be room for dupes[1] -
and for any number of sophisticated variations on the Platonic
professions of Eros (*Symposium* 203D): love the philosopher, en-
chanter, sorcerer and sophist.

Each of the four competent ideal novelists contrives a lover
who is somehow less than heroic. Chariton uses his resources of
irony to ensure that the hero's laments are incurred at the wrong
places;[2] Longus has a suspicion of the mock-heroic on a tiny
scale;[3] Achilles' hero is melodramatic in laments, passive in

87

crises, and thanks to the *Ich-Erzählung*, a self-confessed hypocrite as well;[4] while Heliodorus' is a puppet of the heroine
throughout. All four authors have an ambiguous attitude to the
main theme: Callirhoe's deceived second husband has to be deceived yet again;[5] Chloe never finds out about Lycaenion;[6] Leucippe
and her father are misled by Pan, Artemis, and the careful expurgations of Clitophon.[7] Only in Heliodorus do both parties have
nothing to hide: but there is still the suspicion that chastity is
a fetish to be exploited for something other than its own sake.[8]
And in all four a fair number of minor characters are singled out
for comic treatment.

     Certain topoi recur with monotonous regularity, a fact which
has probably done more than anything else to condemn the ideal
novel in the eyes of the majority of scholars. What is less
often recognised is that many of these belong to a repertoire of
standard jokes: three authors make *impudicitia* an *officium*; three
use the conceit of love as a disease for comic effect;[9] three
make Love the mightiest of the gods, and follow up the paradoxical implications in some form: he must be greater than the kings
of Persia, or more powerful than Zeus - whether seen through the
eyes of the sophisticated lover or the rustic.[10] And in like
manner, as we have noted, *initiamentum* or *Scheintod* scenes, lovers' laments and erotic symposia can all be exploited for the purposes of wit.[11] So too can paradoxography: the manner in which
both Heliodorus and Achilles use their pseudo-learning is easily
contrasted with the gauche decorations of Philostratus in the
Life of Apollonius of Tyana: Achilles' Nile is a river which
tells no lies, keeps its appointments, and does not like to be
unpunctual; Heliodorus's, on the other hand, is a river whose
mystical operations almost all ranks of the pious misunderstand.[12]
The very inclusion of such topics in an erotic context opens the
way for playful incongruity.

     It is important to understand the literary aspirations of
each of the novelists, and to consider the playful effects of
much of their *mimesis*. Each of these writers uses New Comedy as
part of his mixture of genres, with predictable results for all
the others. It is one thing for Phaedrus to rehearse speeches
about love beside the Ilissus; quite another when a New Comic
lover gets his hands on it and sees the possibility of a quick
conquest.[13] The familiar politics of the *Anabasis* and *Hellenica*
crumble into elegant farce when a New Comic heroine moves on
Ionia and Persia.[14] Heliodorus manages to preserve a more

respectable façade than either Chariton or Achilles, with his
ponderous affectations of Homer, Herodotus, and Tragedy; but if
the New Comic idiot Cnemon is relegated to an episode, the techniques of the *Helen* are not.[15] Longus is indeed different, cutting down the world of the novel into the miniature of Theocritus
and the *adoxon*. But there is the same sense of playful incongruity: the *deus ex machina* - or his representative - is still
recognisably a bourgeois parent straight from Menander.[16] How
can we sum up the novelist's outlook? The Greek tragedian has to
leave Iphigenia on the altar and get the fleet to Troy: the novelist will either fake the sacrifice or turn Agamemnon into a New
Comic father.

The major fragments can also be suspected of playful intent.
This should be regarded as certain in the case of Iamblichus, who
stands close to Achilles, and of *Metiochus*, perhaps somewhat
closer to Chariton; but it should also be considered in the case
of *Ninus*, again close to Chariton (and even Longus, in some respects); or Lollianus, somewhere between Achilles and Heliodorus;
and Antonius Diogenes, possibly the same. All have an element of
sabotage, or potential sabotage, directed against something, in
most cases against paradoxography or religious trickery once
more; in the case of *Ninus*, against the lovers' innocence and
anti-heroism. And in each case the author's technique in other
respects is sufficiently sophisticated to enable us to assume
that we have not come upon isolated snatches of humorous material
destined to mislead. All this underlines the need for caution in
the handling of *Iolaus*, which may still come from a humorous
ideal novel. The fringe romances offer no consistent picture or
criterion. The pressure of external commitment and the inade-
quate technique of the writers operate against the consistent use
of humorous material. It is here that the distinction between
'popular' and 'sophisticated' novels can be most readily applied.

Should we attempt to redefine the novel? Reardon has re-
cently produced a new formula: 'we should expect only a light-
weight, fanciful, sentimental tale, something not very serious,
not very *spoudaion*'.[17] I should be tempted to go further. If we
attempt to piece together a standard outline from Chariton,
Achilles, Longus and Heliodorus, we shall be left with something
like the following: 'a young New Comic couple fall in love,
thanks to the whim of Eros; Tyche plays a number of tricks to
prevent their union, though they manage to repay it in kind; they
leave behind them a trail of duped pirates, bogus rituals,

dubious military campaigns, and absurd natural history; a smiling
god wryly connives at their infidelities to rivals, or they over-
play their devotion to chastity. And love and sex are somehow at
variance with the background of history, civic assembly, temple
precinct, or pastoral landscape'. There is more than a subtle
distinction between this paraphrase and Perry's or Weinreich's[18]
evocation of the same standard events. In brief: four out of
five ideal novelists have a light touch, and the personality and
technique to maintain it.

Moreover it is in their techniques of playfulness that the
novelists have displayed their individuality most clearly. Chari-
tons' special interest is in pretences working at cross purposes to reveal charmingly one-dimensional character-types, at
the expense of their historical situation. Longus smiles at the
results of beautiful innocence; while Achilles specialises in a
refined and cynical use of rhetoric and sex, Heliodorus in religious shams succeeding in conventional religious machinery going
wrong. The predominant images are significant: in Chariton love
is a diplomat,[19] in Longus, the traditional little boy;[20] in
Achilles, a sophist;[21] while in Heliodorus, the presiding deities
spend most of their time mocking their characters or producing
sacred tragicomedy,[22] duly criticised by their characters. The
four writers also differ in their sympathy and commitment to the
couple, with Chariton and Longus wholly devoted to their lovers,
though still treating both of them with detached amusement; while
Heliodorus devotes his time to puzzling them and enabling them to
puzzle others with a whole repertoire of religious riddles, and
Achilles is wryly delighted at their physically cruel discomforts.
But most of all the four differ in their degree of sophisticated
ambiguity. Chariton has none, out of choice rather than lack of
skill, I should argue; Achilles' intentions are almost always
clear, yet after V.27 the reader has to look at the narrator in a
rather different light. But in the other two ambiguity is an end
in itself: Longus with his avowed σωφροσύνη can detach himself
from the action and exploit the interplay between ideal innocence
and sexual experiment; Heliodorus constructs a vast maze as a con-
tainer for his religious equivocations.

Such, then, is the general pattern suggested by our extant
evidence. What does it tell us about what is typical and exceptional in the novels, or about their origins and development? On
the face of it Achilles does indeed contrive a sick burlesque of
the basic love story, while Chariton, Longus and Heliodorus

present playful and sophisticated variations on it. The relationship of the four texts is similar to that between Ovid and
the other Elegists: each is capable of smiling at love and lovers,
while still basically committed to their operations; but Achilles
and Ovid stand cynically and skilfully apart. The exception to
this pattern is not Chariton but Xenophon, whose religious commitment, lack of skill and simple earnestness mark him out as a
genuinely naive popular purveyor of the same basic material.

The real question is how we relate this pattern to the question of origins. I am not convinced that *Ninus* is to be classed
with Xenophon rather than Chariton;[23] if that is accepted, we
should also accept that the ideal novel was just as probably a
sophisticated creation as an unsophisticated one. In other
words, there is no particular reason to assume that the first
novelist wrote a humble entertainment like the *Chariton* Mime
rather than, say, a smartly historical version of Menander's
Phasma. The Greek novel may always have been a light, literary
and sophisticated genre, and we may yet find ourselves calling
Anthia and Habrocomes or *Joseph and Aseneth* a *Zersetzung* of romance, rather than Chariton a *Zersetzung* of historiography. We
should not necessarily feel sadder and wiser about such a possibility; we should instead be considerably more amused by the
novels we have, and prepared to examine future discoveries accordingly.

In the so-called comic novel the balance between a romantic
plot and the author's modifications and diversions is equally important, and perhaps even more difficult to determine. I am not
convinced by Perry's insistence that Petronius, the *Onos* and Apuleius are all unique works for unique purposes.[24] They all make
use of the Ideal novel as one of their chief humorous vehicles;
but their smiles, reservations or sabotage at the expense of the
plot do not need to be kept within bounds in the same way; these
writers have produced anti-novels, but the temptation to parody
anything and everything frequently complicates the demands on the
reader.[25] Both Petronius and Apuleius found new and comic uses
for traditionally serious and elevated material; the former emerges as the virtuoso saboteur, the latter as the bizarre individu-
alist. In both cases the balance between romantic plot and the
author's modifications and diversions is crucial, and still difficult to determine. Both play with their mixtures of moods and
materials in a whimsical and elusive way. In both cases I have
argued for a basically comic reading; but it is well to

acknowledge that an able author who sets out to defeat the reader's expectations will be able to hold out indefinitely against scholarly rationalisation. At the end of the *Symposium*, Socrates tries to prove to Aristophanes and Agathon that the tragic poet must be a comic poet as well. Plato lets the comedian fall asleep first. When applied to novelists rather than playwrights, their problem is infinitely longer and more soporific: I leave tragic interpreters of the novel to lose any further sleep over it.

Two Demotic Romances: *Nectanebus* and *Tefnut*

In recent years several scholars have noted the possibility
of Egyptian influence on the Greek novel;[1] and even if the first
novel itself can be adequately explained in wholly Greek terms,
it cannot be ruled out that novelists drew on Egyptian material.
We should note that at least two romantic fragments of demotic
origin contain some suspicion of comic content. The sixty-odd
lines of the Greek version of the *Dream of Nectanebus* break off
just at the point where the sculptor Petesis, commissioned to
complete Nectanebus' temple-inscription, sees the most beautiful
girl he has ever set eyes upon.[2] Since the author has told us in
advance that this man was a wine-bibber by nature, and was bent
on relaxation before work,[3] we can reasonably suspect that the
temple will not be finished. The girl should turn out to be an
amusing diversion, whether or not she ever finds her way into the
arms of Nectanebus himself.[4] We have at least one parallel for
the association of erotic intrigue with an oriental monarch's
founding of a temple, in the hilarious story of Combabus in
Lucian's *de Dea Syria*.[5]

Tefnut is a rather different case:[6] remnants of a Greek re-
working of an original demotic text, in which Hermes (Thoth) persuades the goddess (Tefnut) to return from her self-imposed exile
as a cat in Ethiopia. The intelligible portion of the Greek version opens[7] with what appears to be a variant on the frequent
romantic game of oaths and counteroaths;[8] and to the demotic the
Greek translator has added a joke about the riddle of the sphinx.
In spite of the ingenious and simple style, the array of exempla
from Hermes leaves a suspicion of ironic and rhetorical treatment.[9] What will happen to Tefnut when she is enticed back to
Egypt by these eloquent overtures? We know what nearly happens to
Hermes, who has to counter Tefnut's hostile change into a lion
with a timely fable about the lion and Thanatos,[10] told by per-
sonifications of ἀκοή and ὄρασις. We should compare the sophisticated presentations of fable in Achilles between Conops and Satyrus;[11] and Lucian's conversation between Menelaus and the highly
volatile Proteus: καὶ εἰς λέοντα δὲ εἰ ἀλλαγείης, ὅμως οὐδὲ τοῦτο
ἔξω πίστεως.[12] The succeeding fables maintain the game of politesse between animals: we have some ironic courtesies between a

lion and two terrified wolves rooted to the spot; and respectful
overtures from a mouse to a lion.[13] In the remainder of the action, Hermes (changed into a lynx), rescues Tefnut (changed into
a gazelle) from her impious hunters: such antics of the gods are
reminiscent of Lucianic or Ovidian games with metamorphoses.[14]
This sort of material could conceivably have been accommodated in
the digressions of the normal novel; but it could equally well
have provided the material for a mythical fantasy in the manner
of *Cupid and Psyche*, or for an elaborated fable like the *Onos*
itself.[15] Given the well-established tradition of native Egyptian
animal stories, however, such connexions can on present evidence
only be seen as possibilities.

APPENDIX II:

Some Comparative Approaches to Petronius

The traditional moralist approach to the *Satyricon* has frequently made use of assumptions about the didactic character of
much ancient literature. More difficult to come to terms with
are views which employ analogies with serious, complex and morbid
twentieth century literature to establish the serious and pessi-
mistic world-view of Petronius. Such techniques are illuminating
when used in careful conjunction with available ancient evidence;
but it is worth indicating some pressing problems of criteria to
which they have given rise. Arrowsmith[1] and Bacon[2] well illustrate the complexities and pitfalls when they use quite different
readings of *The Waste Land* to throw light on the *Satyricon*, and
predictably arrive at divergent readings of the latter.

It has often been tempting to impose a perspective from modern literature while leaving available ancient analogies out of
account. Arrowsmith produced the most uncompromising programme of
symbolism, inspired by Eliot: the *Cena* presents an obsessive conjunction of sex, impotence, defecation and death.[3] But too much
of the material is just as readily seen as Cynic cliché at home
in Menippean Satire; and Cynic cliché is easily, often compul-
sively, multiplied by variation. No-one will deny that the result is sometimes black humour, but the fact that it is black
does not mean that it is serious: one might as well argue that
Lucian was obsessed by death or immorality respectively when he
wrote *Dialogues of the Dead* and *Dialogues of Courtesans*.

Zeitlin[4] takes comic and picaresque elements in Petronius
into account, and draws comparisons with subsequent picaresque
fiction; but she still simply assumes that the total effect must
have moral connotations: by portraying chaos, the argument runs,
Petronius is setting out to reflect the chaos of the human condition.[5] This approach is based on the unproven conviction that
every work must have a message, however diffusely or perversely
expressed.[6] But why should stylistic order mirror world disorder?
A basic weakness of Zeitlin's case is that it applies equally
readily - and unconvincingly - to the Greek ideal novel plots as
well. If Petronius mirrors a chaotic world-order dominated by
chance and preoccupied with deception and *trompe l'oeil*, so do

they. And the chaos in Trimalchio's symposium is no more striking
than that in the comic symposia of Horace's Nasidienus or Lucian's
philosophers; while the detached spectator at a banquet is one
more Cynic cliché (like the chaos in world-order itself). It is
difficult to enumerate the distortions created by Zeitlin's approach
to literature: she provides no proof and no criterion to dis-
tinguish the symbolic *cri-de-coeur* from the ironic literary game.

Averil Cameron[7] arrives at similar results by another route,
by comparing the use of myth in Joyce, Pound and Eliot in order
to suggest that Petronius employs a symbolic and serious use of
myth which forms a coherent pattern behind the fun in the *Satyricon*. But her suggestions fall too short of proof to have cumulative force. One example: it is difficult to place much significance on the claim that the most pervasive recurrent motif common
to the *Satyricon* and *Ulysses* is the image of Daedalus.[8] Of the
four instances in Petronius, only two involve direct use of the
name - as a nickname for Trimalchio's chef,[9] and as a misnomer for
the maker of the wooden horse.[10] Is this insistent symbolism,
Freudian slip, or an hilarious reminder that Trimalchio's mythology is *sui generis*? A third appearance of Daedalus has to be
wrenched from a commonplace allusion to the labyrinth, to which
Encolpius compares Trimalchio's house;[11] a fourth from still further afield.[12] There is not much basis for comparison between
Joyce's obsession with Daedalus and Petronius' casual allusions.

Allied to Cameron's use of association is the unproven assumption that tricks and deceit are serious. I can make little of
the following chain of assertions: 'Petronius' use of the Daedalus
image is characteristically sly, but no less serious. Daedalus
is the maker of tricks and deceit. His products are not what they
seem: nor is the *Satyricon*. As the ultimate trick is art itself,
so too the ultimate puzzle or labyrinth here is the work itself,
a blending of form like the blend of man and beast in the labyrinth's inhabitant, the Minotaur'.[13] But the same result could be
demonstrated for Heliodorus, without its following that his work
is wholly serious.[14] And on Cameron's rules of association we
should easily be able to prove that Trimalchio was Odysseus and
the Cyclops and many another, without really establishing more
than that Petronius is a clever opportunist with literary comparisons.

But arguments based on comparative literature and *Zeitgeist*
can be met on their own ground. P. G. Walsh[15] draws attention to

the relationship between American interpretations of Petronius and
the modern urban society which may have helped to condition their
outlook: it is tempting to see Petronius as the prophet of urban
decay and ailing materialism merely because a modern literature
has grown up against it; but comparison is just as able to distort
the scholar's perspective as to broaden it. The difficulty is
that the moment one discovers that the twentieth century can still
produce amoral satire, it can no longer be maintained that its
society must engender protest as a matter of course. Modern urban
culture has not just produced *The Waste Land*: those who compare
it to the *Satyricon* should also compare its parodies as well, from
which moral criticism may be embarrassingly absent: yet their
realism is just as similar to Petronius' as to that of Eliot himself (...*Cloax is the vilest drink, gouging / Pockets out of your
giblets, mixing / Frenzy and remorse, blending Rot-gut and white-
ants. / Jalap has a use, laundering / Colons with refreshing suds,
purging / The lower soul with gentle motion*).[16] If modern con-
cepts of sick humour for its own sake were applied to antiquity
as assiduously as philosophical world-views, then the *Satyricon*
might fall into place with less difficulty.

A Note on the Literary Parodies in Petronius

The question of moralising or mock-moralising is even more difficult to answer in the case of Petronius' literary parodies. The difficulty in parodying a banal moralist such as Seneca is that one person's banalities are much the same as anyone else's by nature. But this does not preclude Seneca from being an obvious target in the elevated meditations of Trimalchio or Encolpius.[1] It is difficult moreover to isolate stylistic parody from that of content; but Petronius is able and entitled to sabotage both together. The role of context and speaker often determines the balance of evidence. It is important that the platitudes on slavery, for example, are assigned to Trimalchio:[2] what comes so glibly in a Senecan epistle has a different nuance when affected by a vulgar ex-slave.

The same questions arise in a slightly different form in connexion with the explicitly literary topics: Encolpius' discussions with Agamemnon and the two large poetic effusions of Eumolpus. Is Petronius laughing at these outbursts, or setting himself up as a literary critic and advocating serious literary ideals? Sullivan argues extensively that Petronius' criticisms represent the author's own reactions and critical principles, while accepting that his view of moral tirades is literary and parodic.[3] This combination of aims is not impossible, though obviously inconsistent. It is of course tempting to see Petronius as the old-fashioned enemy of all that Senecan prose style stood for, but does that automatically make him, as opposed to his characters, an admirer of Cicero or Virgil? It is just as possible for Petronius to be a literary as well as a moral cynic, rejecting what is pretentiously old-fashioned as well as what is pretentiously new.

Sullivan's careful formulation seems to ignore the possibility that Petronius was an opportunist in criticism as in so much else: ('How could an author who offered criticisms of contemporary rhetorical style...write in a style which is consonant with his critical principles, and then not hold them?').[4] But was Petronius' own style governed by 'principles' rather than convenience? He had after all to keep the narrative going in *something*, without necessarily setting out to advocate it, any more than

Aristophanes 'advocates' his own trimeters when he ridicules those
of Aeschylus or Euripides. The fact that Petronius ridicules extremes of style, high and low, may be due to the fact that they
are easy to ridicule, rather than that he approves of the means required to frame and offset them.

In the episode of the rhetorical school Petronius has other
aims which have to be combined with any critical motives we may
wish to ascribe to him. The point of the fun is that a young
rogue and an old one are prepared to compromise their principles
to get dinners - as Ascyltus' reproaches later make only too clear
(*Sat*. 10). Sullivan allows Petronius to identify with the senti-
ments expressed by Agamemnon ('it is clear that Petronius is a
traditionalist'); but how is this compatible with implying that
the author treats Agamemnon's speech with ironic sophistication?[5]
If Petronius so passionately believes these platitudes, then why
does he assign them to someone whose presentation will make their
platitudinous nature all the more obvious? All we can say is that
'it is clear that *Agamemnon* is a traditionalist' content with the
all-time greats. The same applies to the criticism in the *BC*
fragment. The fact that Petronius coined the quotable *curiosa
felicitas* should not blind us to the possibility that it was intended as a banality, or to the hollowness of Eumolpus' pretentions. Again it is important to stress how much so-called literary criticism verges on moral criticism. It is a moral decline
that has brought Agamemnon's decline of rhetoric; and a moral decline that has brought Eumolpus' civil war and the lapse of taste
in present-day handling of it. In Petronius' hands, banal pro-
nouncements on literature belong closely with those on life: they
are no less shallow and not demonstrably different in intention
from the platitudes of the freedmen, for example; and Eumolpus'
literary hypocrisy goes hand in hand with his moral hypocrisy.

The crucial test is the interpretation of the *Bellum Civile*
fragment (119-124). Is it intended as parody or as serious literary criticism? The main problems have been two: Eumolpus' verse
is competent, and we have perhaps insufficient material to establish why it should be seen to be mediocre. Secondly, neither
Westerburg nor his successors have been able to point to any obvious central focus for parody. As a result there has been an impressive consensus that Petronius is setting himself up to 'improve' on Lucan;[6] but this makes Eumolpus a passable poet when the
context suggests that he ought to be an awful one. It also makes
Petronius less than a brilliant critic or artist on his own

account. Collignon's glib sententia has held the field: 'parodier
tout le monde, c'est ne parodier personne'.[7] This has encouraged
a concern to find a single, simple purpose and target for Eumolpus' effusions. But both external and internal considerations
favour a more complex view.

In the first place a parody does not *need* to be so simple:
the infamous parody of Socrates in the *Clouds* confounds him with
his supposed enemies,[8] while Lucian's *Podagra* laughs at encomium
and Tragedy together, and each at the expense of the other.[9] In
the second place, Petronius has given ample indication elsewhere
of his versatility in burlesque. The treatment of Trimalchio is
far from simple, and his pretentious garblings of literature or
mythology are not systematic and predictable travesties, but ec-
lectic and whimsical ones.[10] Nor are we entitled to expect him
to take any particular line here, though he has left us in no
doubt as to the talents and reputation of Eumolpus.[11] The argument that he has no reputable mouthpiece to assign his own ideas
to is unconvincing:[12] Petronius was at liberty to invent a real
poet with a more dignified contribution to the action - if he
really wanted such a poem to be seen in a creditable light. But
the *BC* is still an out-and-out fiasco, if only for one overriding
reason: purple passages have squeezed out the action altogether.
Almost sixty lines - a fifth of the whole - are taken up with
tedious, commonplace, and occasionally lascivious moralising;[13]
the divine council of war between allegories takes up nearly as
long again, and is naturally concerned with expressing the same
moralisings from the opposition point of view.[14] By line 182
nothing has happened: Eumolpus has got as far as a speech by
Caesar, flanked with horrific omens. The only action is that
Caesar takes the decision - to cross not the Rubicon but the
Alps![15] Of course this is an excuse for natural disasters, followed by an equally well-worn *locus* on rumour at Rome; the only
significant action is one line on Pompey's flight. Then a mass
evacuation of deities - as panic-stricken as the population itself - and finally the climax of 294 lines: we are assured
that *Factum est in terris, quicquid Discordia iussit. Parturiunt
montes?* Would Petronius really have put his name to a traditional
Epic with an action of two lines? Or is Eumolpus' effort that
'little thing of my own' to end all such trifles?

The *BC* can therefore be seen as brilliant disaster rather
than competent mediocrity.[16] And within so disastrously ill-
proportioned an action there is no reason why Petronius should not

attempt simultaneously to imitate Lucan in some particulars, contradict him in others, exaggerate him in others yet again, con-
found him with material that does not belong to him (or belongs
as readily to others) - and bring down others along with him. The
whole amalgam will still be a scathing reflection on its author
Eumolpus. If Petronius executes all these possibilities simultaneously, it will not be surprising if some of these legitimate
aims of the parodist begin to get in each other's way. But Lucan
is a lot worse when weighed down by pretentious Virgilian machinery and Horatian moralising, all conveyed by the mouth of an
ageing and lecherous Eumolpus.

An important chiastic relationship between the two long
poems has been persistently missed. In the *Troiae Halosis*, Petronius of course gives us a contemporary Silver handling of the
subject-matter of the *Aeneid* (as from Seneca); here we have a
Virgilian version of contemporary Silver subject-matter. Both
hybrids are equally bizarre and absurd, and should be seen as two
complementary literary disasters.[17] All that is missing here is
the stones which end the *Troiae Halosis*; instead the *BC* is prefaced with the farts of Giton and Eumolpus' servant.

1   *Der griechische Roman und seine Vorlaüfer*, Leipzig 1876.
     References are to the repagination of the third edition
     (ed. Wilhelm Schmid, Leipzig 1914, retained in the fourth
     (ed. K. Kerenyi, 1960; repr. Darmstadt 1974). For excellent
     short accounts, see O. Weinreich, *Die griechische Liebes-
     roman*, Zurich 1962 (= *Nachwort* to R. Reymer, *Heliodor:
     Aithiopika. Die Abenteuer der schönen Charikleia*. Ueber-
     tragen von Rudolf Reymer, Zurich 1950); A. Lesky, *Geschich-
     te der griechische Literatur*[2], Berne 1963, 913-927; B.P.
     Reardon, *Courants littéraires grecs des II*[e] *et III*[e] *siècles
     après J.-C.*, Paris 1971, 309-403. For the latest biblio-
     graphical reports, G. Sandy, *CW* 67 (1974), 321-359; for pre-
     vious reports, O. Mazal, *JOeBG* 11-12 (1962-63), 11-26;
     13(1964), 29-69. The *Acta* of the International Conference
     on the Ancient Novel, held at Bangor, Wales in July 1976,
     are now available (as *Erotica Antiqua*, *ICAN* 1976, ed. B.P.
     Reardon, Bangor 1977; hereafter *Acta*). None of the forty-
     eight papers summarised deals with this subject as such, but
     over half of them have a bearing on it.

2   Novels or romances? B.E. Perry adopts the latter label
     throughout *The Ancient Romances, A Literary-Historical
     Account of Their Origins*, Berkeley and Los Angeles 1967,
     while admitting that the two terms have been used by classi-
     cists interchangeably. I have preferred the term 'novel' to
     'romance', in order to discourage the arbitrary division be-
     tween fantastic and realistic fiction too often used to
     divide Petronius and Apuleius from the Greek examples. It
     also helps to place ancient fiction closer to the modern
     novel than to medieval romance. This has left me with the
     slightly unusual expression 'ideal novel' for what is
     normally described as either 'the Greek novel' or 'ideal
     romance'. But since the 'ideal' element is so often open to
     question, both parts of the latter expression are unsatis-
     factory.

3   By Wilcken's publication of the first fragments of the
     Ninus-text (*Hermes* 28, 1893, 161-193).

4   *AJP* 51 (1930), 93f., cf. *The Ancient Romances* (hereafter *AR*)
     97.

5   *Roman und Mysterium in der Antike*, Munich-Berlin 1962. The
     latest commentator on Achilles Tatius, writing in the same
     year as Merkelbach, claimed that 'there is a touch of humour
     in this book that is totally missing in the other romances'
     (E. Vilborg, *Achilles Tatius, Leucippe and Clitophon: a
     Commentary, Studia graeca et latina Gothoburgensia* XV,
     Gothenberg 1962, 12).

6   Cf. Rohde 184.

7   For humour in Homer, see for example V. Bérard, *Introduction
     à l'Odyssée* II, Paris 1933 ('l'urbanité homérique', 61-104;
     'le gros rire', 105-158). B. pays particular attention to
     ancient editorial awareness of such effects; their existence

was realised, if not always approved. As such features can
be used to establish the individuality of novelists, so they
are now being used to argue afresh the individuality of
Homer: so J. Griffin, *Homer on Life and Death*, Oxford 1980,
183ff. (laughter); 79 (deception).

8   XIV.191-359 (to Eumaeus); XVII.415-444 (to Antinous);
     XIII.254-295 (to Athena). For the whole subject, A.F. Decker,
     Ironie in de Odyssee, Leyden 1955; P. Walcot, *Ancient Soci-
     ety* 8(1977), 1-19, the latter with a popular explanation of
     what he well calls 'teasing'. The Second Sophistic enjoyed
     Homer's lies: Lucian cites Odysseus' tales as authority for
     lying both in *Philopseudes* 1 and *Verae Historiae* I.3.

9   VI.57-70; V.160-191.

10   154-177.

11   For an excellent characterisation see B. Snell, *Die Entdeck-
     ung des Geistes*[3], Hamburg 1955, 353-70 ('Ueber das Spieler-
     ische bei Kallimachos'), especially 359f., mixtures of
     learning and humour; 361, childlike naivety; 364f., rhetori-
     cal fun.

12   See now A. Lesky, *Vom Eros der Hellenen*, Göttingen 1976,
     101-5.

13   See E. Fraenkel, *Horace*, Oxford 1957, 194-196; cf. Lesky
     ibid. 123-129.

14   Lucian, *D. Mar.* 15; Achilles I.1.

15   260-309.

16   III.90-155. The only lengthy treatment of the *Argonautica*
     in the context of the novel is A. Heiserman, *The Novel before
     the Novel, Essays and Discussions about the Beginnings of
     Prose Fiction in the West*, Chicago 1977, 11-40; but he seems
     unaware of this dimension of the poem.

17   III.932-937.

18   IV.948-960. Cf. IV.665-682 (grotesque contents of Circe's
     laboratory).

19   IV.1111-1120.

20   For his contribution to the novel in general, Rohde 33-37.

21   As a somewhat bedraggled and heavily disadvantaged *miles
     gloriosus* (415ff.; 453; 393-396).

22   72-591; 293ff.; 1050,1077.

23   1253ff.; 1278.

24   There is less hope than ever of consensus on the balance of
     elements in the *Helen*. Among recent literature, see espe-
     cially A.N. Pippin, *CP* 55 (1960), 151-163; as Anne Pippin
     Burnett, *Catastrophe survived: Euripides' Plays of Mixed
     Reversal*, Oxford 1971, 76-100; G. Zuntz, 'On Euripides'
     Helena: Theology and Irony', *Entretiens sur l'Antiquité
     Classique* VI, Vandoeuvres-Geneva 1960, 201-242; C. Wolff,

HSCP 77 (1973), 61-84 (all inclining to comic interpretations). A.M. Dale in the introduction to her edition,
Oxford 1967, vii-xvi, and A. Podlecki, *TAPA* 101 (1970),
401-418 still emphasise the tragic dimension.

25   E. Schwartz, *Fünf Vorträge über den griechischen Roman*[2],
     Berlin 1943; cf. Reardon 315; Perry *AR* 32-43.

26   V.1.8ff.

27   V.1.14,18; VI.1.41.

28   II.3.17-20; II.2.6-9; IV.5.54f.

29   I.3.11; I.3.10.

30   II.2.11-16; VIII.4.13-17.

31   Their falsehoods are explicitly parodied by Lucian's *Verae
     Historiae*(I.3).

32   *De oratore* II.240.

33   It is by ignoring this dimension that Perry (*AR* 70f.) seems
     to me to misinterpret the implications of writing a 'histo-
     rical' novel in antiquity. It is not just a matter of tak-
     ing shelter in an established prose genre in order to gain
     respectability; Perry failed to appreciate the amusement
     value of correcting known charlatans with equally false
     corrections; and that was something which any writer of
     fictitious *Persica* or *Babyloniaca* after Ctesias was likely
     to be doing.

34   For illustration of its comic effects, Ph.-E. Legrand, *Daos*,
     Paris 1911, is still useful (comic βωμολοχικά, 585-613;
     character and situation, 624-633).

35   See *infra* 52.

36   Menaechmus II feigns possession by Apollo, (Plaut. *Men.*
     837-875); Menander's *Hiereia* included a pretext of exorcism,
     (Körte-Thierfelder I pp.146ff., II p.82), *Phasma* a heroine
     worshipped in a bogus ritual and mistaken for a ghost (*ibid.*
     I pp. livff., 134); *Deisidaimon, Thettale* and *Trophonius*
     at least suggest similar situations (*ibid.* II pp.45ff.,
     75ff.; 141f.).

37   P. De Lacy, 'Plato and the Intellectual Life of the Second
     Century A.D.', in *Approaches to the Second Sophistic*, ed.
     G.W. Bowersock, Pennsylvania 1974, 4-10.

38   For recent studies on Plato and humour, see e.g. P. Plass
     TAPA 98 (1967), 343-364; G. Ardley, *Philosophy* 42 (1967),
     226-244; H.D. Rankin, *C&M* 28 (1967), 186-213; and now M.
     Mader, *Das Problem des lachens und der Komödie bei Platon*,
     Tübinger Beiträge zur Altertumswissenschaft 47 (1977).

39   *Phaedr.* 230E-234C; 237A-241D.

40   *Phaedr.* 229Bff. (Boreas and Oreithuia); 279BC (token offer-
     ing to Pan), 238CD, 241E, 244Aff. (jokes on divine inspira-
     tion); 235D, 236B (and on divine honours); 278BC (humorous
     directives to the dead).

41   *Phaedr*. 274C-275B.

42   Arist. *Rhet*. III.18.7, 1419b 3.3. For the whole subject,
      see M. Grant, *Ancient Rhetorical Theories of the Laughable*,
      University of Wisconsin Studies in Language and Literature
      21, Madison 1924, especially conclusions, 139-148. But the
      absence of criticism of the novel, and the character and
      context of so many of the ancient discussions, restrict
      their application to such works. For Cicero, see A. Haury,
      L'Ironie et l'humour chez Cicéron, Leyden 1955; K. Geffcken
      Comedy in the Pro Caelio, (*Mnemosyne* Suppl. 30), Leyden 1973.

43   Apart from Petronius' attack (*Sat*. 1.1), cf. Quint. II.10.
      1-12; Tac. *Dial*. 28-35; Sen. *Contr*. IX *praef*. 2ff.; S.F.
      Bonner, *Roman Declamation* Liverpool 1949, 71-83.

44   *Contr*. IV *praef*. 10.

45   *Vitae Sophistarum* 542.

46   *Phalaris*, I.4; for *de Dea Syria*, see my *Studies in Lucian's
      Comic Fiction*, *Mnemosyne* Suppl. 43 (1976), 72-82.

47   For a useful collection of illustrations, A.S. Pease, *CP* 21
      (1926), 27-42.

48   *Infra* 36f., 43.

49   Heliodorus III.5.4/*Phaedr*. 252Dff.

50   Longus II.7.2; IV.18.1.

51   *Quaest. Conv*. II.1.10.

52   For a useful enumeration of erotic topoi, Rohde 155-177.

53   For comparable prose examples, cf. Lucian *D. Meretr*. 9, 13,
      15.

54   Propertius I.16.

55   Plato *Symp*. 194E-197E.

56   I have not treated humorous effect in language and style as
      a separate subject: the deliberate and ponderous rhetoric
      of the novelists is well known, and has been frequently
      condemned as gratuitous affectation; it only becomes comic
      if it is foisted on inappropriate and trivial subject-matter.
      Once the character of the content is itself established,
      stylistic humour follows as a matter of course.

57   As late as the 'fifties L.P. Wilkinson had still to protest
      the very existence of humour in Ovid (*Ovid Recalled*, Cam-
      bridge 1955, 163n.3; since then the subject has been exten-
      sively covered, notably by J.M. Frécaut, *L'Esprit et l'Hu-
      mour chez Ovide*, Grenoble 1972, to which add the discussion
      in G.K. Galinsky *Ovid's Metamorphoses, An Introduction to
      the Basic Aspects*, Oxford (Basil Blackwell) 1975, 158-209.

58   For the *Euboicus*, Rohde 542f.; *Studies* 94-98 (some parallels
      with Lucian).

59   Cf. J. Bompaire, *Lucien écrivain, Imitation et création*,
      Paris 1958, 587-655.

60   *AJP* 51 (1930), 93f.

61   Two contributors came to the problem from English litera-
      ture: S.L. Wolff, *The Greek Romances in Elizabethan Prose
      Fiction*, New York 1912 (repr. 1961), bore the stamp of his
      time and collected some five pages of humorous effects,
      while classifying much potentially playful material as mere
      rhetorical figures tastelessly deployed: but at least he
      recognised humour as a legitimate part of the ancient novel-
      ist's equipment (as did his Elizabethan subjects). There
      is a much fresher and more constructive approach to humour
      in parts of A. Heiserman's posthumous book (*supra* n. 16),
      which I saw only after completing my own text. It appears
      from his footnotes, however, that H. knew the novel exclu-
      sively through translations, and the book is far too erra-
      tic to be serviceable to scholars. But it is a curious
      gloss on the history of this problem that his apparent un-
      awareness of Rohde(!) was probably an advantage. In subse-
      quent chapters I have not attempted to relate my examples
      more than incidentally to those of either author, in view
      of the much wider differences in overall perspective; but I
      have recorded typical instances of disagreement with Wolff.

62   For detailed criticism of Merkelbach's case, see the lengthy
      review by R. Turcan, *RHR* 163 (1963), 149-199; against that
      of his predecessor Kerenyi's *Die griechische-orientalische
      Romanliteratur in religionsgeschichtlicher Beleuchtung*,
      Tübingen 1927, see A.D. Nock, *Gnomon* 4 (1928), 169-175.
      Merkelbach does not sufficiently allow for community of
      material between ritual practices or cult-myths and litera-
      ture as such: see Reardon 396f. He has shown that bread
      and wine or father and brother were sometimes used as mys-
      tical metaphors; on the strength of what he then assumes,
      the whole of English literature would be converted into an
      unfathomable eucharistic drama. His arguments totally fail
      to come to terms with the novels as works of fiction: for
      symbolism to be the only possible explanation, texts have
      to fail to make literary sense. But in any case both
      Kerenyi and Merkelbach have to resort to scholarly alchemy
      to make their case: M.'s effort to project Mithraism into
      Iamblichus (where the name does not occur) is almost as un-
      convincing as his failure to deal with why there is in-
      sufficient mystical content in Chariton. For a further un-
      successful attempt at this latter problem, see R. Petri,
      *Ueber den Roman des Chariton, Beiträge zur klassischen
      Philologie* 11, Meisenheim am Glan 1963.

63   *RM* 89. The difficulty is that while this quality of reli-
      gious writing does exist, so also does outright satire of
      religion. Aristophanes had both at his command, and both
      occur in Egyptian literature, a point very unsettling for
      Merkelbach's thesis. In particular he himself cites a pre-
      Homeric satire on the Egyptian pantheon (cf. J. Barns, *Mit-
      teilungen aus der Papyrussammlung der Oesterreich. Natio-
      nalbibliothek*, Neue Series, 5.folge, Vienna 1956, 34).
      Alexandrian Greek novelists were just as capable of using
      this kind of Egyptian material as they were of using areta-
      logies - without devotional connotations of any kind.

64   Much of the substance of Merkelbach's arguments lies in the
      symbolic correspondence between works of art in the novels
      and the action itself. Of course such contrivances can be
      used as a basis for mystical and not-so-mystical allegory:

one thinks of the classic pseudo-Cebes' *Pinax*. But such
correspondences can be very easily turned into pure fun.
The gallant disguised as a eunuch in Terence, *Eunuchus*
581-591 carries out his seduction with a picture of Jupiter
and Danae beside him for reference.

65   *MH* 22 (1965), 133-154.

66   *Ibid.* 135.

67   *Ibid.* 144.

68   There is also the problem of regression from classical to
      popular works. We happen to know that πρωκτολαλία appears
      in Old Comedy and the *Chariton* mime before it finds its
      way into Lollianus' *Phoenicica* (*infra* 143 n. 68); but the
      Iphigenia in Tauris precedes the *Chariton* mime (whatever
      their relationship), and the trick chastity test in Achil-
      les (IV.13f.) precedes its celebrated popular handling in
      the Tristan Legend (Béroul 4213).

69   We are not concerned with the outlook of ponderous moralists:
      the Younger Seneca could not see the fun in Ovid's flood
      (*Nat. Quaest.* III.27.3); and one may doubt whether he would
      have seen himself in the alleged parodies of his own prose
      style in Petronius (*infra* 99); nor need we be concerned
      with the fantasies of allegorising idiots in late antiquity;
      Fulgentius and his kind were capable of finding edifying
      nonsense in any sort of text.

70   This was a cleverly forged philosophical treatise meant to
      be misunderstood: see G. Strohmaier, *Philologus* 120 (1976),
      117-122.

71   III.7f.; *infra* 36f.

72   H.W. Fowler, *A Dictionary of Modern English Usage*, Oxford
      1926, s.v. humour.

73   For general discussion of humour in antiquity, see e.g.
      W. Süss, *NJklAlt* 45 (1929), 28-45; Id., *Lachen, Komik und
      Witz in der Antike*, Zurich/Stuttgart 1969; E. de St.-Denis,
      Essais sur le rire et le sourire des Latins, Paris 1965;
      J.-Ph. Cèbe, *La caricature et la parodie dans le monde ro-
      main antique des origines à Juvenal*, Paris 1966. There is
      now an excellent Bibliography in Mader *o.c.* (*supra* n.38).

74   For more general surveys, based on a variety of disciplines,
      see e.g. J. Huizinga, *Homo Ludens, A Study of the Play-
      Element in Culture*, English translation by R.F.C. Hull,
      London 1949; J. Feibleman, *In Praise of Comedy: a Study of
      its Theory and Practice*, New York 1939, 123ff.; G. Duckworth,
      The Nature of Roman Comedy, Princeton 1952 (repr. 1971),
      305-330; Ch. Mauron, *Psychocritique du genre comique*, Paris
      1964; and Mader *o.c.* (*supra* n. 38).

75   One thinks particularly of strictures against the use of
      obscenity in declamation: the Elder Seneca makes it quite
      clear that Greek declaimers expected to get off with more
      than their Roman counterparts (*Contr.* I.2.22, cf. 23).

76   L. Radermacher's *Weinen und Lachen, Studien über antikes
      Lebensgefühl*, Vienna 1947, is a series of short and charming

excursions, unfortunately not extending to the novel.
L. Giangrande's *The Use of Spoudaiogeloion in Greek and
Roman Literature*, The Hague/Paris 1972, makes no serious
claims to scholarship, by the author's admission. E.S.
Ramage, *Urbanitas: Ancient Sophistication and Refinement,
University of Cincinnati Classical Studies* III, Oklahoma
1973, deals briefly with the novel (14-39), but only as a
source for gentlemanly attitudes; he does not raise the
connexion, obvious enough in the extant novels, between
urbanity and wit.

77   I adopt that of Eric Partridge, *A Dictionary of Slang and
       Unconventional Usage* II (Supplement), London 1970, sense 5:
       (humour that is) 'often too unreal, or even too ludicrously
       morbid, to carry a deadly sting'.

78   Bergson illustrates the delights of mechanical comedy from
       the chain of events which begins with a horse eating an
       Italian straw hat (*Le Rire. Essai sur la signification du
       comique*[43], 1924, 84); one need only compare Longus' goats
       eating the osier mooring-rope of the Methymnaean ship
       (II.13.4). And there could be few better parallels to the
       antics of Clitandre and Sganarelles' daughter in *L'Amour
       Médecin* (*ibid*. 169f.) than Heliodorus' presentation of
       Calasiris' consultation with Charicleia (IV.5.3ff.). It
       should of course be noted that Bergson's material is drawn
       from the French successors of Classical New Comedy, so that
       his perspective is deceptively close to that of the novel-
       ists themselves.

79   Bergson *ibid*. 94f.; 42; 90ff.; 82; 151.

80   *Ibid*. 5; 28, 69, 78f.

81   For a cautionary tale on the distinction between naivety
       and pseudo-naivety, see K.J. Dover, *Theocritus, Select Po-
       ems*, London 1971, lxviif. His instance (from Corinna) also
       illustrates how readily problems of humour can be entangled
       with those of chronology.

1   Chariton's humour has only been briefly studied, in the im-
     portant article by Perry, *AJP* 51 (1930), 115-127. But
     apart from discussing irony and characterisation, he tends
     to quote long stretches without further comment, and seems
     to imply that any humour must be confined to and insepar-
     able from these categories; while he discusses Theron to
     the detriment of many other touches. Others have ignored
     or denied the existence of any such effects: so for example
     the two recent translators, K. Plepelits, *Chariton von
     Aphrodisias: Kallirhoe*, Stuttgart 1976, and G. Molinié in
     his Budé, Paris 1979 ('un roman d'analyse psychologique bâti
     sur un canevas de tragédie', 35); Heiserman, *Novel before
     the Novel o.c. (supra* 104 n.16), 75-116.

2   On the relationship between New Comedy and the novel, see
     C. Corbato, *Quaderni Triestini sul Teatro Antico* 1 (1969),
     5-44 (on the *Sicyonius*, 15). It should be noted that this
     play also contains a villain Theron; the possibility of
     direct borrowing is attractive.

3   For this last aspect, Reardon, *Phoenix* 23 (1969), 294-297;
     Courants 340-347.

4   *Phoenix* ibid. 295; *Courants* 341f.

5   II.9.1-11.3.

6   Cf. Reardon *G&R N.S.* 23 (1976), 124.

7   II.9.6.

8   II.11.1f.

9   II.11.2.

10   II.11.3: πυθώμεθα σοῦ καὶ τοῦ πατρός· μᾶλλον δὲ εἴρηκεν·
     αὐτὸς γάρ μοι παραστὰς ἐν τοῖς ὀνείροις 'Παρατίθεμαί σοι'
     φησι 'τὸν υἱόν'. Μαρτύρομαί σε, Χαιρέα, σύ με Διονυσίῳ
     νυμφαγωγεῖς.

11   II.4.5; II.2.8.

12   J. Helms, *Character Portrayal in the Romance of Chariton*,
     The Hague/Paris 1966 concerns himself with principles of
     characterisation, but his system allows little recognition
     of humorous effect (e.g. 141f., but not 88-94, on Theron).

13   Cf. Rohde 527f.: 'In solchen und ähnlichen Seltsamkeiten
     spürt man freilich recht stark die Haltlosigkeit des späten
     Graeculus' (528); Reardon 349.

14   I.1.7.

15   VII.1.8ff.

16   II.3.6.

17   III.2.1ff.

18   VIII.5.14.

19   VIII.6.9.

20   III.3.12

21   III.3.17. Other amusing touches at I.12.3, III.3.9 (appre-
      hension about the integrity of his fellow-pirates); III.3.9,
      I.12.1 (mercenary motives for his courteous treatment of
      Callirhoe).

22   I.2.5.

23   VI.1.10; Achilles I.5.7.

24   I.7.6; I.7.5.

25   V.4.4.

26   V.8.10, V.8.6. Cf. the excitement at the assembly at Mile-
      tus (III.4.2), or the improvised beauty contest with Rhodo-
      gyne, which the crowd misjudges (V.3.5ff.).

27   When the case reaches Babylon, the satrapy support Mithri-
      dates against Dionysius, but then the latter against Chae-
      reas (V.4.1; VI.2.1f.). The women divide according to their
      jealousy of Callirhoe (V.4.2), the king and queen according
      to their self-interest (VI.1.6ff.).

28   V.4.11.

29   III.3.8.

30   I.3.3; III.4.4-17; VIII.6.5f.

31   III.4.10. The whole Syracusan assembly wants to go on the
      embassy to Asia; Hermocrates has to point out that five will
      be enough.

32   I.11.6; cf. the banter between Lucian's Athenians and Scy-
      thians, *Theme and Variation* 14, 82; *Studies* 13.

33   I.11.7.

34   To the eunuch Artaxates Greeks are μικραίτιοι καὶ λάλοι
      (when he wants to present Callirhoe as a liability), VI.6.7;
      to Stateira they are ἀλαζόνες καὶ πτωχοί (when she cannot
      bring herself to believe the reports of Callirhoe's beauty),
      V.3.2.

35   *AJP ibid.* (*supra* n.1) 123-127.

36   I.1.12ff.; VII.6.7.

37   II.5.10f.; IV.5.10.

38   V.10.4f.; VIII.4.4.

39   IV.1.1; similarly Callirhoe is busy burying Chaereas in
      Miletus, while he is working in chains in Caria (IV.2.1).

40   III.1.1ff.

41   III.6.4; III.9.1. Cf. the confusion over the couple's stay
      in Babylon (VI.9.6ff.-VII.1.4).

42   Dionysius maintains that Leonas judges Callirhoe by country
      standards, Stateira that Dionysius in turn judges her by
      those of the Greeks (II.1.5; V.3.2).

43   III.6.2f.; IV.1.7-12.

44   V.10.

45   First kiss trick: II.7.7 (Dionysius); excuses to see Calli-
      rhoe: IV.6.2 (Pharnakes), V.9.7 (Artaxerxes). Chaereas also
      seems to take a fancy to Stateira and Rhodogyne, and sugg-
      ests them as handmaids for Callirhoe (VIII.3.1).

46   II.1.6; VI.3.1ff.

47   IV.5.10. Chariton also makes use of conventional ψεῦδος:
      Theron's tall story is a tissue of Odyssean lies, culmina-
      ting in a boast of piety (III.3.17); he has another about
      Callirhoe's departure from Sicily (I.12.8). The suitors
      set in train a whole range of New Comic tricks (I.4.3ff.);
      and even Chaereas himself pretends to be sailing an Egyptian
      merchantman (VIII.6.2,4).

48   For the use of 'historical' material see Perry, *AJP o.c.*
      (*supra* n.1) 100-104; *AR* 137-140; also F. Zimmermann, 'Chari-
      ton u. die Geschichte', *Sozialökonomische Verhältnisse im
      alten Orient und im klassischen Altertum, Tagung der Sektion
      alte Geschichte der Deutschen Historiker-Gesellschaft*, 12-17
      Oct. 1959 in Altenburg, Berlin 1961,329-345. Rohde's atti-
      tude was characteristically condescending (523): 'Er schreibt
      eben einen echten 'historischen' Roman, dergleichen zu meist
      auf sehr naive Leser berechnet zu sein pflegen'; but he re-
      cognises the exact nature of what Chariton has produced:
      'historisch-romanhaften Tragelaphen', 'historische Maske-
      rade'. Reardon (341) stresses that Chaereas' outlook is
      Hellenistic rather than Fifth-century, and so 'apolitique'.
      But Chariton can extract humour from this situation: one
      might almost say that the whole conduct of the novel is
      'anti-politique'. For the Hellenistic world, as R. says,
      Chaereas' love in itself is of no importance: but its tri-
      vialising effect on the facts of history is of interest both
      to the Hellenistic reader and to the Second Sophistic.

49   I.2.3; I.1.11f.

50   Cf. Rohde 527f.; but he does not seem to see the joke.

51   VI.1.11.

52   V.8.8. By a similar mutation of history Chaereas cannot put
      to sea because his wife and the queen of Persia keep talking
      as a pair of inseparable gossips (VIII.4.10). Apollonius
      Rhodius has used bourgeois goddesses; here we have a bour-
      geois Hellenistic queen. M. Braun, *History and Romance in
      Graeco-Oriental Literature*, Oxford (Basil Blackwell) 1938,
      11, misses the point of Chariton's handling of Artaxerxes:
      'When we look back...upon the Herodotean Cambyses episode,
      we can easily judge how strongly the Oriental royal person-
      ages have been humanised, but also trivialised, in the Greek
      romances under the influence of popular philosophical views,

in this case, on the law-abiding king in contrast to the
lawless tyrant'.

53   VIII.7.11.

54   VIII.7.2.

55   VIII.7.2.

56   I.1.4; I.1.12; III.9.4 (cf. also Aphrodite's marriage-
      policies, II.2.8); VI.3.1. Such personification is of course
      a well-established source of amusement in Hellenistic poetry
      and Roman Elegy, and continues in sophistic prose: even
      Xenophon of Ephesus can write a perfunctory ecphrasis of
      Ares without his weapons, being led to Aphrodite by Eros
      (I.8.3), while Lucian describes Cupids playing in the ar-
      mour of Alexander (*Herodotus sive Aetion* 5).

57   VIII.6.12.

58   III.4.18.

59   VII.3.9.

60   V.4.4. K.H. Gerschmann, *Chariton-Interpretationen*, Diss.
      Münster, Frankfurt 1974, p.V recognises the possibility of
      a parodic or ironic treatment of a mystery tradition: but
      the allusion here amounts to no more than Platonic ornament.

61   III.2.15 (nymph); II.3.6 (goddess); VI.3.4f. (both).

62   I.9.4 (she herself mistakes Theron for the same, *ibid.*, or
      Chaereas for an *eidolon*, V.9.4). In the same vein Chariton
      allows amusing rationalisation of dreams, which the magoi
      and Dionysius interpret according to their self-interest and
      wishful thinking respectively (VI.8.3; II.1.2).

63   II.3.9.

64   VI.2.2ff.

65   VI.2.4.

66   VI.2.7.

67   V.7.10.

68   IV.4.1.

69   III.3.4.

70   III.3.5f.; V.10.1.

71   II.3.6f. As is the king's: how can he reject his ancestor
      the sun's gift of Callirhoe (VI.1.10)? Artaxates manipula-
      tes his master's piety accordingly (Callirhoe must be a god-
      dess, VI.3.5); and when things look like going wrong too
      fast, only the king can resist one (VI.3.8).

72   Among erotic topoi, Chariton plays with lovers' oaths (III.
      2.5), cf. Achilles VIII.5.2f., Longus II.39, Heliodorus
      IV.18.6; or with lovers' excessive reverence for the belov-
      ed's name, IV.2.11 (cf. II.5.6). Lovers' distractions

affect the king even at the hunt (VI.4.4), while lovers re-
conciled hear Polycharmus as from the bottom of a well
(VIII.1.10).

73   Cf. Achilles III.3f.;   Longus I.30, III.27.4; Heliodorus
     I.1ff.

74   III.4.6.

75   IV.5.10.

76   I.7.1f.

77   V.6.10; IV.1.12.

78   III.3.7.

79   VIII.2.4.

80   I.5.4.

81   V.10.6.

82   V.3.1-9.

83   V.8.5.

84   V.10.5.

85   I.1.6.

86   III.4.18; 4.7.

87   VI.8.1.

88   VIII.1.4.

89   Rohde misses the point of such phrases as λόγου θᾶττον
     (528f.). Chariton is aware of the absurdity of an action
     in which so much is no sooner said than done, and does not
     hesitate to draw attention to it.

90   Perry emphasises Chariton's sincerity (o.c. supra n.1, 93);
     Reardon (345) speaks of his lack of sophistication. But
     sophistication cannot always be measured by elaboration of
     clauses or the inclusion of ecphrases on amorous plants:
     later Greek literature embraces Atticism of theme and treat-
     ment as well as language. Chariton is sophisticated; and
     like Longus, he is smiling for much of the time (cf. Rear-
     don 348: l'histoire n'est pas en fait si simple, elle le
     paraît seulement. En somme, le récit peut être naïf, mais
     l'auteur ne l'est pas. Il sait ce qu'il fait'.

Notes to Chapter III

1   D.P. Durham, *CP* 33 (1938), 1-19, interpreted *Clitophon and Leucippe* as direct parody of Heliodorus, on the basis of a chronology now disproved by Vogliano's publication of a 2nd or 3rd-century papyrus of Achilles, *SIFC* 15 (1938), 121-130. On the same false chronology Rohde (514f.) and O. Schissel, *Entwicklungsgeschichte des griechischen Romanes im Altertum, Rhetorische Forschungen* II, Halle 1913, 62-81, interpreted Achilles as merely inept and tasteless imitation. Wolff (160ff., cf. 154f.) had already listed a number of humorous touches, many of which he himself did not approve. Others are sympathetic to Durham, but with some qualification: Vilborg, Commentary (*supra* 103 n.5) 12, rejects parody, but allows humour only here among the novels: cf. Perry, *AR* 106 ('close to burlesque'; Reardon 365 (of the chastity test), 'je ne dis pas parodie, mais une de ces grimaces que l'auteur fait partout au thème de l'amour'; R.M. Rattenbury, *New Chapters in Greek Literature* III, ed. J.U. Powell, Oxford 1933, 254-57 ('not exactly parody'). Heiserman, *Novel before the Novel o.c.* (*supra* 104 n.16) 118-130 goes considerably beyond Durham and Reardon in recognising comic effect, and does not hesitate to employ the term comedy as such. His chief contribution is to recognise the humorous side of incongruous rhetoric, as Wolff so often fails to do. But even here his account is too erratic to be illuminating: (the dismemberment of Leucippe is not comic because it has been mistakenly prophesied by Leucippe's mother, 124; nor is there any doubt about the point of Leucippe's chastity, 127).

2   VIII.1.4. Lucian provides comparable slapstick when he bites the proferred hand of Alexander of Abonouteichos (*Alexander* 55).

3   VIII.1.5.

4   VIII.2.3. Heiserman *o.c.* (*supra* n.1) also sees comedy here (127), but I do not see what it has to do with Clitophon's alleged irrational guilt.

5   V.15.4ff.

6   V.11.2. So Heiserman *o.c.* (*supra* n.1) 125.

7   Durham *o.c.* (*supra* n.1) 11; Reardon 365 (cf. Wolff 129f., who is however morally revolted by Leucippe).

8   II.24 (cf. Wolff 161).

9   V.27.2 (Cf. Wolff 155, but again he seems to miss the comic point).

10   VI.21f.

11   V.27.4. There is also a distinct irony about Clitophon's use of the expression εἴ τις ἐστὶ καὶ ἐν ἀνδράσι παρθενία: he first adopts it to assure Leucippe by letter that he has

imitated her chastity (V.20.5). So of course he has, but
the reader knows that he was already sexually experienced
with prostitutes *before* he had her shining example to imitate (II.37.5). And the reader will find out that he sleeps
with Melite very shortly afterwards (V.27.3f.). In the dé-
nouement he is able to assure Leucippe's father that εἴ τις
ἄρα ἐστὶν ἀνδρὸς παρθενία he has maintained it as far as she
is concerned (VIII.5.7). The repetition of the phrase reminds the reader that this oath is as equivocal as the
former, since Clitophon has added Melite to his conquests in
the meantime! There is also deliberate ambiguity in his confession ἔπαθόν τι ἀνθρώπινον (V.27.2). This can be taken as
'I felt some human sympathy' (for the frustrations of Melite); and 'I felt like any other man' (presented with the
prospect of an effortless conquest); for the two senses, see
Rattenbury-Lumb on Heliodorus VII.21.1. Scholars have been
slow to appreciate the cynical implications of this episode.
R.M. Rattenbury, *Proceedings of the Leeds Philosophical and
Literary Society, Literary and Historical Section* 1 (1926),
70 suggests that Achilles 'only ventured to break the tradition (of chastity) with many apologies'. There is no
trace of them when he is cleverly covering up his tracks in
VIII.5.2-7. Of course Clitophon shows a sense of proportion
(Reardon 364) and Melite is realistic (Wolff 154-7); but
neither consideration detracts from the effect of the episode
on the plot as a whole: the hero gives in to a sex-starved
adulteress the moment both of them find out their partners
are alive! Clitophon's comment in V.27.1 says a great deal:
διδάσκει γὰρ ὁ Ἔρως καὶ λόγους: 'Sex is never lost for reasons'.

12   III.15.4f.; V.7.4; VII.3.8.

13   Xen. Ephes. IV.6.2ff.

14   Achilles III.11.7; III.18.2f. (to Wolff's evident disgust,
     161). Heiserman, *o.c.*(*supra* n.1) sees the fun.

15   IV.10.6.

16   IV.9.2.

17   I.1.10f.; III.7.5ff.

18   I.3.4; II.23.5.

19   III.15.4f.; III.8.1ff.

20   V.3; V.5.

21   I.12.5-13.2.

22   *AA* I.321f.

23   III.7.9.

24   Reardon (364) commends the first two books of Achilles for
     their 'psychologie pratique', but adds 'L'on peu se plain-
     dre de la lourdeur de la psychologie théorique d'Achille
     Tatius'. But these displays act as comically incongruous
     flourishes between the business of cynical sexuality; with-
     out them the contrived anti-climax at the end of Book II
     would be impossible; as it is Panthea's dream undoes all the

schemes and erotic meditations at a stroke.

25   II.8.

26   II.37.7ff./38.5, cf. Reardon 365.

27   IV.8.4. Achilles also includes a 'first kiss' trick (II.7).
      By comparison with those of Chariton (II.7.6f.) and Longus
      (I.15.4-17.1) it is much more contrived and piquant, involv-
      ing Clitophon's pretending that he was stung by a bee (after
      ps.-Theocritus XIX).

28   V.27.3f.

29   I.16.1. For the popularity of Plato, see *supra* 105 n.37.

30   II.29.

31   II.35-38.

32   V.22.5.

33   I.10.1; V.27.4; V.27.1.

34   I.8.1ff. Cf. the specious arguments in the debate between
      the two Loves, II.35-38 (Semele's fate; Zeus' coming down to
      earth for women, but taking Ganymede back to heaven).

35   *Ibid.*

36   III.10.3f.

37   I.13f. Again, the moment Leucippe is beheaded, it is time
      for a lecture on 'time the healer' (V.8.2).

38   13-19.

39   θρήνων ἄμιλλα, I.14.1. Other examples of erotic bombast:
      Melite's epigram κενοτάφιον μὲν γὰρ εἶδον, κενογάμιον δὲ
      οὔ, which Clitophon himself considers a memorable joke,
      though half-serious on her part (V.14.4), cf. μετὰ θάνατον
      γάμοι, μετὰ θρῆνον ὑμέναιοι (V.11.2); and Clitophon's extra-
      vagant love-letter (V.20.5). Eros is put into court (cf.
      Chariton *supra* 19f.); while a symposium at which all are
      ashamed is αἰδώς itself (VIII.4.1). For Achilles' exhaust-
      ively rhetorical style, see Rohde 516f.; Wolff 210-235 *pas-
      sim*. This is not the superfluous and tasteless ornament
      both would believe, but reinforces the author's fundamental-
      ly facetious intentions. Achilles' tirades are as mock-
      heroic as those of Petronius' protagonists, as at *Sat.* 9.8
      (cf. P.G. Walsh, *The Roman Novel*, Cambridge 1970, 87; 81).

40   Cf. Seneca *Contr.* I.2.

41   VI.21 (cf. Reardon 365).

42   VIII.9.1. Wolff characteristically disapproves (161); cf.
      Durham, *o.c.* (*supra* n.1) 18; Reardon 365.

43   II.16ff.

44   II.13.2f.; 16.2.

45   VIII.17f. On the other hand there is something a little
        suspect about the happy ending of Calligone's adventure;
        Reardon (363) interprets this as an 'histoire moralisante
        sur la force régénératrice de l'amour'. But there is also
        irony here: while Sostratus accepts this gallant reprobate
        reformer, over the main love-affair both he and Leucippe
        remain deceived.

46   IV.14.8.

47   III.2.1; III.3.2-4.2. Cf. Heiserman *o.c.* (*supra* n.1)123.

48   III.20.2-5.

49   Wehrli (143) notes that *Scheintod* is common both to the ideal
        and the comic novel, but does not see its comic or parodic
        tendencies in all authors except Xenophon.

50   III.15.1-5/II.19-22.

51   III.19.1f.

52   III.22.3.

53   III.21.3-5; 19.3.

54   V.26.7. Durham *o.c.* (*supra* n.1)16 quotes a similar gibe
        from Cleinias (VII.6.2): 'who knows that Leucippe isn't
        alive again? Hasn't she often died? And hasn't she often
        come to life?'.

55   VII.5.3.

56   In the courtroom scenes of the last two books Achilles has
        the opportunity to compound the absurdities of school rhe-
        toric in its most familiar surroundings. The innocent man
        accuses himself of murder (VII.7.6, cf. Chariton I.5.4);
        and Melite confounds the opposition (VII.7.4f.), affording
        splendid opportunities for Cleinias: 'what murderer is so
        fond of love, what kind of hatred is as loving as this?'
        (VII.9.6f., among many examples). Moreover Thersander finds
        himself in the position of accusing Clitophon of the murder
        of Leucippe, whose corpse has returned in person: this leaves
        Achilles free to concentrate on his uninhibited *psogos* of
        Thersander, incongruously put into the mouth of the priest
        of Artemis (VII.9.1-5).

57   III.25. For the details, see now R. van den Broek, *The myth
        of the Phoenix according to Classical and early Christian
        traditions*, Leyden 1972, index *s.v.* Achilles.

58   Herod. II.73; Achilles III.25.4.

59   III.25.1. For the rhetorical use of the peacock, Bompaire
        718ff.

60   III.25.7. Cf. *supra* 25, of Ἔρως.

61   *Quomodo historia conscribenda sit* 25f. Achilles is also
        interested in the ecphrasis of stones, in which again his
        preoccupations are revealing: he chooses to talk about the
        ballistic properties of the Egyptian clod (III.13.3), with
        its superb capacity for horrific wounds; contrast Heliodorus'

choice of the *pantarbe* (V.14).

62   By Rohde (511f.) and Wolff (202-210).

63   I.8.1-9.

64   II.35-38 (to Wolff's horror, 162); Reardon 365.

65   II.35.1. Wehrli (142) well compares the unhealthy conversa-
      tion on board Lichas' ship (the 'Widow of Ephesus' story).
      He rejects parody of the ideal novel on Petronius' part in
      favour of community of theme: but parallel parodies by
      Achilles and Petronius should not be ruled out.

66   IV.7.3ff.

67   IV.7.7.

68   IV.3ff.

69   *AA* I.219-228. Merkelbach (*RM* 133) notes that the hippopo-
      tamus was used as a type of ἀναιδεία; to know that is to
      appreciate still better the comic implications of the
      general's speech. But M. is then forced to assume that
      there must be a correspondingly innocent Egyptian symbolism
      behind the elephant, without being able to produce it. This
      will not do.

70   IV.19.5f.

71   I.15-18.

72   *AA* I.465: *quis, nisi mentis inops, tenerae declamat amicae?*

73   In this category we should also include the excursus on
      Conops. The servant's treachery is not developed in the
      usual way: unlike that of Gnathon in Longus or Artaxates in
      Chariton, Achilles' servant is next to a sophist in his own
      right, engaging in a virtuoso piece of adoxography in praise
      of his own name - only to be outdone by Satyrus both in word
      and deed (II.20ff.: Wolff 161 misses the point). For the
      details of the fable, cf. Lucian's *Muscae Encomium*).

          There is also more than mere irrelevance in the general
      Chaerephon, who digresses from the oracle under discussion
      to fishing for gold in Libya - only to agree with his sub-
      ordinate's interpretation of the oracle in the end (II.14.6-
      15.1). Rohde found this particularly hard to take (513 n.1),
      but its effect in establishing the character of a pompous
      and bumbling soldier should be considered.

74   II.11.

75   II.12ff. Cf. the elaborate description of the suitability
      of the Egyptian ox for sacrifice, doomed to failure for the
      same reason (II.15.3); and of the convoluted marriage
      arrangements - all in vain, since the Fates had other plans
      (I.3.1f.). Further anticlimax is provided by Clitophon's
      attempted seduction of Leucippe, when the pair are disturb-
      ed by Satyrus (II.10.3); or the elaborate attempt to reach
      Leucippe's bedroom, circumvented at the last moment by the
      most cynically contrived of divine interventions (II.19.2ff.).

76   Clitophon is caught in the middle of the debate on his loyal-
      ty to Calligone or Leucippe - by Leucippe herself (II.6.1,
      cf. Wolff 161).

77   II.3.

78   II.2.4.

79   II.23.5. Cf. Wolff 161.

80   VIII.6, 12. See also *infra* n.108.

81   VIII.5.2.

82   VIII.5.5ff. Cf. Melite's mixture of truth and falsehood to
      Thersander (especially on her rescue of Clitophon from the
      sea (VI.9.2-10). Cunning servants and agents are once more
      the experts in *pseudos*: Thersander's spy in prison puts up
      a good show of pretended groaning (VII.2.1ff.), and Sosthenes
      lays on his share of lies for Thersander's benefit (VI.15.2;
      VI.3.4).

83   VI.9.7.

84   V.27.

85   VI.9.4; VI.9.5, cf. Wolff 155.

86   V.16.1f.

87   V.23.5.

88   VIII.10.12.

89   VIII.7.5.

90   VI.10.4.

91   Other examples: comedy of errors in V-VI, when Melite mis-
      takes Leucippe for a Thessalian witch and instructs her to
      win Clitophon for her (V.22.2f.-26.12); ironic misunder-
      standing by Sosthenes of Leucippe's wishing him the good
      luck he is bringing her (VI.12.1).

92   II.24.28; VIII.7.3.

93   II.20ff.; V.17.4.

94   IV.2-7.

95   Rohde 509, cf. 511: 'Man ist haüfig in Zweifel, ob ihre gro-
      teske Abgeschmacktheit ihnen vom Dichter mit bewusster Ab-
      sicht gegeben sei, oder einfach dessen eigene Gemütsart und
      die der ihn umgebenden Graeculi dieser späten, bereits stark
      zum Byzantinertum hinüberneigenden Zeit abspiegle'.

96   II.8.1.

97   II.23.6.

98   Moreover having abducted Leucippe he finds out three books
      later that it was all unnecessary anyway - now that she has
      apparently died (V.11.1f.).

99   V.23.5ff.

100   VI.1.3.

101   Rohde (508f) dismisses Achilles' use of religion with little
        interest or comment, since the wrong date involves discuss-
        ing it only in relation to Christianity. For the rational
        approach to religion in the novels, cf. Wehrli 144, 147;
        U. Schneider-Menzel in F. Altheim, *Literatur und Gesell-
        schaft in ausgehenden Altertum* I, Halle-Saale 1948, 88.

102   I.2.1.

103   I.5.7.

104   VIII.13f.

105   VIII.2.1.

106   VIII.2.3.

107   Cf. Sen. *Contr.* I.2.

108   For wry use or abuse of a chastity test in literature, cf.
        Propertius IV.8: after twelve lines of describing the snake
        cult at Lanuvium and its ritual, we are told that a visit
        there was used by Cynthia as a cover for an amorous esca-
        pade. The episode is rightly treated as humorous by J.P.
        Sullivan, *Propertius, A critical introduction*, Cambridge
        1976, 153f.; M.L. Currie, *Latomus* 22(1973), 617; P.J.
        Connor, *Ramus* 5(1977), 104f. (*contra* M. Hubbard, *Propertius*,
        London 1974, 154, who questionably regards Cynthia as super-
        stitious).

109   II.6.2f.

110   Cf. *supra* 30.

111   III.17.4-18.5; cf. Satyrus as a messenger from Hades, when
        he brings a letter from Leucippe (V.19.2). For Leucippe
        herself as a pretended witch, V.25.2f., cf. V.22.7. The
        contemptible servant Sosthenes embroiders Thersander's
        escape with suitable miracles (VI.13.2).

112   *RM* 114-160.

113   II.19.1.

114   V.25.6.

115   V.27.2. For interpretation of the explicitly mystical
        pomegranate at III.6.1, see my note in *AJP* 100 (1979), 516-
        518: (Achilles' cleverness may have extended as far as con-
        triving a collapsible fake fruit to anticipate Leucippe's
        collapsible fake stomach - not the most devotional of sym-
        bolisms).

116   V.23.6.

117   For comedy in Achilles' Byzantine imitator Eustathius
        Macrembolites, see now M. Alexiou, *Byzantine and Modern
        Greek Studies* 3 (1977), 23-43 (cf. *Acta* 55f.).

Notes to Chapter IV

1   Wolff (158f.) (cf. Wehrli, *MH* 22, 1965, 152) thought that
    Heliodorus allowed humorous material almost exclusively in
    his episodes, and did not think much of it ('such humour as
    H. is capable of'). Maillon was more optimistic (Budé,
    introduction xcii: 'une réelle gaîté et de style et de
    pensée'), but still accuses his author of unintentional hu-
    mour. On the whole however scholars have followed Rohde in
    stressing the hieratic *Tendenz* of the work, which can in it-
    self be interpreted in widely different ways. For Rohde
    himself (473), the religious dimension is mere artifice; so
    Rattenbury-Lumb (Budé, introd. xx); for Reardon (385f.) and
    Perry (*AR* 107), as inevitably for Merkelbach, it is all a
    serious business. After this chapter was written I was glad
    to see two further explorations of Heliodorus' ambiguity:
    J.J. Winkler, 'The Mendacity of Calasiris and the narrative
    Technique of Heliodorus' (*Acta* 29ff.), which stresses H.'s
    prowess as manipulator and illusionist; and J.R. Morgan,
    'Realism and the Historiographical Pose in Heliodorus',
    (*Acta* 138f.), which explores his veneer of verisimilitude.
    Both aspects can be seen as part of the author's mischievous
    technique and personality.

2   I.1.6.

3   III.14.1. R. Helm, *Der Antike Roman*², Göttingen 1956, 41,
    rightly takes the episode as an example of *Scheingelehrsam-
    keit*; but it is not just a matter of sophistic display or
    Calasiris' local patriotism.

4   III.14.4.

5   *RM* 296f., (after Kerenyi *o.c.*, *supra* 107 n.62). For Ratten-
    bury-Lumb (III.14.4) this is merely 'un curieux exemple des
    légendes parfois puériles qui couraient au sujet d'Homère'.

6   See my note in *JHS* 99 (1979), 149.

7   III.13.1.

8   III.13. Cf. Lucian's joke on Homer as a Babylonian hostage
    (*VH* II.20) - or a camel (*Gall.* 17). For bogus temple-legends,
    cf. the more piquant story of Combabos in *de Dea Syria* 19-26
    (*Studies* 78-81).

9   I.7.2, cf. V.32.4 (the pirates think Charicleia's arrows
    come from heaven).

10 IX.22.7-23.1. For humour at willingness to worship men, cf.
    Lucian, *Toxaris* 1-4.

11 I.18.5; I.30.4. So at II.36, where all the interpretations
    offered to Charicles for the oracle at Delphi are wrong.
    For the oracular games with names (χάρις - κλέος ; θεᾶς -
    γενέτην II.35.5), cf. Lucian, *Alexander* 11. Cf. also
    II.16.5 (Charicleia accepts Cnemon's inept interpretation of
    a dream about Theagenes); X.3.1 (Persinna gives a symbolic
    interpretation for a dream which is obviously literally
    correct).

12   VIII.11.4.

13   V.2.5-3.1.

14   V.3.2; V.2.4.

15   VI.1.2.

16   III.16.2f., cf. 17.1.

17   III.16.4; cf. III.17.1ff.; IV.5.3; IV.6.4f. Rattenbury-Lumb
      (ad IV.7.7) see in the treatment of love as a disease 'une
      légère satire du ton doctoral qu'affectent parfois les
      practiciens'. But the emphasis is rather on fun at the
      expense of Charicles' credulity. Cf. Calasiris' deceit of
      the shifty Nausicles (V.13.2) with a touch of prestidigita-
      tion.

18   *Met.* II.13f.

19   *Philopseudes* 15, cf. the activities of Alexander of Abonou-
      teichos, *Theme and Variation* 124-127; and Regulus, Pliny
      Ep. II.20.

20   Even when it is clear to Charicles that Calasiris has duped
      him with religious hocus-pocus, he believes it must be in
      punishment for seeing a prohibited sight in the shrine.
      But he is still as irrational as ever: though he admits it
      is useless to fight providence, he still goes off with the
      Delphians on their wild goose chase (IV.9.3).

21   For the last, X.39.3f., cf. IV.21.1f.

22   Note the characterisation of Calasiris as Proteus, (II.24.4).
      Rattenbury-Lumb insensitively condemn the simplest irony
      (IV.16.4), along with II.7.3 and II.11.3.

23   Comparisons with Philostratus' so-called *Life of Apollonius*
      of Tyana are instructive (Maillon lxxxvif.); but it is
      important to notice that the two authors manipulate the
      clichés of sagecraft in opposite directions (*pace* Reardon
      390). Apollonius has many credentials similar to those of
      Calasiris, but while he will smile at superstitions, it
      would be inconceivable for him to abet a love-affair, let
      alone compound his falsehoods in the same way. Maillon well
      compares Calasiris to the hero of Lucian's *Vita Demonactis*.

24   IV.17.3ff. *Pace* Reardon 389, Heliodorus allows his religious
      spectacle to border on charade; he is good at having things
      both ways.

25   IV.21.1f. For comic decrees, Bompaire 637ff.; *Theme and
      Variation* 104ff.

26   V.1.1. Nor does he omit to add that he doesn't know how the
      Delphians got on with their search!

27   I.3.2. Cf. Hydaspes' melodramatic rhetoric over Charicleia
      about to be sacrificed (V.16.4ff.): he hoped that his mob-
      oratory (δημηγορία) would have no effect on the assembly,
      as indeed it did not (X.17.1). Charicleia herself delivers
      a deliberately hollow harangue to hold off the pirate
      Thyamis - as she assures Theagenes (I.21.3-22; 25.5-26.3).

Maillon rightly suspects parody of Euripides in her monologue at V.2.7. Of course he takes it as showing 'un pathé-
tique de mauvais aloi'. But it is introduced in order to be
misunderstood point by point by Cnemon.

28   X.9-39.

29   V.18.4ff. Cf. Wolff 159.

30   But the joke may once more be a standard one. When Lucian's
      hired professor is asked 'Who is the king of the Achaeans?'
      he replies 'they had a thousand ships' (*de Mercede Conductis*
      11).

31   II.30.1.

32   V.1.3 (cf. Lucian *Lexiphanes* 16).

33   III.1.1; 2.3; 4.7ff.

34   Rattenbury (xx) claims that the purpose of Heliodorus' eru-
      dition is 'non pour faire l'éducation de ses lecteurs, mais
      parce qu'il est toujours agréable aux ignorants d'être mis
      en contact avec le savoir'. But their effect on the well-
      informed has also to be taken into account; and it is not
      to reinforce what they already know.

35   III.7.2ff.

36   III.8. Theagenes' love, on the other hand, is related to
      drunkenness, in yet another variation on the 'comic sym-
      posium' (III.10.5).

37   V.27.2ff. (*Resp.* 488B).

38   IX.17.1. Cf. Dionysus' kettledrums and cymbals in battle,
      Lucian *Bacchus* 4 (with ass's bray for trumpet).

39   IX.18, cf. 15 (cf. the witch transfixed by a spear in the
      groin as a result of her *danse macabre*, VI.15.5); IX.18.6.

40   IX.19.4. For satyrs in paradoxical battles, cf. Lucian
      Bacchus 1-4; for weapons of fishbone, *VH* 1.36f. Even the
      siege of Syene is a little suspect: of course there is
      pathos and suspense in these operations besides the rhe-
      torical novelties (at IV.4.2 or IV.5.5); but in the end the
      Persians simply leave by putting planks across the mud
      (IX.11.1ff.): a case of *parturiunt montes*?

41   I.5.4. I am unable to see why Maillon (xciii n.1) should
      cite this as an example of bad taste. Rattenbury-Lumb (ad
      III.4.6) complain that 'Héliodore a la fâcheuse inspiration
      de terminer une description, d'ailleurs réussie, par une
      pointe de mauvais goût', referring to the snakes soothed
      with the pleasure of wreathing round Charicleia's breasts
      in the description of her cuirass (III.4.4). But that ex-
      ample might be seen as a facetious reference to Hesiod
      Scutum 233ff. Elsewhere the Budé editors acknowledge the
      possibility of deliberate bad taste (ad I.12.3).

42   IX.11.6. Children were unscrupulously used to arouse pity
      in Greek law-courts: both Chariton (V.10.4f.) and Apuleius
      (III.8.1-5) smile at the abuse.

43   V.14.2ff. The description is flanked by another smart ety-
       mology (amethysts keep one sober at symposia, V.13.4); and
       a conceit (the artist uses stone to represent rock, to avoid
       simulating stone on stone, V.14.4).

44   VI.1.2.

45   VI.3.3.

46   X.27 (cf. *Theme and Variation* 45f.); X.29.1.

47   IV.6.3.

48   IV.17.3. Other topoi: Eros as master and judge of the Pythia
       (IV.1.1);   Charicleia comes to the games in obedience to
       ancestral custom, or perhaps, Calasiris suspects, in the hope
       of seeing Theagenes (IV.1.2). The joke of lovers' pretexts
       is frequent in Chariton (*supra* 113 n.45).

49   Chastity is the object of the Delphians' prudish decree
       (IV.21.1). There are perhaps mischievous implications even
       to the chastity test at X.7.7: victims for the sun and moon
       must be chaste, but for Dionysus it doesn't matter; but of
       course they must undergo the test just the same, and have
       the added indignity of getting the soles of their feet burn-
       ed (X.8.2)! Theagenes himself notes that for the Ethiopians
       sacrifice and slaughter are the prize of chastity (X.9.1).

50   V.22.2f., cf. Achilles VIII.13.2f.

51   VI.9.7. It is perhaps true that Charicleia sometimes be-
       comes more human (Maillon xc), but Perry's view succinctly
       sums her up (*AR* 107): 'she is more interested throughout in
       managing things by means of deceptions and roundabout meth-
       ods, in which she is an expert, than in love or loving, al-
       though she is willing to marry under priestly guidance after
       all the proprieties of courtship have been rigidly and
       ostentatiously observed'.

52   IV.18.6.

53   VI.8.6.

54   II.6.4-7.2.

55   II.13.2.

56   Even the immaculate Theagenes will play a trick on the over-
       sensitive Achaemenes (VII.27.2f.); or will not be averse to
       wearing Persian dress (VII.27.1).

57   V.11.2, 25.3, cf. 12.1, 13.2f. (merchants); VII.5.1 (crowds).
       Note also the cowardice of Petosiris when challenged by the
       return of Thyamis: Rattenbury-Lumb ad VII.5.3 rightly com-
       pare the treatment of Irus at *Od.* XVIII.75ff.

58   I.32.4.

59   IX.7.2.

60   IX.22.7.

61   X.25.2.

62   V.18.19. Theagenes for his part has a touch of the anti-
      hero: cf. Rattenbury-Lumb ad I.25.1. He is an easy prey to
      the hocus-pocus of Calasiris (III.17.2f.), and makes the
      usual laments, especially at V.6.2ff. (cf. Achilles
      IV.9.5ff.). Charicleia on the other hand emerges as some-
      thing of a sophist (cf. Rattenbury-Lumb ad I.25.6, I.26.3,
      6).

63   For quasi-scientific instances reported in antiquity, Rohde
      476 n.4.

64   III.14.2, X.14.7.

65   V.2.5-3.1.

66   X.39ff. For Maillon (xci) the final scene 'ne manque pas de
      grandeur'. But the Ethiopians do not emerge better than
      other religious crowds in Heliodorus, clamouring for sacri-
      ficial victims but expecting Charicleia to be saved (X.7.1;
      9.5). For Hydaspes' stupidity, see Rattenbury-Lumb ad
      X.39.1; X.18.3 (cf. Rohde 475); and there is still Charicles
      to come (X.34.5ff.).

67   For comparison to Grand Opera as such, Rohde 478.

68   Charicleia doesn't know whether Calasiris is serious or
      making fun of her, when he encourages her to dupe his own
      son a second time (IV.9.7-10.1). Often ambiguities and
      equivocations follow fast on one another, as in the danse
      macabre over Thisbe's body (II.1.2ff.-II.11.2f.). See also
      infra n.72.

69   E.g. VII.8.1 (Calasiris' intervention transforms the spect-
      acle from tragedy to comedy); I.8.7 (Cnemon's New Comic bed-
      room farce introduced as a tragedy). On the whole Heliodorus
      can neither resist the trickery of comedy nor the grandiosity
      of tragedy, and never wants to commit himself.

70   III.7.1ff., cf. III.5.3ff./Eum. 34-45; X.39.3/Eum. 566f.
      It should not be argued that the Eumenides was now too
      recondite a work to be in the sophistic repertoire: it had
      a special interest in an archaising age for its treatment of
      the Areopagus, and was clearly a model for Lucian's Piscator.

71   So E. Feuillatre, Étude sur Héliodore, Poitiers, 1966,
      120 n.4 (Helen 1590ff./V.32.3ff.); Wehrli also compares both
      Helen and Iphigenia in Tauris, 152.

72   The text of Heliodorus' religious allusions is thick with
      erudite equivocation. Maillon (ad VIII.9.2) notes his
      tendency to juxtapose a 'Socratic' explanation to a religious
      one, but I am not so sure that it is 'au lecteur de choisir,
      selon ses sentiments'. Sometimes H.'s vacillations seem to
      be appropriately Herodotean affectations, as in IX.9.4,
      (dismissal of Isiac interpretation of the worship of the
      Nile, cf. Lucian, de Dea Syria 8), or IX.10.1 (Herodotean
      reticence, cf. Herod. II.48, de Dea Syria 28). Sometimes it
      seems part of the author's rationalist manner (III.34.8:
      'whether they are deluding themselves or whether their claim
      is the truth'. But sometimes this rationalism borders on
      mischief: in a brief mention of cockcrow (I.18.3), H. finds
      time to ask if the cock awakes in response to providential
      instinct from Apollo or whether it requires to be fed!

Would an Aelian or an Aristides have bothered to ask?

Merkelbach was puzzled by the concentration of oddities
in Heliodorus: therefore, he concludes, they must be mystical
(*RM* 298). Rohde (473, *contra* Reardon 385) does more justice
to the evidence by regarding him as an expert at virtuoso
displays of piety and rationalism: the tone is well summed
up by Perry, from whom I take part of my chapter title:
'religious mysticism, sacerdotal solemnities and strategies,
and the implication that a grandiose epic scheme of things
is being worked out by the design of an inscrutable Providence' (107). One might add 'and a still more inscrutable
author'.

73   We have still to review Heliodorus' credentials as priest
     of Emesa. Without supporting evidence we have no more rea-
     son to believe him than we have to accept that Iamblichus
     was a Babylonian magician. Rohde (473) still regarded his
     claim as bona fide, and Chariton's name and provenance is
     actually attested, however *voulu* it may sound (see Kerenyi's
     addendum to Rohde 520 n.2). All we can say is that a
     connoisseur of religious deceit has a *prima facie* motive for
     affecting to be a priest.

74   Heliodorus' style is consistent with this verdict: it is
     important to distinguish between sheer κακόζηλον and comic-
     ally ponderous effects: Maillon (xcii) condemns his labor-
     ious balancing members, rare expressions and involved syntax
     as 'le mauvais goût d'une époque de décadence'. But he
     admits that H. is capable of considerable variation, and he
     is right to see the comic effect of the author's pomposity:
     ('Il a l'air de faire la caricature des belles et nobles
     monodies du théâtre grec'). Rohde (489ff.) was less sym-
     pathetic. But a comically nuanced style exactly fits his
     handling of the subject-matter. Like Achilles, Longus and
     Chariton, Heliodorus knew what he was doing.

75   Wolff's description of the *Aethiopica* as a nest of boxes
     (193) might also be adapted: Heliodorus has contrived a nest
     of jack-in-the-boxes.

Notes to Chapter V

1   So in essence G. Rohde (always distinguished by initial),
    RhM 86 (1937), 23-49; H.H.O. Chalk *JHS* 80 (1960), 32-51;
    O. Schönberger, *Longus: Hirtengeschichten von Daphnis und
    Chloe, Schriften und Quellen der alten Welt*, Berlin 1960);
    M.C. Mittelstadt, *C&M* 27 (1966), 162-177; Reardon, *Courants*
    374-81, cf. Phoenix 23 (1969), 301f. Although P. Turner
    (in his introduction to the Penguin translation , Harmonds-
    worth 1968,11) neatly characterises the work ('Longus is
    always smiling'), he too forces a very mild spiritual quest
    into the treatment of evil elements working together for
    good; cf. *Id.*, *G&R N.S.* 7 (1960), 117-123. M. Berti, *SCO* 16
    (1967) refutes Chalk and Merkelbach (349-353) before seeking
    Longus' inspiration in New Comedy (though she has little to
    say about humorous effects as such, which she tends to ascribe
    too readily to comic sources, 358). But she adequately
    establishes that literal and literary interpretation offers
    a self-sufficient and artistically satisfying explanation of
    the work. I refer to the editions of Schönberger *supra*
    and Dalmeyda (Budé, 1934) by name throughout.

2   *Praef*. 4.

3   Longus' pastoral sources have been carefully studied: see in
    particular G. Rohde *ibid*. 26-36; M.C. Mittelstadt, *RhM* 113
    (1970), 211-227; but some humorous implications in his *mime-
    sis* have still to be drawn. His Daphnis is not the son of
    Hermes, as in Aelian *VH* X.18, Diodorus IV.84; but of worldly
    bourgeois parents. A mere change of genre and environment,
    or a comic and amusing contradiction of tradition? Still
    less does this Daphnis have anything to do with Artemis, or
    try to fight against love, like the Daphnis of Theocritus;
    nor is there any blinding or tragic death when he lies to
    Chloe! The plot may also stand in an equally incongruous
    relationship to Sositheus' pastoral drama Δάφνις ἢ Λιτυέρσης
    (*TrGrF* p.270 Snell, = 821 Nauck). Daphnis does not this time
    rescue the kidnapped girl with the help of Heracles; a comic
    Pan does everything for him. For the effect of prose 'trans-
    position' of the idyll, cf. Lucian's *Dialogi Deorum* and *Dia-
    logi Marini*, and Bompaire 375-378; as well as Dio Chrysostom's
    Euboicus (*Or*. VII), and the relevant tableaux of Philostra-
    tus' *Imagines*. Dio finally applies his tale to the explicit-
    ly serious end of advocating moral contentment; the others
    do not (cf. Rohde 542f.). For humour in Theocritus, see
    A.E-A. Horstmann, *Ironie und Humor bei Theokrit, Beiträge zur
    klassischen Philologie* 67, Meisenheim am Glan 1976.

4   I.30.

5   I.15ff.; II.15ff.

6   III.27.3f.

7   II.17.3.

8   II.19-29. For the topos of 'comic battles' see *Theme and
    Variation* 37 and index *s.v.* In the νυκτομαχία οὐ παρόντων
    πολεμίων (II.25.4), Puech-Vieillefond *apud* Dalmeyda complains
    that 'l'imagination de Longus s'attarde trop complaisamment'.

But it is the very effortlessness of the whole operation
which is so amusing. The pun on δελφῖνες (*Id.* ad III.26.2
(lead missiles/dolphins) also contributes to the effect.

9   I.20f. Schönberger *o.c.* (*supra* n.1) *ad loc.* well compares
the Dorcon episode to the *Doloneia* and its doublet in
Rhesus 208; and the tearing by dogs to the *sparagmos* of the
Bacchae. But Epic and Tragedy are reduced to ludicrous
vanishing point in a pastoral landscape; the substitution of
Pan for Dionysus in the treatment of the pirates is also an
amusing reduction in scale from that even of the *Homeric
Hymns*. In the light of such reductions we have still less
reason to doubt the amusing effect of loading Platonic re-
miniscences on to a Hellenistic putto.

10   IV.7.3.

11   IV.10ff.

12   IV.7.3.

13   Lycaenion, III.15ff.

14   II.1.4. There is nothing odd about this detail, as Brunck
and Dalmeyda maintained (see the latter *ad loc.*).

15   III.21ff., II.34.

16   II.34.3.

17   IV.2f.

18   II.37.1f. Cf. IV.15.2f. (Daphnis); II.36 (Dryas).

19   IV.14.3/*D. Mar.* 8.2.

20   I.30.6. There is no ground whatever for treating this passage as an interpolation (Castiglioni, *RFIC* 34, 1906, 312,
followed by Dalmeyda). P. Turner (Penguin *l.c.*, *supra* n.1,
11), rightly realises that it is fully consistent with
Longus' sense of humour. He has surely no real interest in
natural history for its own sake, *contra* G. Rohde *o.c.*
(*supra* n.1) 30. For parallels to the cattle escaping from
the pirates, see Schönberger *ad* I.30.1f.

21   I.16. Cf. Lucian's pastoral on the judgement of Paris,
D.Deor. 20 (*Dearum Iudicium*): Paris is only competent to
judge goats or heifers, not goddesses (20.7). In both cases
the judge is won over by amorous considerations (Longus
I.17.1; *D.Deor.* 20.13ff.). Much of Longus' rhetoric is
amusingly incongruous because of its miniature scale and
context: cf. the short exchanges in Daphnis' soliloquy
(III.6.3f.), or his dialogue with Chloe (III.10.3f.), both
comparable to the courtroom exchanges in Chariton (V.8.5).
These exchanges should be related not only to Comedy (Berti
o.c., *supra* n.1, 358) or declamation (Schönberger *ad*
III.10.3), but to Hellenistic dialogue-epigram. Note also
the comic incongruity of Dryas' unlikely speech to Dionysophanes, with Dalmeyda *ad loc.* (IV.30.3f.).

22   Cf. *Theme and Variation* 19, 37, 82; *Studies* 85.

23   Lucian also develops this nuance, exploiting Ganymede's
      rustic innocence at the hands of Zeus, or a young girl's
      bewilderment when faced with advances from a Lesbian
      (*D. Deor.* 4; *D. Meretr.* 5).

24   I.21.5.

25   II.7.1.

26   I.13, 17f.

27   I.13; 23f.

28   II.22.2.

29   III.18.2.

30   III.20.1.

31   III.24.3.

32   III.25.2.

33   III.18.3f. I am not convinced, with Reardon (377), that
      'Les pastorales ne sont point une histoire licentieuse'.
      It seems on the contrary part of Longus' delightful sense
      of fun that they should be. The sexual episode with
      Lycaenion should come as a complete surprise to the first-
      time reader; and it has the same value of wry anti-climax
      as the Melite episode in Achilles. Nor is such a scene
      necessarily 'avant tout naturel'; it is not Chloe who is
      Daphnis' partner. As Reardon admits (380), 'l'on peut
      même penser que L. a trop insisté sur la psychologie; que
      cette intrigue amoureuse a un peu trop l'air d'une expéri-
      ence clinique contrôlée'. Wolff (162) well observes that
      Longus' pervasive humour depends on 'the incongruity between
      the children's innocence and the piquancy of their experi-
      ments'.

34   III.20.2.

35   I.31.2. In fact both of them have already made up a story
      (I.12.5) to cover up the loss of the sheep.

36   IV.31.3. There is double irony here: he is amused or de-
      lighted (ἥσθεις) at Daphnis' seemingly innocent assurance
      that there have only been kisses and oaths; and has evident-
      ly no inkling of what his son has been up to.

37   For the latter, *supra* 23.

38   III.12.2; I.3.

39   For this nuance, cf. the treatment of Philemon and Baucis,
      Ovid *Met.* VIII.629-724.

40   III.32.1.

41   I.11.2.

42   XI.34-42.

43   IV.40.2f. So Berti, *o.c.* (*supra* n.1), 348: 'E un osserva-
      zione maliziosa, che contrasterebbe col presunto tono mis-
      tico della scena'; Wolff 162.

44   II.12.4.

45   I.3.1. Schönberger *ad loc.* compares Daos' action in *Epitr.*
      250ff. *Contra*, Dalmeyda ad III.31.3: 'ces attitudes de
      campagnards, tour à tour généreuses et égoïstes, sont notées
      avec beaucoup de réalisme'. But that realism is harnessed
      to produce comic incongruity.

46   IV.25.3. Both Lamon and Dryas were disappointed when in-
      structed in parallel dreams to bring up the children,
      having assumed that they would turn out to be more elevated
      (I.8.1). And each tries to maintain his hope of superiority
      at the expense of the other because of the birth-tokens
      (III.25.3, Dryas; III.30.5, Lamon).

47   IV.16.4. Cf. IV.29.4: he will die of hunger if Daphnis bans
      him from his table!

48   Moreover the two fathers seem to justify their exposure of
      Daphnis and Chloe just a little too easily: Dionysophanes
      has enough heirs (IV.24.1), while Megacles thinks warships
      and plays more important than daughters, (IV.35.3ff.).

49   IV.38.4.

50   III.2.5. While there is an obvious contrast between town
      and country, one need not agree with Schönberger 12 that
      the 'verderblichen Einfluss der Stadt' comes off badly in
      contrast to the countryside: Longus is prepared to smile at
      human motives and human nature in either.

51   IV.29.3.

52   II.20.2; IV.28.2f. For other instances, see Dalmeyda xxxii.
      But this is more than the presentation of children: it is
      another variation on the characteristic anti-hero of the
      novel.

53   For this and other anti-eclogue, see J.-Ph. Cèbe, *La Cari-
      cature et la Parodie o.c.* (*supra* 108 n.74) 329.

54   I.22.1f.

55   III.27.4; IV.1.3. Rohde's comment is misleading (546): 'er
      malt uns keine parfümierten Salonschäfer hin, wie so viele
      seiner Nachahmer, aber den Stall- und Mistgeruch erspart er
      uns ebenfalls'.

56   IV.38.4.

57   III.8.2.

58   III.6.2.

59   III.23.3.

60   I.29.1; Achilles I.12.5-13.2 (despite Reardon 378).

61   III.19f.; Achilles IV.7.6ff.

62   But the differences are also illuminating: Plutarch indulges
        in ponderous didacticism, which Longus avoids; cf. Schön-
        berger 18.

63   I.3.1, cf. I.6.1. I cannot see what is mystical about Daph-
        nis' boast that he was nourished by a goat just like Zeus
        (I.16.3); at most it is the amusing manipulation of a
        mystical motif, if that (*contra* G. Rohde *o.c.*, *supra* n.1,
        47).

64   I.26. Other examples: Daphnis' winter meeting with Chloe is
        brought about by the bolting of Dryas' dog (III.7.1f.),
        which also undercuts his tragic lament (cf. Puech-Viellefond
        apud Dalmeyda *ad loc.*); and the invasion from Methymna is
        triggered off by goats' eating the vital hawser (II.13.4).

65   IV.39.2. Daphnis and Chloe have their own children suckled
        by animals; but this is not necessarily the action of a
        mystic rite (G. Rohde *o.c.* *supra* n.1, 47). It is comedy on
        its own terms: rustic habits die hard. Longus' *adoxa* are
        not confined to animals: Philetas pronounces wind and sea
        the guilty parties in the 'trial' of Daphnis (II.17.1); and
        the latter feels that the sea has helped him to marry Chloe,
        when he finds the purse in the wreck of the Methymnaean
        yacht (III.28.3).

66   IV.12 2f.

67   II.22.2.

68   II.20.3; IV.12.2f. So the villagers swoop down on the
        Methymnaeans like a flock of starlings or jackdaws (II.17.3);
        or Dryas pursues his thieving dog just like a dog himself
        (III.7.2).

69   III.14.2-5.

70   III.29.2. The oath Chloe swears by the sheep must also be
        comic (II.39.4); it seems special pleading to add that it
        also 'die Bedeutung der Tiere dokumentiert' (Schönberger
        ad loc.). But S. rightly compares Lucian's presentation of
        Pan (*D. Deor.* 22.4) (*ad* 39.2).

71   *Georg.* IV.219-27. Cf. the fly as proof of the soul's im-
        mortality (Lucian, *Musc. Enc.* 7); or the parrot lecturing
        the good birds, in Elysium *si qua fides dubiis* (Ovid *Am.*
        II.6.57f.; 51).

72   The allegory of the seasons is undoubtedly there (Chalk *o.c.*,
        supra n.1, 39-44; Reardon 378f.); but it neatly coincides
        with the standard technique of anticipatory ecphrasis so
        frequently employed by the novelists. It is perhaps not
        quite necessary to press the symbolism of every detail, as
        Chalk seems in danger of doing; cf. Reardon 379f.

73   Chalk *ibid.* 35f.

74   Much rests on the interpretation of ἀνάθημα in the prologue
        (3): τέτταρας βίβλους ἐξεπονησάμην, ἀνάθημα μὲν Ἔρωτι καὶ
        Νύμφαις καὶ Πανί, κτῆμα δὲ τερπνὸν πᾶσιν ἀνθρώποις. Chalk
        ibid. 32 emphasises the force of ἀνάθημα μέν, but its effect
        should in any case be judged in the light of the subsequent
        course of events. Berti (*o.c.*, *supra* n.1, 343) seems just

as entitled to see the prologue as a literary joke in itself.
An appropriately teasing translation would be 'as an offering to the gods, to be sure, but also as a delightful
possession for all men'. We should bear in mind that Longus
is elegantly paraphrasing both κτῆμα ἐς ἀεί (Thuc. I.22.4)
and the introduction to Agathon's discussion of Ἔρως at
Plat. Symp. 197E: οὗτος ... ὁ παρ' ἐμοῦ λόγος, ὦ φαῖδρε, τῷ
θεῷ ἀνακείσθω, τὰ μὲν παιδιᾶς, τὰ δὲ σπουδῆς μετρίας, καθ'
ὅσον ἐγὼ δύναμαι, μετέχων. Longus' version cleverly inverts
the order of the terms; but in any case the force of the
prologue can only be judged in retrospect from the rest of
the work.

It is worth noting the impact of offerings elsewhere
in Longus. Pan receives a temple as a warrior at the end,
but his exploits are delightfully trivial. Nor are offerings to Pan so very serious in Plat. Phaedr. 279BC, or in
Lucian, D.Deor. 4.1f., where it is the simple and innocent
Ganymede who wants to sacrifice to him, unaware of the
greater power of Zeus. In general Longus uses offerings in
order to smile at a child's rustic piety. The milkpails
offered to the nymphs are in the same category as the various
love-objects - from knapsacks, pails and pan-pipes down to
the cage for Chloe's grasshopper (IV.26.3; III.4.3; I.10.2).
And Daphnis is prepared almost to worship Chloe's parents
when he is allowed to stay under the same roof as Chloe; or
promises offerings to his cunning initiatrix Lycaenion
(III.9.2; III.18.1f.).

75   III.4.2. Contra Mittelstadt C&M o.c. (supra n.1) 172. I fail
      to see why the phrase Ἔρωτος ληστήριον (I.32.4) 'makes alle-
      gorization of I.28-32 certain'. It only makes it certain
      that Longus took the opportunity for appropriate and amusing
      metaphor in I.32.

76   IV.13.1; Chalk o.c. (supra n.1) 43.

77   For the latter, Chalk ibid, 33. But he overstates his case
      by continuing: 'a short extract is sufficient to show what
      type of god we are dealing with: one which is paralleled in
      numerous syncretic monotheisms of the early centuries of
      our era; a competitor with the Great Mother in all her forms,
      with Mithras, and with many others, for the office of sup-
      reme controller of the cosmos'.

78   Schönberger ad loc. rightly relates Philetas' speech to
      literary topoi on the power of love (Ps.-Menander apud Spen-
      gel, Rhetores Graeci III.401). Berti rightly protests
      against mystical interpretation of it, o.c. (supra n.1),
      348: it is an ecphrasis presented as a mystery, but with
      obvious irony. The same applies to the 'mysteries' of
      Lycaenion (ibid. 349). G. Rohde (38), Chalk (33) and Schön-
      berger and Mittelstadt (C&M 173) (all occ. supra n.1) insist
      on the sublimity of Eros, most of them citing the classic
      passages from the Phaedrus and Symposium (Dalmeyda ad II.7.1
      wrongly denies the connexion with Phaedrus 349D). To these
      add Menander fr. 235 Körte-Thierfelder; Lucian D. Deor. 2.1.
      But the composition and setting of Philetas' speech have to
      be carefully weighed: it is a clever pastiche of passages on
      Platonic love, combined with the motif of Ἔρως δραπετής,
      and the remedies for love in Theocr. XI.1ff. The contexts
      of none of these passages suggest a serious rather than
      delightful treatment of love. Schönberger and Mittelstadt

both compare Lucian's imitations of Plato in *D. Deor.* 2.1.
Here there is a distinct humour in putting the most familiar
Platonica into the mouth of a rather mealy-mouthed rustic
who can't really bring himself to tell Daphnis and Chloe the
facts of life. Cf. G. Rohde 49, Schönberger *ad loc.* (*contra*
Mittelstadt *CM* 169, who however accepts ironic interpretation at *RhM* 217, following G. Rohde 27). Longus has struck
a delightful balance between humour and pathos: the lovely
lie and clever literary *adoxon* embody a basic truth of human
experience.

79   Schönberger (18) accepts the operations of providence
        through Lycaenion (*contra* Berti *o.c.*, *supra* n.1, 349), but
        is more cautious in his commentary *ad loc.*: 'Lykainion
        selbst behauptet aber (III.17.2), die Nymphen hätten ihr
        befehlen, Daphnis die Liebeswerke zu lehren, was aus ihrem
        Munde als reiner Vorwand gelten muss. Wenn Daphnis aber
        (III.18.2) die zu lernende Kunst als gottgesandt ansicht
        möchte auch der Leser (trotz der vorhandenen Ironie) das
        Motiv des göttlichen Befehles nicht nur als Vorwand empfin-
        den'. For a similar view, D.N. Levin, *RSC* 25 (1977), 5-17
        (cf. *Acta* 129f.); but are we entitled to make any such
        assumption? Longus is not entirely committed to other gods
        either: Pan is a little dubious - unable to win Syrinx even
        with a bribe of twins for her flock (II.34.1f.), and is
        certainly not a suitable god for Chloe to swear by (cf.
        II.39.4ff.: she prefers the sheep and goats!). The nymphs
        have to commission Pan in a crisis (II.23.4). And shepherds
        and goatherds only *imagine* that the cattle are mourning for
        Dorcon (I.31.4).

80   Cf. the divine pretexts alleged by Achilles' Melite, *supra*
        32.

81   *Pace* Reardon, Phoenix *o.c.* (*supra* n.1), 301: 'there are no
        travels, because there is no special point in travel; no
        great dangers, because life is dangerous enough; no mecha-
        nism of circumstance to set the story on its way, because
        the ineluctable passage of the seasons is dynamism itself'.

82   G. Rohde 39; Mittelstadt *C&M* 170 (both *o.c.*, *supra* n.1).
        The effect of saying that αὐτὴ ἡ φύσις taught him τὸ
        πρακτέον is an ironic way of saying that he didn't need
        lessons.

83   *Contra* Reardon, *Courants* 379. Cf. Puech-Vieillefond *apud*
        Dalmeyda II.10.3: Longus uses persistent delays to tantalise
        the reader. When the plot does advance, Providence and
        Chance also move in a comically simplistic sort of way:
        Daphnis starts his sexual explorations when removing a fugi-
        tive grasshopper from Chloe's bosom; the Methymnaean War is
        motivated by a goat's gnawing a hawser (II.13.4); appro-
        priate dreams control the behaviour of Daphnis and the
        Methymnaean general when Chloe is abducted (II.23.2-5; 27);
        and treasure is provided for Daphnis' dowry, conveniently
        guarded by a stinking dolphin (III.27.4). Pan actually
        breaks the dramatic illusion in the middle of the Methym-
        naean war: will Bryaxis abduct a woman ἐξ ἧς Ἔρως μῦθον
        ποιῆσαι θέλει (II.27.2)? Longus' σωφροσύνη strikes a care-
        ful balance between the naively absurd and the natural
        order of things.

84   Lucian *D. Deor.* 4.4f.; 4.1-4; Longus, *supra* n.74.

85   *D. Mar.* 15.3. For the αἴνιγμα ἔρωτος in Philostratus *Ima-*
      gines I.6, see Chalk, *Acta* 133ff. Love is presented as an
      αἴνιγμα - but by a guide to a child. The sketch resembles
      Philetas' speech in circumstance as well as ethos: it pro-
      duces a charming and sympathetic presentation of childhood
      innocence, rather than a serious religious experience in
      the sense known to writers of Apocryphal *Acts.*

86   II.7; III.18.3f.; IV.40.3.

87   IV.38.2-4.

88   IV.39.2. Having stressed the role of Eros, Chalk seems to
      have unnecessary difficulty in explaining why he is men-
      tioned so seldom. It is scarcely necessary to cast him in
      the role of a recessive high god (Chalk *o.c.*, *supra* n.1,
      34); he manifests himself in all the amorous activities of
      Daphnis and Chloe, and indeed is explicitly in charge of the
      plot (II.27.2).

89   For innocence and experience, see P. Turner, *G&R o.c.* (*supra*
      n.1), 119-123.

90   IV.40.3; 39.2.

91   IV.39.2. Longus might of course have had a rustic cult of
      Eros in mind at this point, as suggested by G. Rohde *o.c.*
      (*supra* n.1) 47f., but a realistic or quasi-realistic de-
      tail could still have been selected to occasion a smile.

92   Schönberger admits the literary constituents of Longus'
      work (17), but does not think it possible 'die Grenze
      zwischen echter Religiosität und Spielerisch verwendeten
      Ehrfurchsschauer zu zuchen'. Perhaps this is the safest
      course. The important thing is to appreciate how carefully
      and consistently Longus has contrived the impasse for
      artistic ends.

93   IV.19.4; II.5.5.

Notes to Chapter VI

1   B. Lavagnini, *Eroticorum fragmenta papyracea*, Teubner,
     Leipzig 1922; F. Zimmermann, *Griechische Romanpapyri und
     verwandte Texte*, Heidelberg 1936 (a different selection,
     with excessive supplementation); I have included references
     to both, to the *editio princeps*, and to the running comment-
     ary by R.M. Rattenbury, in *New Chapters in the History of
     Greek Literature* III, ed. J.U. Powell, Oxford 1933, 211-
     263; further bibliography will be found in R.A. Pack, *The
     Greek and Latin Literary Texts from Graeco-Roman Egypt*[2],
     Ann Arbor 1965.

2   *Bibl. Cod.* 94 (Ed. R. Henry, *Collection Byzantine*, Paris
     1960); the Teubner edition of the fragments (ed. E. Habrich,
     1960) also contains facing text of Photius. I cite Bekker's
     pagination of Photius, then Habrich's numbering of the frag-
     ments. There is valuable discussion of their position, and
     of the character of the work, by U. Schneider-Menzel in F.
     Altheim, *Literatur und Gesellschaft im ausgehenden Altertum*
     I, Halle-Saale 1948, 48-92.

3   See *Studies* 44ff.

4   Fr. 5 Habrich.

5   Fr. 70 Habrich.

6   *Cod.* 94.76b - 78a.

7   fr. 100 Habrich.

8   But by an instinctive editorial procedure Hercher failed to
     see the joke and deleted καὶ ὠμὸν after ἐφθόν! We should
     also note the farcical situation in Fr. 101 Habrich (which
     may however be from a declamation by Hadrian of Tyre): mer-
     cenaries claim their reward for a military victory, having
     cheated, so to speak, by diverting a river and not fighting
     a blow! Whoever the author, the effect seems facetious.

9   Fr. 51 Habrich. Cf. the comic context of πολὺς ὁ βορβορ-
     υγμός, Lucian *Lexiphanes* 20.

10   *Theme and Variation* 45f. (monkeys throw off their perform-
     ers' costumes in pursuit of nuts or figs); cf. also *Batra-
     chomuiomachia* 82-88 (the frog throws its mouse passenger in
     a sudden descent to avoid a water-snake). Schneider-Menzel
     (*supra* n.2) 86 recognises the ironic tendency in the camel
     episode, as in the treatment of the treasure and its super-
     natural detection; she rightly notes that Iamblichus is a
     contemporary and fellow-countryman of Lucian. The role of
     animals elsewhere in the *Babyloniaca* is suspect (nor is
     their use by novelists unique to him, as she maintains, 88:
     as in Longus and Achilles they may have helped to trivialise
     the action). On the analogy of the camel, we might suspect
     the poisoned bees which kill the pursuers while the lovers
     escape with tummyache from the poisoned honey (74ab, cf. also
     the poisoned beetles, 75b). I am also inclined to suspect

the amorous goat which appears in a dream to Sinonis (74a):
this may not necessarily be a satyr, (Schissel, *Entwicklungsgeschichte o.c.*, *supra* 117 n.1, 35 n.2), or Semitic
colouring (Schneider-Menzel 88 n.38, cf. Rohde 367 n.1).
For the ceremonial horses see *infra* 53. The possibility
remains of course that such episodes were used to produce
cheap and tasteless horror. It is the cumulative effect of
other evidence that raises suspicion: when the camel episode
is clearly comic, and Iamblichus' religious attitudes are
sophisticated, then we are entitled to question all such
material.

11   77ab.

12   74b.

13   *Ibid.*

14   75a.

15   75b/76a. The couple pretend equally readily to be ghosts of
the robbers' victims, 74b. For the usual jokes against
barbarians, cf. frr. 27, 85.

16   78a. Cf. the pious stupidity of Garmus' men, 74b.

17   76a; 77b; 78a.

18   75b. It is not divination by mice themselves that gives
Iamblichus away, but his insistence πρώτην γὰρ εἶναι τὴν
τῶν μυῶν μαγικήν.

19   Fr. 1 Habrich.

20   See *supra* 29. For ludicrous ecphrasis in bogus histori-
ography, see Lucian, *Quomodo historia conscribenda sit* 19
(Vologesus' breeches or bridle, Osroes' hair; cf. also
Theme and Variation 59ff.).

21   P. 5, on the strength of an unconvincing parallel with
Chariton VI.4. Schneider-Menzel *o.c.* (*supra* n.2) 68 takes
the occasion to be the final coronation of Rhodanes; this
seems possible, but again rather ineffectual.

22   P. 56 Habrich, Phot. *Cod.* 94.77a. So V. Hefti, *Zur Erzäh-
lungstechnik in Heliodors Aethiopica*, Vienna 1950, 144.

23   Fr. 35 Habrich.

24   This is an opportunity for the husband's absurd courtroom
rhetoric (ἡ νικηθεῖσα μὲν ἀδικεῖ, ἀτυχεῖ δὲ ὁ νικήσας
κ.τ.λ., fr. 35, p. 27 lines 16f. Habrich). There is perhaps
a hint that the outraged husband had himself taken a fancy
to the slave (μοιχὸν ἀνὴρ ἐπαινῶ, καὶ ταῦτα τῆς μεμοιχευ-
μένης ἀκουούσης *ibid*. p.29 lines 28f.; cf. p.31 lines 6f.
There is also a suspect false analogy in the husband's evidence from dreams (the archer dreams of a bow, she of her
lover!), used to suggest that she was caught red-handed
through the dream (*ibid*. p.31, lines 15ff.).

25   *Alexander* 50; cf. *Theme and Variation* 126f.

26   Cf. Melite's chastity test, Achilles VIII.12.

27   At least some of the shorter fragments contain a hint of
       comic effect. Apart from explicit mention of laughter (111,
       112) or deceit (31), there is an amusing *adynaton* to illus-
       trate the avarice of the τελώνης handing the necklace to
       the jeweller (93): οὐκ ἤδη καὶ λύκοι θήσουσιν ἄρνας ἐκ τῶν
       στομάτων καὶ λέοντες ἀπὸ τῶν ὀδόντων ἀπολύσουσι νεβροὺς
       ταῖς μητράσιν, ὀπότε καὶ τελώνης ἀφῆκεν ἄγραν τηλικαύτην;
       and some kind of pastoral trick (to elude Garmus' agents?),
       in which the shepherds tinkle bells (in imitation of the
       Curetes protecting Zeus?)(91).

28   Photius *Cod.* 166; for the text of the Myrto-fragment, see
       Zimmermann *o.c.* (*supra* n.1).

29   As the Lucianic scholia suggest, ad *VH* II.12 (ed. H. Rabe,
       Teubner 1906, 21).

30   *Vita Pythagorae* 10 (in A. Nauck, *Porphyrii philosophi plato-
       nici opuscula selecta*[2], Leipzig 1886).

31   Lucian often parodies comic works by carrying their absurd-
       ity a stage further, as in the case of Aristophanes' *Birds*
       and *Clouds*, both used in *VH* (Bompaire 668). Porphyry may
       have relied on Antonius because of his supposed antiquity,
       based on the author's claim that his evidence was discover-
       ed by a soldier of Alexander the Great (Phot. *Cod.* 166.111b);
       but this claim may have been deliberately false: Antonius
       knew how to be πιθανώτατος (*ibid.* 111a).

32   Antonius Diogenes has been all things to all men. Rohde
       placed him wrongly at a crucial point in the 'development'
       of the novel (209-309); K. Reyhl, *Antonius Diogenes: Unter-
       suchungen zu den Roman-Fragmenten der 'Wunder jenseits von
       Thule' und zu den 'Wahren Geschichten' des Lukian*, Diss.
       Tübingen 1969, 129f., makes him a serious Pythagorean author,
       as of course does Merkelbach, *RM* 225-233. For reservations
       see now W. Fauth, *Hermes* 106 (1978), 220-241. Wehrli 135
       emphasises the folk-element in his material; but Photius'
       account implies considerable sophistication.

33   *Cod.* 166.109b; cf. Reardon 371. The enemies of the Iberians
       presumably had some mischief played on them by Astraeus'
       flute-playing (109b), cf. Longus I.30.1-4.

34   *Cod.* 166.110b.

35   *Cod.* 166.109b; *ibid.*; 110ab. For the last, cf. Achilles'
       treatment of Clitophon's lament for Leucippe in a coma
       (IV.9.4ff.); or the inconvenience of Castor and Pollux'
       arrangements for immortality (*D. Deor.* 26).

36   *Cod.* 166.111a.

37   Reyhl *o.c.* (*supra* n.32) 18 plausibly guesses that *P. Mich.
       Inv.* 5 (C. Bonner, *TAPA* 52, 1921, 111-118; Pack 2636) should
       be attributed to Antonius. E.R. Dodds, *Phoenix* Suppl. 1
       (1952), 133-38 had already argued convincingly for a novel,
       and the extract would certainly fit Paapis very well. It is
       a variant on the locus 'although I am supreme in my own field,
       I cannot use my (in this case magic) arts to conquer love'
       (cf. Ap. Rhod. IV.59-64, of Medea). Like *P. Mich. Inv.*3378
       (*infra* n.73), it underlines the potential of themes of
       superstition for paradox.

38   *P. Berol.* 21179, published by H. Maehler, *ZPE* 23 (1976), 1-20,
        cf. *Acta* 49ff.).

39   Whether this process in itself was impertinent enough to be
        amusing, we can scarcely say from what remains; but if
        Chariton is anything to go by, that is certainly what we
        should expect (*supra* 17f.). Lucian's story of Kombabos shows
        how readily two loose ends of Herodotus can be manipulated
        into a spurious erotic tale (*de Dea Syria* 19-26; *Studies*
        79).

40   Col. I (*P. Berol.* 9588+21179 lines 1-3).

41   Col. II (*P. Berol.* 21179 fin.+7927).

42   Col. II.6-26. For the comic treatment of this theme, cf.
        Alexis fr. 20K: λέγεται γὰρ λόγος / ὑπὸ τῶν σοφιστῶν μὴ
        πέτεσθαι τὸν θεὸν / τὸν Ἔρωτα, τοὺς δ'ἐρῶντας·

43   Col. II.26f.

44   *Ibid.* 28f.

45   *Ibid.* 32ff.

46   *Supra* 25.

47   Lucian's *Convivium* also presents a philosopher talking about
        love in a quasi-Platonic way, in the midst of his colleagues'
        (disreputable) amours (*Conv.* 39). One might be tempted to
        suspect that Anaximenes is some kind of mentor, real or
        pretended, to the couple, and that he subsequently acted out
        a role similar to that of either Calasiris or the amorous
        magician Paapis (*supra* 35ff., 141 n.37).

48   U. Wilcken, *Hermes* 28 (1893), 161-193; Lavagnini 1-15;
        Zimmermann 13-35; Rattenbury 213-23; Perry *AR* 53-73; for
        further, extensive, bibliography, Pack 2616.

49   Fr. A.II.8-17.

50   Frr. A.IV.20-V.6; V.27-36.

51   *Apud* Diodorus II.1-20.

52   *AR* 164. But his ideas of ancient patriotism are too clear-
        cut: when did any Greek writer *need* to be patriotic about
        Babylon? Certainly Chariton did not. Here as there we
        have conventional rhetorical fun at the expense of barbar-
        ians.

53   IV.9.33-60.

54   P.J. Parsons, *BICS* 18 (1971), 53-68; *Oxyrynchus Papyri* XVII
        (London 1974) 34-41. In the latter P. notes a detailed
        comic reconstruction by E.R. Dodds, who explains the verses
        as a deliberate mixture of the obscene and arcane as a
        travesty of the lore of the galli. There is further dis-
        cussion of the ritual in Merkelbach, *ZPE* 11 (1973), 81-100.
        Parsons (*BICS o.c.*63) dismisses the possibility that the
        fragment is from an ideal novel.

55   III.15-22.

56   *Supra* 33-35.

57   Phot. *Cod.* 166.109a.

58   See *Studies* 68-82.

59   *Infra* 57f.

60   Cf. Parsons *BICS o.c.* (*supra* n.54), 61.

61   III.22.3ff.

62   Cf. Terence, *Eunuchus* 604ff.

63   E.g. Chariton VI.6.5; Heliodorus VIII.15.4.

64   A. Henrichs, *ZPE* 4 (1969), 205-215; *id.* 5 (1970), 22; *Die
      Phoinikika des Lollianos, Fragmente eines neuen griechischen
      Romans, Papyrologische Texte und Abhandlungen* 14, Bonn 1972,
      to which subsequent reference is made. H. Notes the erotic
      associations of Phoenicia ('dem üppigen orientalischen
      Leben', 20); we are in the same world as the *Milesiaca*.

65   But G.N. Sandy, *AJP* 100 (1979), 376 notes how much of his
      additional parallel material comes mainly from Petronius
      and Achilles Tatius.

66   Fr. A2 recto 9f. (Henrichs 108).

67   Fr. Bl verso 14, 15 (Henrichs 121): 'Hier zeigt sich wieder
      das künstlerische Unvermögen des Lollianos, der die tradi-
      tionellen Stilelemente der gehobenen Romanliteratur zwar
      kannte, aber nicht sicher beherrschte'.

68   Fr. Bl verso 11-13 (Henrichs 120).

69   *Ibid.* 9f. (Henrichs 119). The subsequent account of the
      initiates painting their faces and dressing up in two groups
      can be accounted for in ritual practice: but we are entitled
      to suspect that the whole account, like the procedures of
      Quartilla or Oenothea in Petronius, or the priests of
      Atargatis in the *Onos*, is not told for ritual instruction,
      but by an unsympathetic observer - with a touch of voyeur-
      ism so characteristic of Achilles: when they strip the
      corpses they make sure to include mention of the girls'
      ταινία.

70   Achilles IV.7.7.

71   But cf. Henrichs *o.c.* (*supra* n.64) 7: 'Der drastische Real-
      ismus und die derbe Komik der Darstellung, sowie die platte
      Sinnlichkeit, die nicht wie bei Platon, Apuleius, Longos
      und Achilleus Tatios durch geistreiche Brillanz gedämpft
      wird, kennzeichnen die Ph. also ein unterhaltungsprodukt
      billigster Art'. It should be stressed however that the
      linguistic arguments adduced by H. in support of this claim
      apply just as readily to the *Onos*; that weakens them con-
      siderably.

72   The Glauketes fragment rightly attached to this novel (*P.
      Oxy.* 1368; Lavagnini 33f.; Pack 2620; Henrichs *o.c.*, *supra*
      n.64, 8ff.) does not contain specifically comic content.
      But Glauketes riding through the night is addressed directly

by a ghost.   In view of the rest of the novel this is as
likely to be a hoax (cf. Iamblichus, Phot. *Cod.* 94.74b) as
the real thing.

73   The fragments of most other known novels are too short to
      offer much evidence either way, and we must be content mean-
      time with possibilities.   There may have been a frivolous
      debate on the princess' marriage in the Chione-text
      (Wilcken *APf* I, 1901, 254-264; Lavagnini 24-27; Zimmermann
      40-45), whether by a council of suitors (Wilcken; Zimmer-
      mann, *Aegyptus* 11, 1931, 45ff.), or a council of state
      (Rattenbury 233f.).   Such a possibility may also have been
      realised in *P. Oxy.* 435 (Lavagnini 28f.; Zimmermann 62f.,
      guessing that it belongs to Metiochus; Rattenbury 245; Pack
      2623), where Demosthenes - orator or more likely general -
      was involved in a marriage-question.   Odysseus' αἰδώς is
      once more in question in *P. Lond* 2239 (Rattenbury 245, not
      in Pack) (but neither of the latter has been decisively
      shown to have been from a novel).   Possibilities of fun with
      superstition appear in the Herpyllis-fragment (*P. Dublin Inv.*
      C/3; J.G. Smyly, *Hermathena* 11, 1901, 322-30; Lavagnini 16-
      20; Zimmermann 68-78; Rattenbury 234-37; Pack 2621), where
      the sailors' explanation of St. Elmo's fire is in question,
      or in *P. Mich. Inv.* 3378 (Pack 2629, *APf* II.283); C. Bonner,
      Aegyptus 13 (1933), 203-207, where a man recounts in the
      first person that a ghost ordered him to commit suicide.
      This last episode presupposes a nexus of motifs similar to
      those used by Iamblichus (Phot. *Cod.* 74b), Achilles III.18-
      23, or Apuleius' Thelyphron (II.21-30) or Lucius (II.32-
      III.12); the implication is that one ought to check the cre-
      dentials of people who tell one to commit suicide!   The
      literate nature of the work is underlined by an echo of
      Demosthenes: the narrator kills himself φα[ι]δρὸς καὶ
      γεγηθώς (*De Corona* 223) (so Bonner, who cannot bring himself
      to see anything more than childish absurdity in the whole
      idea, *ibid.* 206).

74   For similar doubts cf. Reardon, *Novels and Novelties*, or
      Mysteriouser and Mysteriouser, in *The Mediterranean World:
      Papers presented in honour of Gilbert Bagnani*, Peterborough,
      Ontario 1976, 94.

1   Texts of Apocryphal *Acts* are cited from the edition of
R.A. Lipsius - M. Bonnet, *Acta Apostolorum Apocrypha*, Leipzig 1889-1903 (hereafter *AA*). The starting-point in this
sub-literary no-man's land is W. Schneemelcher's revision
(Tübingen 1964) of E. Hennecke's *Neutestamentliche Apokryphen* II, which contains valuable introductory and bibliographical information on the nature of *praxeis*-literature and
on the individual Apocryphal *Acts* (including the *pseudo-
Clementines*). Early attempts to come to grips with this
material include R. Reitzenstein's *Hellenistische Wundererzählungen*, Leipzig 1906, repr. Stuttgart 1963); F. Pfister
in Hennecke[2] (*supra*) (1924) 163ff.; R. Söder, *Die apokryphen
Apostelgeschichten und die romanhafte Literatur der Antike,
Würzburger Studien zur Altertumswissenschaft* 3, 1932; R. Helm,
Der Antike Roman[2], Göttingen 1956, 53-61; see also Reardon
303-330, who places them in the perspective of 2nd and 3rd
century writing as a whole.

2   *Acta Pauli et Theclae* 26 (*AA* I.254); so in *Acta Thomae* IX.
98 (*AA* II.ii.211), where the chief courtier's wife runs off
naked in the middle of the night (but cf. Mk. 14.51f.).
What would Achilles Tatius have made of such a motif?

3   *Acta Pauli et Theclae* 36 (*AA* I.261).

4   Cf. Ovid. *Met.* XIII.477ff.; Apuleius, *Met.* VIII.12.

5   *Acta Pauli et Theclae* 35 (*AA* I.261).

6   *Recognitiones* I.8.3 (text in B. Rehm, *Die Pseudoklementinen,
I Homilien*, Berlin 1953; II *Recognitiones* 1965); cf. Ar. *Nub.*
156-167, and compare its sophistic imitations at Achilles II.
21f.; Heliodorus III.8; Lucian, *Musc. Enc.* 3. The case of
the obedient bugs in the *Acta Johannis* 60f. (*AA* II.ii.180)
is no doubt a conscious variation on 'go to the ant, thou
sluggard' (*Prov.* VI.6).

7   *Homilies* XII.21.4; XIV.6.2-7.3; XIV.8.1.

8   I.1-2 (*AA* II.2.100ff.).

9   I use the text (of the short recension) by M. Philonenko,
Joseph et Aseneth, Studia Post-Biblica XIII, Leyden 1968.
For the longer versions and their relationships, see C.
Burchard, *Untersuchungen zu Joseph u. Aseneth*, Tübingen 1965.
S. West, *CQ N.S.* 24 (1974), 70-81, joins Philonenko (*contra*
G.D. Kilpatrick, *Novum Testamentum* 12, 1970, 233f.), in em-
phasising the affinities to Greek novels (while remaining
rightly non-committal about its place in the development of
the genre). T. Szepessy, *Acta Classica Universitatis Scientiarum Debrecensis* 10-11 (1974-75), 121-131 stresses its
devotional links with genuine religious literature, particularly apocryphal *Acts*. But the sheer variety of humbler
novelistic material makes rigid classification impossible,
as Szepessy himself admits.

10   I.10.

11   IV.14.

12   VII.11. He had already put a less reputable interpretation
      on her watching him from her bedroom window (VII.8-10); and
      promises, all unsuspecting, to love her as a sister (VII.11).

13   XXVII.8. There are also some rather underdeveloped cases of
      pseudos: (false claims of Pharaoh's son, XXIII.4, XXIV.8).

14   Text: A. Riese, Teubner[2] 1983; for the problems, E. Klebs,
      Die Erzählung von Apollonius aus Tyrus, Berlin 1899.

15   19-22; 34f. There is also an inept attempt at irony:
      Apollonius handles the negotiations with the suitors, without
      knowing that he is the object of the princess' affections
      (20).

16   33.

17   *O.c.* (*supra* n.14) 280ff. (verbal imitations of Ovid, Apuleius,
      Roman Comedy); 305f. (humour).

18   Text of the A version in W. Kroll, *Historia Alexandri Magni
      (Pseudo-Callisthenes)* I: *recensio vetusta*, Berlin 1926. For
      the relationship of the extant versions, R. Merkelbach, *Die
      Quellen des griechischen Alexanderromans*, (*Zetemata IX[2]*)
      Munich 1977.

19   Nectanebus masquerades as Ammon and seduces Olympias, I.4ff.

20   II.14.9 (Alexander impersonates his own ambassador, cf.
      III.3.3 (B[1], Armenian). But falsehood in the work has to
      be treated carefully, as noted by M. Braun, *History and
      Romance in Graeco-Oriental Literature*, Oxford 1938, 33f.:
      'Thus the Alexander-romance belongs spiritually to the
      common people who cannot clearly and consciously differenti-
      ate between truth (ἀλήθεια), lies (ψεῦδος), and literary
      fiction (πλάσμα)... In the Alexander Romance, truth and fic-
      tion are inextricably interwoven. The categories ψεῦδος
      and πλάσμα cannot be applied at all to the case of untrue
      and fantastic statements. To apply them would be unjust to
      the anonymous author and to his readers, because the stand-
      ards and categories of the historian are not applicable to
      their intellectual capacities'.

21   Military slapstick: III.3.4 (heated bronze men burn the
      mouths of the Indian animals); III.4.4 (Porus killed through
      the bowels; contrast Heliodorus' treatment of the Persian
      cavalry, *Aeth.* IX.18.2).

22   III.19.2; 22.12.

23   Reardon 189f.; Solmsen *s.v.* Philostratus 2, *PW* 20.2   152-159.

24   IV.11; VI.27.

25   Apollonius mistaken for a spirit (by a eunuch, I.21; by
      Domitian, VII.23); or hailed by Damis as resurrected (III.43;
      VII.41); frequent examples of barbarian irrationalism or
      misunderstanding (e.g. II.34; III.3; III.10; IV.44; VI.3;
      VI.19).

26 Philostratus cultivates a wide range of Platonic graces,
    from a charming myth on Aesop to a joke on the *Phaedrus*
    grasshoppers (V.15, VII.11); and accumulates witty exchanges
    against trivial pursuits (e.g. dancing IV.21; export of
    images of gods, V.20; training birds to talk, VI.36).

27 For the latter episode, *Heroicus* 212 (p.71 de Lannoy), to
    which compare *VA* IV.25, VII.42.

28 For the latter possibility, see now H. Gärtner, *PW* Suppl.
    IX A2, 1967, 2072-80; T. Hägg *C&M* 27 (1966), 118-161.

29 I.1.4-I.4.4.

30 III.5-IV.21.

31 I.1.6.

32 Xenophon I.2.9; Chariton I.1.12.

33 I.6.

34 In Longus the couple do not slight Eros, but do not know
    him either; the discovery of Love is instead a chance to
    smile at their innocence (I.13f.; 17f., and *passim*).

35 E.g. Ovid *Met.* VIII.217-220.

36 I.2.7.

37 II.3.6.

38 I.7.2.

39 Phot. *Cod.* 94.75b/76a.

40 E.g. IV.1.1, IV.2.1 (Chaereas), cf. III.1.1 (Dionysius).

41 *Supra* 29f.

42 Xenophon III.8.3; Achilles III.10.2f.; Heliodorus I.3.2.

43 As held by Merkelbach, *RM* 339f.; R. Petri, *Ueber den Roman
    des Chariton*, Meisenheim am Glan 1963.

Notes to Chapter VIII

1   The doxography of Petronius is now daunting; many of the con-
     tributions of the late 'sixties and early 'seventies appear-
     ed almost simultaneously and could not take account of one
     another; I have sought to illustrate points of view, rather
     than produce voting lists of their proponents. As it
     happens, the three large-scale works of these years all opt
     for a basically 'literary' approach which sees Petronius as
     an amusing entertainer (J.P. Sullivan, *Petronius, A Literary
     Study*, London 1968; E. Stöcker, *Humor bei Petron*, Diss.
     Erlangen 1969; and P.G. Walsh, *The Roman Novel, The Satyricon
     of Petronius and the Golden Ass of Apuleius*, Cambridge 1970).
     Both the English contributions as well as Stöcker devote sub-
     stantial discussion to humour *passim*; I have tried to avoid
     duplication, directing my attention for the most part to
     'moralist' positions which have survived their arguments or
     emerged since. For more recent summaries of Petronian
     questions, see M. Coffey, *Roman Satire*, London and New York
     1976, 178-203; Sullivan, *Helikon* 17 (1977), 137-154.

2   These are well surveyed, e.g. by Sullivan 225-228; Stöcker
     ibid. 54-62; and in the new commentary on the *Cena* by M.S.
     Smith (Oxford 1975). H. Petersmann, *Petrons urbane Prosa:
     Untersuchungen zu Sprache und Text (Syntax), Sitzungsbe-
     richte der Oesterreichischen Akademie der Wissenschafte,
     Phil.-Hist. Klasse* 323, 1977, pays special attention to lin-
     guistic levels. To the valuable study of style and charact-
     er in P.A. George, *Arion* 5 (1966), 336-358, add now R. Beck,
     Phoenix 33 (1979), 239-253 on Eumolpus.

3   For the extension of the problem to the literary episodes in
     Petronius, see Appendix III.

4   For material common to Petronius and Lucian, *Studies* 99-106.

5   *Hermes* 34 (1899), 494-519 (= *Vom Geist des Römertums*[3], Darm-
     stadt 1960, 417-439. Recent discussions continue to divide
     on the balance of genres: Sullivan accepts the novel only
     distrustfully as a possible subsidiary component (96f.),
     while at the other extreme, R. Astbury, *CP* 72 (1977), 22-31,
     would transfer to novels like *'Iolaus'* the credit usually
     accorded to Menippean Satire. There is a similar tendency
     to exclusive interpretation in G. Sandy, *AJP* 90 (1969), 299f.;
     and A. Scobie, *Aspects of the Ancient Romance and its Heri-
     tage (Beiträge zur klassischen Philologie)* 30, Meisenheim am
     Glan 1968, 86-90, in favour of Satire and the novel respect-
     ively. I prefer the more inclusive position of Walsh 29;
     for more cautious formulations, Smith *o.c.* (*supra* n.2),
     xv-xviii, Coffey *o.c.* (*supra* n.1) 183-194.

6   I accept the traditional arguments for identifying our
     Petronius with that of Tac. *Ann.* XVI.18f., as set out by
     Sullivan 21-33, (cf. K.F.C. Rose, *Arion* 5, 1966, 275-301).
     If he is not the author then a Petronius of the same capabili-
     ties and temperament clearly is. There is sufficient internal
     evidence to enable us to form a picture of the author's
     intentions without assuming Tacitus' portrait: if the

Satyricon were by Seneca, it would throw new light on *him*, not vice versa.

7   For the strong colouring of mime, see M. Rosenblüth, *Beiträge zur Quellenkunde von Petronius' Satiren*, Berlin 1909; G. Sandy, *TAPA* 104 (1974) 329-346 (with intervening bibliography). In *AJP* 102 (1981), 50-53 I have suggested that Petronius knew a version of the *Alexander-Romance*, and so used yet another stratum of popular fiction.

8   E.g. by Sullivan 92-98; G. Sandy *o.c.(supra* n.5) 299f.

9   Sullivan (95) curiously admits it as an ideal novel but compares it only with Xenophon's *Cyropaedia*, where the *Liebespaar* play only a peripheral part. But Ninus' amours clearly place him in the same category as Clitophon or Theagenes rather than the tragic and already-married Abradatas.

10 Sullivan (93, cf. 43) does not explain why it is improbable that Giton was with Encolpius from the beginning. Even if he was not, however, other disreputable amours could have served equally well to negate the ideals of the ideal novel.

11 Walsh 10.

12 So Wehrli 136f.; G. Sandy, *o.c.* (*supra* n.5) 299.

13 E.g. Sen. *Ep.* 47.7.

14 Longus IV.11f., cf. 16ff.; *contra* Sandy *o.c.* (*supra* n.5) 299 and n.16.

15 I.7-14; II.35-38.

16 I.14ff.; III.2.

17 Cf. Sullivan 95 (Eumolpus as hypocritical philosopher or importunate poetaster); he is also close to a Calasiris gone wrong.

18 So Sullivan 95f.

19 *Sat.* 83ff.; Sullivan 96.

20 *Sat.* 126ff.; Sullivan 119-122, 96.

21 *Sat.* 126ff. Sullivan (216f.) compares *Am.*III.7. As well as the parallels in Longus (II.9ff.; III.14), cf. the rather more trivial hitches in Achilles' erotic garden, where the lovers are first interrupted by Leucippe's maid, then by Satyrus, (II.8.1; 10.4f.).

22 On the other hand a number of episodes in the *Satyricon* have been claimed to have no obvious connexion with the ideal novel. But these do not exclude Heinze's theory: most of the ideal novels have an overall literary colouring, be it Plato or Pastoral, which determines the choice of digressions. Here the topoi of Satire provide such a background, and the amorous adventure is interwoven with them. The positioning of such digressions would have contributed to the tension of the love-affair: the initial diversion at the rhetorical school allows Ascyltus to slip away and get a head start with Giton (*Sat.* 6.1-9); the *Cena*, for all its length, goes on its

way while the reader is wondering how Encolpius will shake
off Ascyltus. Its length does not upset Heinze's case, as
objected e.g. by Sandy *o.c.* (*supra* n.5) 299: even if our
information about the length of the novel is mistaken, dis-
proportionate digressions do occur in the ideal novels.
The siege of Syene in Heliodorus does not turn his novel
into history.

23   There is now a wide spectrum of such positions: I have
        focussed on the classic statement by Highet in *TAPA* 72
        (1941), 176-194, because it illustrates the tendency to
        apriorism in moralist argument ('it cannot be a satire if
        Petronius is not a moralist'; 'if Petronius is a moralist,
        his work is a satire', 177). Few would now accept his the-
        sis that Petronius aims to reform through disgust, but many
        allow some element of detached resignation in the human
        condition (e.g. Perry *AR* 200; Stöcker *o.c.*, *supra* n.1, 53,
        151-154; W. Arrowsmith, *Arion* 5, 1966, 330). For views
        like the last, founded on comparative material, see Appen-
        dix I. Against interpretation of Petronius as an Epicurean,
        see Sullivan's qualification (107-110) of Highet and of O.
        Raith, *Petronius ein Epikureer*, Nuremberg 1963. I am uncon-
        vinced by the revival of this position by C. Piano, *Rendi-
        conti dell' Accademia di Archeologia, Lettere e Belle arti
        di Napoli* 51 (1976) 3-30: there is little in the allegedly
        Epicurean ethos that cannot be just as easily explained as
        amused scepticism.

24   Highet *ibid.* 188f. No other writer who aims to practise
        spoudaiogeloion is much help. Horace can experiment with
        quite equivocal combinations: both *Sat.* II.4 and II.7 em-
        body familiar satirical material on dining and human con-
        duct respectively, yet the results do not necessarily amount
        to committed Satire (see N. Rudd, *The Satires of Horace*,
        Cambridge 1966, 213,196); Lucian tends to works with only
        a facade of seriousness, as Highet points out (*The Anatomy
        of Satire*, Princeton 1961, 42f.). We are thrown back on
        the evidence of the *Satyricon* itself. (I am not convinced
        that Menippean Satire is automatically the medium for
        allusiveness to other genres, *contra* E.C. Courtney, *Philo-
        logus* 106, 1962, 96-100).

25   Highet *ibid.* 182f.

26   Highet *ibid.* 187 cites the parasite's speech at Ter. *Phorm.*
        339; for Gnathon, *supra* 44; for Lucian's Simon, Bompaire
        607ff. The same line of argument applies to the treatment
        of superstition in the *Satyricon*, whether of Lichas or
        Trimalchio himself; Theophrastus' *Deisidaimon* and Lucian's
        Philopseudes offer at least as much literary entertainment
        as satire, as does Heliodorus' Cnemon.

27   *Carmm.* 23, 67. For humour in Catullus' invective, see
        J.-Ph. Cèbe, *La caricature et la parodie o.c.* (*supra* 108
        n.73) 180-184; 188-190. Another comparable case is that of
        the more obscene mimes of Herodas (II, V, VI, VII): it would
        be absurd to suggest that the clever and eloquent brothel-
        keeper of II was intended as any kind of satire on hypo-
        crisy, any more than that his counterpart in *Apollonius of
        Tyre* was meant as an attack on immorality.

28   Another cornerstone of moralist argument is that the
        character of the speaker can be detached from his subject-

matter: if a hypocrite or a homosexual is made to deliver
moral sermons, their moral content must be allowed to stand
(Highet *o.c.*, *supra* n.23, 179). One might cite Horace's
slave interlocutor (*Sat.* II.7) on the servitude of fools,
the foolish Stoic delivering a serious sermon (*Sat.* II.3),
or Apollodorus as the reporter in Plato's *Symposium*. But
there are no inflexible rules: a Horatian money-lender can
also praise the country, undoing the effect when he reveals
his identity in the closing lines (*Ep.* II.127ff.; E. Fraenkel, *Horace*, Oxford 1975, 60f.); or the Platonic Socrates
can bring himself to mimic the questionable style and
subject-matter of Lysias (*Phaedr.* 237B-241D). Moreover
none of the characters cited by Highet are out-and-out
reprobates; in Petronius it is consistently amusing that
they are. In these circumstances there is not much point
in citing examples of idyllic melancholy from the fragments,
as Perry does: he has to admit that they were 'probably
uttered by such characters as Encolpius or Eumolpus against
a background of farce' (*AR* 201). At least one of Perry's
short selection has an uncomfortable resemblance to the
effusions over the body of Lichas (fr. 49, and possibly
fr. 32 Ernout), and must be treated as equally suspect (see
infra 71f. A third is about Midas' secret (fr. 28), and
could well relate to the divulging of the secret of one of
the dubious mysteries (cf. *Sat.* 17).

29   Sullivan 90.

30   For the relationship of the *Satyricon* to the *Priapeia*, see
      H.D. Rankin, *CM* 26 (1965), 233-245 (*Petronius the Artist,
      Essays on the Satyricon and its author*, The Hague 1971,
      52-67).

31   *Priapeium* 49.1f. (*Carmina ludicra Romanorum*, ed. E. Cazza-
      niga, Paravia 1959).

32   For the Wrath, see Sullivan's general index *s.v.* Priapus;
      Walsh 76f. I am unconvinced by the attempt of B. Baldwin,
      CP 68 (1973), 74-76 to localise and minimise the effect of
      each individual reference to the god.

33   Cf. Lucian's projection of Priapus into an imitation of
      Socrates and Alcibiades, *D. Deorum* 23.

34   See *supra* 56ff. R. Astbury *o.c.* (*supra* n.5) carefully uses
      Iolaus to reduce the link between Petronius and Menippean
      Satire; though the *prosimetrum* in itself could always have
      enabled P. to claim that he was using the form. If he did
      in fact absorb it into his general amalgam, there is still
      no telling whether he twisted it in the process.

35   Fr. B1 verso 9f.

36   For the parallels, Parsons *BICS* 18 (1971), 65f.; Merkelbach
      ZPE 11 (1973), 83-86.

37   Chariton III.4.18.

38   Longus I.29f.

39   *Supra* 38.

40   *Supra* 24.

41   *Supra* 31.

42   The elusive *Ich-Erzählung* in the *Satyricon* cannot be used to
      exclude its connexion with the ideal novel, as argued by
      P. Veyne, *REL* 42 (1964), 301-324; Achilles at least dis-
      covered that humiliations are funny in the first person,
      a feature which Perry underlines for the comic novels (*AR*
      325-329). I intend to discuss this vexed question else-
      where. For the moment it must suffice to say that I am not
      wholly convinced by the explanations of Smith *o.c.* (*supra*
      n.2) and R. Beck, *Phoenix* 27 (1973), 42-61; *ibid.* 29 (1975),
      271-283 on Encolpius' reactions. Smith ad 41.5 stresses
      that Encolpius makes a number of stupid mistakes which any
      normal person would have been able to avoid; but it must
      be remembered that the whole affair is an obstacle course,
      of increasingly ominous duration. The reader might reason-
      ably be expected to be embarrassed for Encolpius as he
      finds he cannot quite keep pace with the proceedings, and
      does not see himself able to last them out. Petronius
      succeeds in communicating Encolpius' sophisticated superi-
      ority and subservient fear at the same time. It might be
      argued that his very sophistication is conducive to his
      being caught out: *because* he is rightly shocked by the
      vulgarity of the porter and the bird, he is caught out over
      the canine *trompe l'oeil*.

43   Walsh *G&R* *o.c.* (*supra* n.1) 184f. suggests four criteria:
      the author's character and title; the shifting moral view-
      point, and the constant comparison with mime. The last
      three are all comic effects in their own right: P. puns on
      his title, as cleverly as he puns on the common material of
      incompatible genres; the shifting moral viewpoint produces
      an anti-hero still more clearly drawn than Clitophon; and
      comparisons with dramatic performance can be used to comic
      effect in Heliodorus.

44   Cf. Walsh *ibid.* 186ff., who discusses the Circe-episode and
      the misleading preoccupation of scholars with the *Cena*.
      For ironic literary presentation of the sexual episodes,
      C. Gill, *CP* 68 (1973), 177-179.

45   *Sat.* 16-26.

46   E.g. *supra* 27 (Achilles); 34f.(Heliodorus). For the Roman
      colouring of Quartilla, see Walsh, *Roman Novel* 89f.

47   Cf. Hor. *Sat.* I.8; Heliodorus VI.14f. (real rituals gone
      wrong).

48   Arrowsmith *o.c.* (*supra* n.23) 307, cf. 309.

49   *Sat.* 22.1, cf. 26.6.

50   *Sat.* 85-87.

51   *Sat.* 17.8, cf. 104.1, 137.1f, 139.2.

52   *Sat.* 77.7-78; Arrowsmith *o.c.* (*supra* n.23) 306ff.

53   *Apocolocyntosis* 12.3-13.1.

54   Echoes are well established by Averil Cameron, *CQ N.S.* 19
      (1969), 367-70.

55   *Sat.* 101ff.

56   *Sat.* 104f.

57   Cf. Longus II.23-29.

58   *Sat.* 115.7ff.

59   Fr. 115 Merkelbach-West.

60   E.g. Averil Cameron, *Latomus* 29 (1970), 411f., cf. Arrow-
      smith *o.c.* (*supra* n.23), 327f.

61   Achilles III.4.5.

62   *Ibid.* VI.9.4f.

63   Cf. Lucian *de Luctu* 12-20.

64   I.13f.

65   *Sat.* 116f.

66   *Sat.* 116.6; 117.1.

67   *Sat.* 117; Heliodorus VI.11.3-12.1.

68   *Sat.* 140; Highet *o.c.* (*supra* n.23) 181.

69   *Met.* IX.7.

70   52.

71   Cf. also Lucian, *D. Meretr.* 5,6 (mother sends her daughter
      out as a prostitute).

72   *Sat.* 141. Highet *o.c.* (*supra* n.23) admits the weakness of
      moralist argument here ('if we could only recover a frag-
      ment telling us how they solved their problem, and how
      Eumolpus' party escape'). Even if he escapes with consider-
      able discomfiture, is Petronius likely to have made that
      discomfiture anything but amusing? Again we are dealing
      with lovable villain versus unlovable, without any moral
      differentiation between them.

73   For underlying literary tradition, see H.D. Rankin, *Hermes*
      97 (1969), 381-389 (= *Petronius the Artist* 100-105).   To
      Rankin's parallels we should add the polite irony of the
      Greek in Lucian's *Toxaris* 8f.: Scythian 'friendship' con-
      sists of eating their fathers; the Scythian suggests that
      the discussion be postponed!

74   25.

75   Achilles III.15.5; Lollianus fr. B1 verso.

76   So Cameron *o.c.* (*supra* n.60), 413f.; but I am not convinced
      by her insistence that such a presentation of the evil city
      must be morally earnest.

Notes to Chapter IX

1   For the problem of the two surviving versions and their
       relationship to the lost *Metamorphoses* attributed to Lucius
       of Patras, see P. Vallette's introduction to D.S. Robert-
       son's Budé Apuleius[2], Paris 1956; H. van Thiel's introduc-
       tion to his synoptic text of the *Onos* and Apuleius, *Der
       Eselsroman* I (*Zetemata* 54.1), Munich 1971; and now H.J.
       Mason, 'Fabula Graecanica: Apuleius and his Greek Sources',
       in B.L. Hijmans - R. van der Paardt, *Aspects of Apuleius'
       Golden Ass*, Groningen 1977, 1-15, to which add *Studies*
       34-67.

2   So K. Bürger, *Studien zur Geschichte des griechischen Romans*
       I: *Der Lukiosroman und seine litteratur-geschichtliche
       Bedeutung*, Gymnasialprogramm, Blankenburg 1902, 21.; van
       Thiel *ibid*. 190-194. One could argue that the normal situa-
       tions of the ideal novel do not correspond to Lucius'
       experience. It is not to Palaestra he returns when he re-
       gains his human shape; and the ideal heroine he comes
       across in the middle is encountered only in passing. But
       there is a limit to the amount of correspondence that *can* be
       achieved: he cannot return to the house at Hypata, having
       since been accused of complicity with the robbers; and hav-
       ing suffered once he does not want another encounter with
       Pamphile either.

3   *Onos* 16ff.

4   *Onos* 24.

5   *Onos* 25f.

6   *Onos* 35-41; 12-14.

7   *Onos* 50-52.

8   *Onos* 6-11.

9   *Onos* 50-52.

10   *Onos* 53-55.

11   *Onos* 56.

12   *Onos* 25, 28.

13   *Onos* 33.

14   *Onos* 51.

15   *Onos* 53.

16   *Onos* 38.

17   *Onos* 53.

18   *Onos* 32.

19   *Onos* 33.

20   *Onos* 24.

21   *Onos* 25.

22   Cf. *Studies* 48f.

23   His approach to altering the original has been intensively
        studied: for a useful summary of its less controversial
        aspects, see van Thiel *o.c.* (*supra* n.1) 9-21; on humour,
        ibid. 14-16. Apuleius prefers explicit irony, heightens
        the human identity of the ass with a polite and 'philo-
        sophic' personality, and humorously overloads the texture
        of the humble fable with poetic and rhetorical flourish and
        mythological comparison (on the latter see especially
        Walsh, *Roman Novel* 148-76 *passim*). Two 'running comment-
        aries' pay particular attention to humorous effect: Walsh
        ibid., and now J. Tatum, *Apuleius and the Golden Ass*,
        Ithaca and London 1979, deal sympathetically with its com-
        plexities, placing humour in a broad literary, philosophi-
        cal and religious perspective, but opting for much more di-
        dactic interpretations than the present author. F.J.J. Feld-
        brugge, *Het schertsende karakter van Apuleius' Metamorphosen*,
        Diss. Nijmegen 1938, Utrecht 1939, provides a more mundane
        catalogue of humorous 'effects' (1-87), followed by an in-
        ventory of stylistic witticisms (88-126). For the problems
        of book XI, see *infra* n.65.

24   Warren Smith Jnr., *TAPA* 103 (1972), 522 neatly characteri-
        ses the ingredients as surprise, mock-naivety and incon-
        gruity, and rightly suggests that the reader has been deli-
        berately misled before bk. XI.   But he goes on to accept
        a serious significance (526ff.).

25   So Walsh 171.

26   I.19.9f.

27   II.30.7.

28   III.9.9-10.1.

29   III.15.3-18.7.

30   IX.29ff.

31   VIII.4.1.

32   VIII.12: cf. the rather demure suicide pose of Polyxena,
        Ovid *Met.* XIII.477ff.

33   II.21.6.

34   II.26.5.

35   II.30.9.

36   I.12.7-13.1; I.18.4f., 6f. Lucius' own pretensions also come
        to grief when he defends himself in increasingly absurd
        rhetoric for killing the robbers, only to find himself the
        butt of the *Risus*-festival (III.9.9-10.2).

37   H. Riefstahl, *Der Roman des Apuleius, Frankfurter Studien
      zur Geschichte und Kultur der Antike* 15 (1938), 90, and
      F. Pfister, *PhW* 60 (1940), 540 fail to see it.

38   Lamachus nailed to a door (IV.10.3); Alcimus pushed from a
      window (IV.2.7); Thrasyleon caught in a bear costume
      (IV.19.5-20.5).

39   IV.11.5. The resourceful adulterer does no better, for all
      the bawd's praises of his quick thinking (IX.16-21); he
      himself is caught and painfully humiliated first by Lucius,
      then by the outraged husband (IX.27.2). J. Tatum, *TAPA* 100
      (1969), 487-527 finds such tales didactic and admonitory as
      much as amusing, and considers it depressing (525) that such
      characters ignore the warnings; but in company with R. Heine,
      'Picaresque Novel versus Allegory' in Hijmans-van der Paardt
      o.c. (*supra* n.1) 30, I find the ignoring of such warnings
      amusing in itself (cf. *infra* n.76).

40   X.33.

41   *Gall.* 25; 18.19.

42   In particular Perry *AR* vii.

43   *O.c.* (*supra* n.37), 540.

44   For Plato's popularity, see De Lacey *o.c.* (*supra* c.I n.37)
      4-10.

45   C. Schlam, *TAPA* 101 (1970), 477-87, illustrates the dangers
      very well. If we try to connect Lucius' misfortunes with
      Plato's transmigrations of gluttons into asses (*Phaedo* 81E;
      Schlam 480), the effect need still be no more than one of
      mock-moral, elegant amusement; and such an allusion is just
      as likely to underlie the original Greek story. Schlam also
      draws attention to the juxtaposition of tales involving
      doctors with those of the cooks, and cites the famous con-
      trast in *Gorgias* 463E-466A (482). But if we accept an allu-
      sion here, the contrast between the two doctor-stories would
      not simply 'seem to show that even a true τέχνη is not se-
      cure against corruption' (Schlam *ibid.*); it would also turn
      Platonic values upside down: the doctor now plays the cook's
      game, and cannot heal himself either. Apuleius' allusion
      to *Apol.* 41B (X.33; Schlam 485f.) does indeed bring us full
      circle back to Socrates, but again he is used incongruously:
      Lucius' allusion to Palamedes, Ajax and the trial of Socra-
      tes is now applied to the corrupt judgement of Paris. We
      should note that the majority of instances suggested by
      Schlam are *literary* Platonica, the common property of a
      sophistic education (e.g. *Apol.* 12; *Symp.* 180Dff.). Apu-
      leius need not be playing the professional Platonist, as
      opposed to the Platonic connoisseur on holiday. Nor does
      it follow that because Apuleius states a belief in so many
      words in his philosophical works that it is upheld (rather
      than used for some other purpose) in the *Metamorphoses*.
      This difficulty affects most Platonising interpretations of
      the work, e.g. Walsh 184; Grimal's commentary on *Cupid and
      Psyche* (Paris 1963) 14; R. Thibau, *Studia philosophica
      Gandensia* 3 (1965) 89-144. Nor are Apuleius' *philosophica*
      themselves consistently serious or free from literary diver-
      sion, as usefully noted by J. Beaujeu, *Bulletin de l'Asso-
      ciation Guillaume Budé* 4 (1975), 94.

46   *Symp*. 189C-193D.

47   *De feriis Alsiensibus* III.8-12 (pp. 216-19 van den Hout).

48   *Ibid*. III.9f.

49   *Symp*. 174E; *Met*. I.6.1.

50   *Met*. I.7.7ff.; I.12.4ff. R. Helm, in the preface to his
     edition, Teubner 1931³ xxxii, rightly suspected that the name
     Socrates is used κατ' ἀντίφρασιν.

51   *Phaedr*. 229b; I.19.9. A. Scobie, *Apuleius Metamorphoses* I,
     A Commentary, Beiträge zur klassische Philologie 54, Meisen-
     heim am Glan 1975, accepts the correspondence in the preced-
     ing note, but misses this one; Thibau *o.c.* (*supra* n.45)
     105f., 112 notes both, but tries to impose a serious inter-
     pretation throughout.

52   *Phaedr*. 242BC; *Met. ibid*. Other details can be suspected of
     an 'anti-Platonic' colouring: Socrates' discussion of Ory-
     thuia rationalises the robber as the wind (*Phaedr*. 229C);
     Lucius' robbers turn out to be bags of wind (III.12). Soc-
     rates condemns rhetoric for making the weak man claim in
     court that he could not have attacked the strong, and making
     the coward say he was attacked by more than one man (*Phaedr*.
     265Ef.); both arguments are used by Lucius in court (III.
     8.6; III.5.2). I am less sure about two passages in the
     Symposium: Socrates' opening remark on arrival is that he
     wishes wisdom could be drained from one person to another;
     (175D); Apuleius' Socrates has his life-blood drained
     (I.19.9). The first tale in Plato's *Symposium* may have
     been travestied by Thelyphron's tale (179B-180B; *Met*. II.
     21-30). But Apuleius' approach to Plato is clear enough.

53   On the question of folktale origins, I agree with D. Fehling,
     Amor und Psyche: Die Schöpfung des Apuleius und ihre Ein-
     wirkung auf das Märchen: eine Kritik der romantischen
     Märchentheorie, Akademie der Wissenschaften und der Litera-
     tur (Mainz), Abhandlungen der Geistes- und Sozialwissen-
     schaftlichen Klasse, Wiesbaden 1977, who revives Helm's
     theory of literary origins, *NJklAlt* 33 (1914), 170-209
     (= Binder-Merkelbach, *Amor und Psyche*, Darmstadt 1968, 175-
     234), in contrast to the attempts of Reitzenstein and Merkel-
     bach to force an Iranian or Isiac origin on the material
     (*Das Märchen von Amor und Psyche bei Apuleius*, Leipzig 1912
     = Binder-Merkelbach *ibid*. 87-158; *Philologus* 102, 1958,
     103-116 = *id*. 392-407). But F. does not do justice to Pla-
     tonic elements (cf. the review by J. Tatum, *AJP* 101, 1980,
     110f.).

54   The many humorous touches in *Cupid and Psyche* seem to re-
     flect the likely diversity of material and tone which Apu-
     leius has used. There are a number of variations on con-
     ceits familiar in the ideal novel: the heroine's rivalling
     Venus herself (IV.29.3f.); the 'mournful marriage' topos
     (IV.33, cf. Achilles I.13); pretended divination (by Pan!)
     that the heroine is in love (v.25, cf. Heliodorus IV.10.4f.).
     But there are also touches of comic realism appropriate to
     fable or (quasi-) folktale, as when the sisters lament their
     husbands' baldness and senility, or gout and impotence
     (V.9f.). But here as so often sources converge: the help of
     ant, reed, eagle and tower (VI.10, 12, 15, 17) suggests

fable; but it is used in a comparably charming way to help
the lovers in Longus. *Cupid and Psyche* also exhibits a wide
variety of Ovidian mannerisms, as befits any subsequent
Latin *Metamorphoses*: besides the frequent mixture of Hellenistic frippery and Roman institutions, the similarities
range from fun with the absurdities of Allegory (e.g. *sic
ignara Psyche sponte in Amoris incidit amorem*, V.23.3, cf.
Ovid *Met.* X.526) to garrulous fowls (for the moralising
gull, V.28.1-6; cf. the officious crow and raven of Ovid
Met. II.534-632).

55   See the excellent characterisation in Perry, *AR* 236-240.

56   This debate still carries on from one generation to the
      next. In the late 'thirties the conflicting interpretations
      of Apuleius are well illustrated by Feldbrugge, *o.c.* (*supra*
      n.23), and by Riefstahl *o.c.* (*supra* n.37); followed by the
      compromising positions of F. Pfister *o.c.* (*supra* n.37) 538-
      541, and P.J. Enk, *Acta Classica* I 1958), 85-88, both of
      whom draw attention to comic elements in devotional litera-
      ture. But little progress has been made. J. Gwynn Grif-
      fiths, *Apuleius of Madauros, The Isis-Book, Edited with an
      introduction, translation and Commentary*, Leiden 1975
      (*Études Préliminaires aux Religions Orientales dans l'Empire
      Romain* 39), 48 is right to invoke the use of σπουδογέλοιον
      here; but once more the term in itself admits of too many
      ambiguities. But the mixture of comic and serious in the
      service of religion advocated by Pfister and Enk does not
      easily explain this case: there seems to be just too much
      comic and too little serious.

57   For the problems, see J. Bompaire, *Lucien écrivain*, Paris
      1958, 509-12; a mannered imitation of Plato's Menexenus is
      also involved: see E.J. Smith, *AJP* 18 (1897), 339-341. It
      is useful to note that scholars have gone as far as to
      postulate revisions of both the *Nigrinus* and the *Metamor-
      phoses* because of this striking disparity: so M. Caster,
      Mélanges offers à M. Octave Navarre, Toulouse 1935, 471-85;
      P.G. Walsh, *Phoenix* 22 (1968), 148f. This course is now
      discounted in Lucian's case; it is equally superfluous in
      that of Apuleius. For still more experiments of the same
      sort, cf. Philagros' combination of encomium and *epitaphios*,
      Philostratus *Vit. Soph.* 579; and the ps.-Lucianic *Demos-
      thenis Encomium*, with its serious historical dialogue on
      the orator's suicide, appended to a long playful prologue
      about the writing of encomium (1-26; 27-49).

58   *Nigrinus* 12-34.

59   *Or.* 36.39-61.

60   *Ibid.* 61.

61   *Phaedr.* 246A-257B; *Symp.* 202D-204C.

62   *Phaedr.* 274C-275B; *Symp.* 213A-220B.

63   A. Wlosok, *Philologus* 113 (1969) 83f. usefully points to a
      connexion between Platonism and Isiac religion in Apuleius'
      own experience: Plutarch's *de Iside* seems the natural
      reason for the allusion to Plutarch himself at I.2.1; hence
      substitution of Isiac material for that of *Phaedrus* and
      Symposium seems all the more acceptable.

64   Ovid *Met*. XV.75-478; 745-851.

65   The two latest commentators continue to take opposing views.
      Gwynn Griffiths, *o.c.* (*supra* n.56) 48 makes only a limited
      concession to comic elements in Book XI, while J.-C. Fre-
      douille, *Apulée Metamorphoseon* XI, Paris (*Érasme*) 1975 goes
      further than most in attempting to undermine the serious
      contents of the book. Older approaches to the problem are
      summarised in Feldbrugge, *o.c.* (*supra* n.23) 127-153. Since
      then F. Norwood, *Phoenix* 10 (1956), 1-12 and Perry *AR* 234,
      244, have argued against repeated opposition that Book XI
      is a mere concession to a serious pose, an obligatory gest-
      ure in any work which claims literary respectability. Perry
      went no further than unconvincing dogma; but his views of
      the *Isis*-Book as exuberant *epideixis* has much to commend it.

66   XI.8.4. Note also the bizarre descriptions of hierogly-
      phics (XI.22.8) and vestments with animal patterns (XI.24.
      2f.). In each of these cases one has to consider what Apu-
      leius is trying to do: is his purpose to name the objects
      for the instruction of potential converts, or is he simply
      evoking a smile at the exuberant circumlocutions for ob-
      jects perfectly familiar to his audience? Ecphrasis of
      mystic rites was legitimate for purely literary ends: cf.
      Lucian, *Nekyomanteia* 7ff.; *D. Meretr.* 4.4f. Descriptions
      of Bacchic ritual had the same appeal, following Eur. *Bacch.*
      216-251 (cf. Lucian, *Bacchus* 1f.). Compare also Apuleius'
      treatment of the masque in X.30-32.

67   XI.15.

68   Cf. the finale ensemble of *Don Giovanni*, setting up the
      don's damnation somewhat flippantly as a warning (and fre-
      quently omitted in 19th century performances for that
      reason).

69   XI.23.7; Fredouille *o.c.* (*supra* n.65) *ad loc.*

70   XI.27.7; Fredouille *ad loc.* It should be noted that a lame
      priest ought not to have conducted such an initiation;
      Gwynn Griffiths *ad loc.* is prepared to use this as evidence
      to prove that normal practice admitted exceptions. But did
      Apuleius want a priest who was not only asinine but down-
      at-heel as well? For the pun, note that another assman in
      an equally famous comic fantasy also puns on his name when
      he looks back on his mystical experience: 'The eye of man
      hath not heard...what my dream was: ...it shall be called
      'Bottom's Dream', because it hath no bottom.' (*A Midsummer
      Night's Dream*, Act IV, scene I).

71   XI.28.6; XI.30.2; Fredouille 12f.: 'Les questions matéri-
      elles, et, plus précisément, pécunaires, occupent d'ailleurs,
      dans le livre XI, une place qui semble peu compatible avec
      la ferveur ou la pureté du sentiment religieux'.

72   *Madaurensem* (XI.27.9) is now generally accepted as a *sphra-
      gis* (H. Werner, *Hermes* 53, 1918, 242). There may have been
      a comic surprise in the original, where Lucius gives himself
      specific relatives (*Onos* 55).

73   *Phaedr.* 278E-279B. Thibau also notes this analogy (*o.c.*
      supra n.45) 141; but does not comment on its significant
      positioning in the text.

74   *Phaedr.* 279C; *Met.* XI.30.4f.

75   *Somnium* 14-18.

76   Other aspects of Apuleius' arrangement can also be seen in
      terms of sophistic experiment. We might suspect that the
      placing of *Cupid and Psyche* was intended in itself as a
      facetious effect. The frame tale downgrades the motifs of
      the love-romance, while the inset tale sublimifies them; we
      have two 'versions' of romance grotesquely at odds with one
      another in a whimsical literary counterpoint.

      Apuleius' technique of anticipation has often been dis-
      cussed, and it is easy to trace the similarities between the
      fortunes of Lucius and those of Aristomenes, Thelyphron or
      Diophanes (I.20.5; II.15.1ff.; II.31.3), whose humiliations
      he ignores to his cost. But such anticipation is familiar
      in the ideal novels as a literary decoration without moral
      force; it is difficult to prove that Lucius' sight of the
      statue of Actaeon before his transformation (II.4.10) is
      any more 'earnest' or 'meaningful' than Clitophon's sight
      of pictures of Prometheus or Procne before disaster strikes
      Leucippe (Achilles III.8; V.3f.); Apuleius has scarcely
      taken the trouble to make it appear so.

      The problem is most pronounced in the priest's sermon
      to Lucius (XI.15.1-4): are his remarks, some eight books
      after the metamorphosis itself, really sufficient evidence
      that the whole work is a serious fable (e.g. Walsh 176f.;
      Tatum *o.c.*, *supra* n.23, 82-86)? But the reader's reaction
      has also to be gauged: Apuleius' public did not read the
      Metamorphoses backwards, and after all his other interpola-
      tions it would be difficult to correct one's prior impres-
      sion of the other ten books. It is particularly difficult
      to force *Cupid and Psyche* into a prefiguration of the pro-
      logue *Isis*-book, or to see the prologue as a mystical pro-
      gramme for the whole work. Nor need the obvious correspond-
      ence of *Cupid and Psyche* and the story of Lucius have any
      interior significance more profound than the literary
      counterpoint already suggested: that is what corresponds to
      practice in the ideal novels and in sophistic experiments.
      Allegorical and semi-allegorical interpretations have pro-
      liferated. But such approaches as Scazzoso's only serve to
      show the subjectivity or ambiguity to which symbolism gives
      rise. Against his claims for such phrases as *papyrum
      Aegyptiam* and *Nilotici calami* in I.1 (*Le Metamorfosi di
      Apuleio, Studio critico sul significato del romanzo*, Milan
      1951, 19) see Scobie (*supra* n.51) *ad loc*. Even in the light
      of book XI there is nothing to stop a Milesian tale written
      on Egyptian papyrus from being a playful description of a
      hybrid composition. The same reservation can be made against
      R. Thibau's exegesis of the same passage (*supra* n.45) 92-101.
      Among less extreme attempts, Walsh (176-182) and Tatum *o.c.*
      (*supra* n.23) 21-91 provide useful accumulations of the warn-
      ings and anticipations that underlie the case for an *Ent-
      wicklungsroman*. But two basic objections must be faced
      after all such material has been assembled. Heine *o.c.*
      (*supra* n.39) 30 rightly asks whether the warnings are real-
      ly serious, or merely set up to be ignored - they can in
      effect just as easily be used to show that he is a practical
      joker, or at least a master of ambiguity. Secondly, the
      Entwicklung in Apuleius' additions is not an *Entwicklung* at
      all: the same progress could just as easily have been

claimed had the stories of lust and adultery *preceded* those
of magic (cf. G.N. Sandy, *Phoenix* 28, 1974, 235, who points
out the incongruity of the additions in books VII-X to any
overall scheme).

It is perhaps useful to note that Apuleius' successful
formula for the arrangement of material has emerged in
another medium. In Walt Disney's *Fantasia* ghoulish and
magical episodes ('A Night on the Bare Mountain', 'The
Sorcerer's Apprentice') are among the variety of episodes
grouped round a pastoral centrepiece (Beethoven's *Pastoral
Symphony*); but the final episode is a pilgrims' procession
to Schubert's *Ave Maria. Plus ça change*?

77   Walsh 189. But I find it particularly difficult to envisage
      the *Metamorphoses* as propaganda of the kind he suggests,
      Phoenix 22 (1968), 151-157; *Roman Novel* 185-189. A grimace
      against Christianity is not excluded; but if this is a
      committed missionary enterprise or defence on the part of
      Isis, then the Christian victory of a Tertullian or a Cyp-
      rian was already assured.

Notes to Chapter X

1 Cf. Reardon, *G&R* 23 (1976), 127f.: 'amused reference to a cast of mind, a spiritual mode, which the writer does not share'.

2 E.g. IV.1.1; III.6.2f.

3 E.g. II.20.2; IV.28.2f.

4 Melodramatic laments: e.g. III.10.3f.; VII.5.3. Passivity in crises: especially V.23.5ff.; VIII.1. Hypocrisy: VIII.5.

5 VIII.5.14.

6 III.20.2; cf. IV.40.3.

7 Pan and Artemis, VIII.13f.; expurgations, VIII.5.

8 *Supra* c. IV nn.49, 51.

9 *Impudicitia-officium*: Achilles I.5.7; Chariton II.11.3 (Callirhoe), VI.1.10 (Artaxerxes); Longus III.17.2. *Eros-nosos*: Achilles I.6.2ff.; Longus I.13f., I.17f.; Heliodorus III.7ff.

10 Achilles I.1.13-2.1; Longus II.7.2; Chariton VI.3.2.

11 *Initiamentum*: Longus III.18.3f.; Achilles V.27.3f. *Scheintod*: Achilles III.15-22, cf. Longus III.4.2; Chariton I.9. Erotic symposia: Achilles VIII.4-7; Metiochus, *supra* 55; Heliodorus III.10f.; Chariton IV.3.7; IV.5.10.

12 Achilles IV.12.2; Heliodorus IX.9.

13 Achilles I.16.1.

14 E.g. Chariton V.8.8.

15 *Supra* 39.

16 IV.13.1f. and *passim*.

17 *O.c.* (*supra* n.1) 119.

18 E.g. Perry *AR* 33; Weinreich *apud* Reymer *o.c.* (*supra* 103 n.1) 337.

19 Cf. *supra* 114 n.56.

20 Longus II.4.1; 6.1.

21 Achilles I.10.1.

22 E.g. I.1.6; V.6.3f. For the numerous variations, cf. J.W.H. Walden, *HSCP* 5 (1894), 1-43.

23   For the view that the early novel was humble and demotic,
        see Perry, *AR* 33, following B. Lavagnini, *Le origini del*
        romanzo greco, Pisa 1922, 12-25; and compare M.D. Reeve, *CQ*
        N.S. 21 (1971), 538: 'this view has an air of profundity
        about it, but unless it is borne out by a lack of literary
        ambition on the part of the novelists themselves, it is
        really no more than a projection of the writer's own evalua-
        tion. Authors who avoided hiatus and took trouble over
        rhythm would have been surprised to hear that their works
        were addressed to the 'juvenile' and 'poor in spirit'.
        Authors who took pains to cultivate nuances of wit might
        have felt the same way.

24   *AR praef.* vif.

25   The exception is Lucian's *Verae Historiae*. For a good
        characterisation of this skit, see Bompaire 658-677; for the
        identifiable targets, A. Stengel, *De Luciani Veris Historiis*,
        Rostock 1911. Against K. Reyhl's attempts to attribute too
        much to Antonius Diogenes, *Studies* 1-7; for the composition
        of some of the fantasies, *Theme and Variation* 23-28; Lucian's
        parodies are often as complex as his intentions are simple.
        Too often however *Verae Historiae* is implied to be the only
        kind of novel he was interested in or capable of writing.
        Yet he seems among the best equipped to sabotage the ideal
        novel: as a near contemporary of Achilles, Longus and Iam-
        blichus, he is the only figure who might have been expected
        to excel them at this kind of activity. I suggest that he
        did not do so as a matter of choice, but divided his roman-
        tic parodies into two, concentrating on the literary extra-
        vagances in *VH*, and making fun of the erotic theme in the
        Onos. It is also a real possibility that he had been pre-
        empted: if he knew either Achilles or Iamblichus, or any
        similar work, he may have chosen to embark on more radical
        travesties of the form.

            It is also worth pointing out a technical difficulty in
        VH. Lucian may have felt that with an ideal heroine to take
        account of it would have been difficult to do full justice
        to his own role in the work as a latter-day Odysseus. Now
        since he is usually a good deal more interested in Homer
        than, say, Apollonius of Rhodes, a pastiche closer to the
        shape of the *Argonautica* would probably have interested him
        less. Of course there is no lack of erotic episodes in *VH*,
        as in Philostratus' *Life of Apollonius*, but having made use
        of Antonius Diogenes Lucian may have felt that he had suffi-
        ciently exploited the traditions of the ideal novel.

Notes to Appendix I

1   The cultic significance of Egypt makes it central to the
theories of Kerenyi and Merkelbach. See also J.W.B. Barns,
*Mitteilungen aus der Papyrussammlung der Oesterreich.
Nationalbibliothek*, Neue Serie, ed. Gerstinger, 5. Folge,
Vienna 1956, 29-36; Reardon 327-332.

2   V.1-4 Lavagnini.

3   IV.19-22.

4   Perry's reconstruction is arbitrary, *TAPA* 97 (1966), 327-
333.

5   19-26.

6   *P. Lond*. II.274; R. Reitzenstein, *Die griechische Tefnutlegende, Sitzungsberichte d. Heidelberger Akademie d. Wissenschaft, Phil.-Hist. klasse* 1923.2; Pack 2618.

7   Col. III.37ff.

8   Cf. Longus II.39.

9   Reitzenstein *o.c.* (*supra* n.6) 27 (III.55ff.).

10   VIa. Here the translator seems to miss the opportunity of
comic personification inherent in the demotic, where both
the allegories are birds (cf. Reitzenstein 17).

11   Achilles II.21f.

12   Lucian *D. Mar*. 4.1.

13   VIIb.65ff.

14   For the former, *D. Deor*. 7.2.

15   Cf. Barns *o.c.* (*supra* n.1) 34; Reitzenstein *o.c.* (*supra* n.6)
('Kunstmärchen').

Notes to Appendix II

1 *Arion* 5 (1966), 304-331 (= *Essays on Classical Literature*, ed. N. Rudd (Cambridge, Heffer 1972, 122-149).

2 *Virginia Quarterly Review* 34 (1958), 262-276.

3 Arrowsmith *ibid*. But the defecation theme (307) is at least as comic and literary in Theophrastus, *Char*. 20; cf. also Lucian, *Symposium* 35 (both without moralist implication).

4 *TAPA* 102 (1971), 631-684.

5 *Ibid*. 658ff. Such interpretations can just as easily be angled in a more optimistic direction, e.g. by L. Callebat, *REL* 52 (1974), 294 ('perception baroque de l'univers').

6 Z. begins by postulating among her aesthetic criteria that 'fusion of form and content should result in some significant statement, implicit or explicit, about the human condition as perceived by the artist' (632). Such reformulation of the ancient preference for didactic literature would not have surprised Petronius; but he was under no obligation to follow it.

7 *Latomus* 29 (1970), 397-425.

8 *Ibid*. 405ff.

9 *Sat*. 70.2.

10 *Sat*. 52.2.

11 *Sat*. 73.1.

12 I do not think the reader can be expected to keep Daedalus in the front of his mind as he connects the sibyl at *Cena* 48 with her role in *Aeneid* VI, as Cameron seems to imply. The passage in which Daedalus' name occurs may spring to mind, but there is nothing to draw the reader's attention to his appearance in it. Nor could Daedalus be taken out of *Sat*. 83 (the picture gallery), which does indeed recall *Aen*. VI. 14ff., but contains a list of artists in which Daedalus himself does not appear. Cameron goes further, claiming that the labyrinth in 73.1 symbolises death. No doubt the hapless Encolpius by now regards further exposure to Trimalchio as a fate worse than death, but have we anything more morbid than that? Strepsiades at the *phrontisterion* thinks he is going to be sacrificed, like Athamas (*Nub*. 256f.), then enters the Cave of Trophonius (*ibid*. 505f.); does he then have an obsession with death, or is Aristophanes smiling at his innocent discomfiture?

13 Cameron *ibid*. 40f.

14 *Supra* 39f. For themes of concealment and pretence in the *Satyricon*, see H.D. Rankin, *Latomus* 28, (1969), 99-119, who

remains carefully uncommitted and views the general literary
perspectives of such material. Cynic satire seems to have
been very fond of them, and indeed they are inherent in the
nature of satire itself. Cf. L. Callebat, *REL* 52 (1974),
292 ('dynamique joyeuse d'un "jeu de duperie"').

15   *G&R* 21 (1974), 181-190. But J. Wright, *ibid.* 23 (1976), 32-
      39 points out the literary conditioning of so many contempo-
      rary American responses.

16   'Myra Buttle', *Sweeney in Articulo*, in *Parodies, An Anth-
      ology from Chaucer to Beerbohm and after*, ed. D. Macdonald,
      London 1960, 220.

Notes to Appendix III

1   For examples, Sullivan 129-138 (Trimalchio); 193-213 (Encolpius, Eumolpus).

2   *Sat.* 71.1/Sen. *Ep.* 47 *passim* (Sullivan 132-135).

3   This amounts to wanting parody of Seneca but constructive emulation of Lucan; but the two would have formed a very obvious and tempting pair of targets.

4   Sullivan 159f. (after E.T. Sage, *TAPA* 46, 1915, 47-57).

5   *Ibid.* 165, cf. Walsh 84. G. Kennedy, *AJP* 99 (1978), 178, well sums up the overall effect: 'Encolpius is out dangling his literary line, and Agamemnon is dancing at the end of it'.

6   For the convoluted history of 'improvement versus Parody' see now Sullivan 170-186, G. Guido, *Dal Satyricon: Il Bellum Civile*, Bologna 1976, 344-351; both are themselves supporters of the former (Guido 351-362), as is G. Luck, *AJP* 93 (1972), 133-141, and Coffey *o.c.* (*supra* 149 n.1) 192-194. The latter has found recent support in P.G. Walsh, *CP* 63 (1968), 208-212, *Roman Novel* 49f.; P.A. George, *CQ* 24 (1974), 119-133 (the latter however strongly against specific parody of Lucan); and R. Beck, *Phoenix* 33 (1979), 240-245. Walsh and Beck both rightly stress the intervening complication of Eumolpus' own character: it is perhaps easiest to say that there is really double parody here: Eumolpus parodies Lucan; he himself is a parody of the pompous ass who likes to 'show how it ought to be done' and fails miserably.

7   *Étude sur Pétrone*, Paris 1892, 178.

8   K.J. Dover, *Aristophanes' Clouds*, Oxford 1968, lxv.

9   J. Bompaire, *Lucien écrivain*, Paris 1958, 641-44.

10   For details see M.S. Smith *o.c.* (*supra* 149 n.2) on 55.5; 52; 59.4f.; and Stöcker 77-104.

11   See P.A. George, *Arion* 5 (1966), 346ff.

12   Sullivan 171.

13   Lines 1-60.

14   Lines 76-121.

15   Lines 183f.

16   Here too moralising interpretations have been applied: A.F. Sochatoff, *TAPA* 93 (1962), 449-58, stresses the moralising interpretations which have accompanied the *BC* fragment in transit. But Medieval moralists were quite prepared to misread anything into instruction: this is a counsel of despair. Zeitlin's approach, *Latomus* 30 (1971), 56-82, reveals

the *petitio principii* on which moralising interpretations
tend to work. She well demonstrates that both the *BC* and
Troiae Halosis are at odds with Eumolpus and with their
contexts, and that Petronius makes ironic misuse of Virgil
(*ibid.* 62-67; 76-79); but because neither poem had the
glories of a golden age to follow, they are seen as a subtle
comment on the time which had not such moral and political
ideals to offer: there are no longer hopes, only despair
(*ibid.* 80). But the moralist interpretation does not follow from the ironies so well demonstrated. In common with
Sullivan, who opposes moralist interpretation, she assumes
that Petronius *likes* Virgil, and imitates him accordingly.
But the evidence she supplies does not preclude Petronius
from laughing at Virgilianism as such, and making fun of
laudatores temporis acti. On present evidence Petronius
might just as readily have had a world-view similar to
Ovid's, that the initial Augustan values are pretentious
and passé.

17   Other contrasts between the poems have been suggested:
      Sullivan's position is unsatisfactory: the *BC* fragment is
      serious criticism of Lucan (*supra* n.6), yet the *Troiae
      Halosis* is parody of Seneca (cf. H. Stubbe, *Die Verseinlagen
      im Petron, Philologus* Suppl. 25, 1933, 24f., who wants the
      parodic effect of the latter poem to reside only in its
      context). I am unconvinced by recent attempts to alter the
      chronological relationship of Lucan and the *BC* fragment;
      that Lucan wrote in the light of Petronius (P. Grimal, *La
      Guerre Civile de Pétrone dans ses rapports avec la Pharsale,*
      Paris 1977); or that Petronius wrote after Silius Italicus,
      (R. Martin, *REL* 53, 1975, 182-224). Both expose in extreme
      forms the difficulty of detecting and evaluating linguistic
      parody without completely certain chronology. But neither
      disposes of the inherent probability of the relationship
      suggested by *Sat.* 118, nor produces a more acceptable al-
      ternative.

ABBREVIATIONS

AJP	*American Journal of Philology*
APf	*Archiv für Papyrusforschung*
BICS	*Bulletin of the Institute of Classical Studies*
C&M	*Classica et Medievalia*
CP	*Classical Philology*
CQ	*Classical Quarterly*
CW	*Classical World*
G&R	*Greece and Rome*
HSCP	*Harvard Studies in Classical Philology*
JHS	*Journal of Hellenic Studies*
JOeBG	*Jahrbuch der Oesterreichischen Byzantinischen Gesellschaft*
NJklAlt	*Neue Jahrbücher des klassische Altertum*
MH	*Museum Helveticum*
PhW	*Philologische Wochenschrift*
RhM	*Rheinisches Museum für Philologie*
RSC	*Rivista di Studi Classici*
RFIC	*Rivista di Filologia e di Istruzione Classica*
SCO	*Studi Classici e Orientali*
SIFC	*Studi Italiani di Filologia Classica*
TAPA	*Transactions and Proceedings of the American Philological Association*
ZPE	*Zeitschrift für Papyrologie und Epigraphik*

The titles of several works of Lucian have been abbreviated, as follows: *VH = Verae Historiae*; *D. Deor. = Dialogi Deorum*; *D. Mar. = Dialogi Marini*; *D. Meretr. = Dialogi Meretricum*; *Musc. Enc. = Muscae Encomium*.

SELECT BIBLIOGRAPHY

The following is an abbreviated list of works cited. It reflects the interests of this study in a ruthlessly arbitrary way, particularly in the case of the Latin novels. A full bibliography would have been impractical: even the *BC* fragment and *Cupid and Psyche* need doxographies in their own right. Out with *l'Année Philologique* the latest bibliographical surveys, with directions to their predecessors, will be found in G. Sandy, *CW* 67 (1974), 321-359 (the ancient novel); G. Schmeling, *CW* 62 (1969), 157-164 (Petronius); and C. Schlam, *CW* 64 (1971), 285-309 (Apuleius). G. Schmeling and J. Stuckey, *A Bibliography of Petronius (Mnemosyne* Suppl. 39, Leyden 1977), is unfortunately marred by frequent inaccuracy.

My *Lucian: Theme and Variation in the Second Sophistic* and *Studies in Lucian's Comic Fiction (Mnemosyne* Suppll. 41, 43, Leyden 1976), are referred to as *Theme and Variation* and *Studies* respectively. The following are referred to by author and/or cue-title only:

Acta
Erotica Antiqua, Acta of the International Conference on the Ancient Novel, Bangor (Wales) 1976, ed. B.P. Reardon, Bangor 1977.

Bompaire,
J. Bompaire, *Lucien écrivain, Imitation et création, Bibliothèque des Ecoles françaises d'Athènes et de Rome* 190, Paris 1958.

Merkelbach, RM
R. Merkelbach, *Roman und Mysterium in der Antike*, Munich/Berlin 1962.

Perry, AR
B.E. Perry, *The Ancient Romances, A Literary-historical account of their Origins*, Berkeley, California and London 1967.

Reardon
B.P. Reardon, *Courants littéraires grecs des IIe et IIIe siècles après J.-C., Annales littéraires de l'Université de Nantes* 3, Paris 1971.

Rohde
E. Rohde, *Der griechische Roman und seine Verlaüfer^5*, Darmstadt 1974 (with pagination of the third edition, ed. Wilhelm Schmid, Leipzig 1914).

Sullivan
J.P. Sullivan, *The Satyricon of Petronius, A Literary Study*, London 1968.

Wehrli
'Einheit und Vorgeschichte der griechisch-römischen Romanliteratur', *Museum Helveticum* 22 (1965), 133-154.

Walsh   P.G. Walsh, *The Roman Novel: The Satyricon of Petronius
           and the Metamorphoses of Apuleius*, Cambridge 1970.

Wolff   S.L. Wolff, *The Greek Romances in Elizabethan Prose
           Fiction*, Columbia 1912 (repr. Burt Franklin, New York
           1961).

           I have adopted the text or numeration system of the following
editions:

Achilles Tatius: E. VILBORG, *Leucippe and Clitophon*, (*Studia graeca
     et latina Gothoburgensia*, I, Gothenburg 1955 (text); XV, *ibid.*
     1962 (commentary).

Chariton: W.E. BLAKE, *Charitonis Aphrodisiensis de Chaerea et
     Callirhoe amatoriarum narrationum libri octo*, Oxford 1938.

Heliodorus: R.M. RATTENBURY-T.W. LUMB, *Héliodore, Les Éthiopiques
     (Théagene et Chariclée)*, Paris, *Les Belles Lettres*, 1935-43
     (with translation and second introduction by J. MAILLON).

Longus: G. DALMEYDA, *Longus, Pastorales (Daphnis et Chloé)* Paris,
     Les Belles Lettres, 1934 (including additional notes by
     A. PUECH and J.-B. VIEILLEFOND).

Xenophon of Ephesus: A.D. PAPANIKOLAOU, Teubner 1973.

Petronius: K. MUELLER[2] (with German tr. by W. EHLERS), Munich 1965.

Apuleius: D.S. ROBERTSON[2], (with introduction and tr. by P.
     VALLETTE, Paris, *Les Belles Lettres* 1956).

The *Onos*:   M.D. MACLEOD, *LCL* Lucian VIII, London and Cambridge
     (Mass.) 1967, 52-144.

Iolaus: P. Parsons, 'A Greek Satyricon?', *BICS* 18 (1971), 63-68;
     Oxyrynchus Papyri XLII, London 1974, 34-41.

Lollianus: A. Henrichs, *Die Phoinikika des Lollianos, Fragmente
     eines neuen griechischen Romans, Papyrologische Texte und
     Abhandlungen* 14, Bonn 1972.

Metiochus: H. MAEHLER, 'Der Metiochus-Parthenope-Roman', *ZPE* 23
     (1977), 1-20.

Iamblichus: E. HABRICH, Teubner 1960.

Other fragments: B. LAVAGNINI, *Eroticorum fragmenta papyracea*,
     Teubner 1922; F. ZIMMERMANN, *Griechische Romanpapyri und
     verwandte Texte*, Heidelberg 1936.

Apocryphal Acts: R.A. LIPSIUS/M. BONNET, *Acta Apostolorum Apocrypha*
     I-II, Leipzig 1889-1903.

Pseudo-Clementines: B. REHM, *Die Pseudoklementinen* I: *Homilien*,
     Berlin 1953; II: *Recognitiones*, 1965.

Joseph and Aseneth: M. PHILONENKO, *Joseph et Aséneth, Studia Post-
     Biblica* XIII, Leyden 1968.

Apollonius of Tyre: A. RIESE, *Historia Apollonii regis Tyrii*,
     Teubner, Leipzig 1893.

Alexander Romance: W. KROLL, *Historia Alexandri Magni, (Pseudo-Callisthenes)* I: *recensio vetusta*, Berlin 1926.

Philostratus, 'Life' of Apollonius of Tyana: C.L. KAYSER, (*editio minor*), Teubner 1870.

Tefnut: R. REITZENSTEIN, *Die griechische Tefnutlegende, Sitzungs-berichte d. Heidelberger Akademie d. Wissenschaft. Phil.-Hist. klasse* 1923.2.

The novels have not hitherto been well provided with comment-aries, nor has the identification of humorous elements been the immediate interest or priority of commentators.   Schönberger on Longus (Berlin² 1974) is an exception; The Budés of Dalmeyda (Longus) and Rattenbury-Lumb-Maillon (Heliodorus) (both *supra*) have also come to grips with the problem; but neither the Budé of G. Molinié (1978) nor the commentary by Plepelits (Stuttgart 1976) does justice to this aspect of Chariton; still less does that of Vilborg (Stockholm 1962) on Achilles. Text and language have been the natural priority of the many commentators on the Latin novels, in particular of the Groningen Series on Apuleius; the commenta-ries of Scobie on I (Meisenheim am Glan, 1975) and Gwynn Griffiths on XI (Leyden, 1975) reflect their authors' special interests in folklore and Egyptian religion respectively. In Petronius' case the identification of irony and humour is most closely integrated with problems of language and *Realien*; M.S. Smith's new Commentary on the *Cena* (Oxford 1975) offers a judicious, if reticent, blend. But the artist/moralist controversies of the last two decades have yet to find their commentator; J.P. Sullivan's promised commentary on the whole of the extant *Satyricon* is eagerly awaited.

The Greek Novel:

ALEXIOU, M.: 'A Critical Reappraisal of Eusthathios Makrembolites' *Hysmine and Hysminias'*, *Byzantine and Modern Greek Studies* 3 (1977), 23-43.

ANDERSON, G.: 'The Mystic Pomegranate and the Vine of Sodom: Achilles Tatius 3.6', *AJP* 100 (1979), 516-518.

'Two Notes on Heliodorus', *JHS* 99 (1979), 149.

BARNS, J.W.B.: 'Egypt and the Greek Romance', *Mitteilungen aus der Papyrussammlung der Oesterreich. Nationalbibliothek, Neue Serie*, ed. Gerstinger, 5. Folge, Vienna 1956, 29-36.

BERTI, M.: 'Sulla Interpretazione mistica del romanzo di Longo', *Studi Classici e Orientali* 16 (1967), 343-358.

BRAUN, M.: *History and Romance in Graeco-Oriental Literature*, Oxford (Basil Blackwell), 1938.

CHALK, H.H.O.: 'Eros and the Lesbian Pastorals of Longus', *JHS* 80 (1960), 32-51.

'Longus Revisited', *Acta* 133-135.

CORBATO, C.: 'Da Menandro a Caritone. Studi sulla genesi del romanzo greco e i suoi rapporti con la commedia nuova', *Quaderni Triestini sul Teatro Antico* I (1968), 5-44.

DODDS, E.R.: 'A Fragment of a Greek Novel', *Phoenix* Suppl. I (*Studies in honour of Gilbert Norwood*), 1952, 133-138.

DURHAM, D.B.: 'Parody in Achilles Tatius', *CP* 33 (1938), 1-19.

FAUTH, W.: 'Astraios und Zamolxis, Ueber spuren pythagoreischer Aretalogie im Thule-Roman des Antonius Diogenes', *Hermes* 106 (1978), 220-241.

GERSCHMANN, K.H.: *Chariton-Interpretationen*, Diss. Münster, Frankfurt 1974.

HEISERMAN, A.: *The Novel before the Novel: Essays and Discussions about the Beginnings of Prose Fiction in the West*, Chicago 1977.

HELM, R.: *Der Antike Roman²*, Göttingen 1956.

HELMS, J.: *Character Portrayal in the Romance of Chariton*, The Hague 1966.

KERENYI, K.: *Die griechische-orientalische Romanliteratur in religionsgeschichtlicher Beleuchtung*, Tübingen 1927 (repr. Darmstadt 1962).

KLEBS, E.: *Die Erzählungen von Apollonius aus Tyrus*, Berlin 1899.

LEVIN, D.N.: 'The pivotal role of Lycaenion in Longus' Pastorals', *RSC* 25 (1977), 5-17.

MERKELBACH, R.: 'Fragment eines satirischen Romans: Aufforderung zur Berichte', *ZPE* 11 (1973), 5-17.

MITTELSTADT, M.C.: 'Bucolic-Lyric Motifs and Dramatic Narrative in Longus' *Daphnis and Chloe*', *RhM* 113 (1970), 211-227.

'*Daphnis and Chloe* and the Pastoral Tradition', *C&M* 27 (1966), 162-177.

MORGAN, J.R.: 'Realism and the Historiographical Pose in Heliodorus', *Acta* 138-139.

PERRY, B.E.: 'Chariton and his Romance from a Literary-Historical Point of View', *AJP* 51 (1930), 93-134.

PETRI, R.: *Ueber den Roman des Chariton, Beiträge zur klassischen Philologie* 11, Meisenheim am Glan 1963.

RATTENBURY, R.M.: 'Chastity and Chastity Ordeals in the Ancient Greek Romances', *Proceedings of the Leeds Philosophical and Literary Society, Literary and Historical Section* 1 (1926), 59-71.

'Traces of Lost Greek Novels', in *New Chapters in the History of Greek Literature* 3, ed. J.U. Powell, Oxford 1933, 211-263.

REARDON, B.P.: 'The Greek Novel', *Phoenix* 23 (1969), 291-309.

   'The Second Sophistic and the Novel' in G.W. Bowersock (ed.)
   *Approaches to the Second Sophistic, Papers Presented at the
   105th Annual Meeting of The American Philological Association,*
   University Park, Pennsylvania, 1974, 23-29.

   'Novels and Novelties, or Mysteriouser and Mysteriouser',
   in *The Mediterranean World, Essays presented to Gilbert
   Bagnani,* Peterborough, Ontario 1975, 78-100.

   'Aspects of the Greek Novel', *G&R* 23 (1976), 118-131.

REEVE, M.D.: 'Hiatus in the Greek Novel', *CQ N.S.* 21 (1971),
   514-539.

REITZENSTEIN, R.: *Hellenistische Wundererzählungen,* Leipzig 1906,
   repr. Stuttgart 1963.

REYHL, K.: *Untersuchungen zu den Roman-Fragmenten der 'Wunder
   jenseits von Thule' und zu den 'Wahren Geschichten' des
   Lukian,* Diss. Tübingen 1969.

ROHDE, G.: 'Longos und die Bukolik', *RhM* 86 (1937), 23-49.

SANDY, G.N.: 'Notes on Lollianus' *Phoenicica*', *AJP* 100 (1979),
   367-376.

SCHISSEL von Fleschenberg, O.: *Entwicklungsgeschichte des griechischen Romanes im Altertum, Rhetorische Forschungen* II,
   Halle 1913.

SCHNEIDER-MENZEL, U.: 'Iamblichus' Babylonische Geschichten', in
   F. ALTHEIM, *Literatur und Gesellschaft im Ausgehenden Altertum,* I, Halle-Saale 1948, 48-92.

SCHWARTZ, E.: *Fünf Vorträge über den griechischen Roman²,* Berlin
   1943.

SCOBIE, A.: *Essays on the Ancient Romance and its Heritage, Beiträge zur klassischen Philologie* 30, Meisenheim am Glan 1969.

SOEDER, R.: *Die apokryphen Apostelgeschichten und die romanhafte
   Literatur der Antike, Wurzburger Studien zur Altertumswissenschaft* 3, 1932.

SZEPESSY, T.: 'L'histoire de Joseph et d'Aséneth et le roman
   antique', *Acta Classica Universitatis Scientiarum Debrecensis*
   10-11 (1974-75), 121-131.

TURNER, P.: 'Daphnis and Chloe: an Interpretation', *G&R N.S.*
   7 (1960), 117-123.

WEINREICH, O.: *Die griechischen Liebesroman,* Zurich 1962 (= *Nach-
   wort* to R. Reymer, *Heliodor: Aithiopika. Die Abenteuer der
   schönen Charikleia, Uebertragen von Rudolf Reymer,* Zurich
   1950).

WEST, S.: 'Joseph and Asenath: a neglected Greek Romance', *CQ N.S.*
   24 (1974), 70-81.

WINKLER, J.J.: 'The Mendacity of Calasiris and the Narrative
    Technique of Heliodorus', *Acta* 29-31.

ZIMMERMANN, F.: 'Chariton u. die Geschichte', *Sozialökonomische
    Verhältnisse im alten Orient und im klassischen Altertum,
    Tagung der Sektion alte Geschichte der Deutschen Historiker-
    Gesellschaft* 12-17 Oct. 1959 in Altenburg, Berlin 1961.

Petronius:

ANDERSON, G.: 'Trimalchio at Sousa-on-Sea', *AJP* 102 (1981), 50-53.

ARROWSMITH, W.: 'Luxury and Death in the Satyricon', *Arion* (1966),
    304-331.

ASTBURY, R.: 'Petronius, *P. Oxy.* 3010, and Menippean Satire', *CP*
    72 (1977), 22-31.

BACON, H.H.: 'The Sibyl in the Bottle', *Virginia Quarterly Review*
    34 (1958), 262-276.

BALDWIN, B.: 'Ira Priapi', *CP* 68 (1973), 294-296.

BALDWIN, F.T.: *The Bellum Civile of Petronius*, New York 1911.

BECK, R.: 'Some Observations on the Narrative Technique of
    Petronius', *Phoenix* 27 (1973), 42-61.

    'Encolpius at the Cena', *Phoenix* 29 (1975), 271-283.

    'Eumolpus *poeta*, Eumolpus *fabulator*: A Study of Character-
    ization in the *Satyricon*', *Phoenix* 33 (1979), 239-253.

CALLEBAT, L.: 'Structures narratives et modes de représentation
    dans le *Satyricon* de Pétrone', *REL* 52 (1974), 285-303.

CAMERON, Averil M.: 'Petronius and Plato', *CQ N.S.* 19 (1969),
    367-70.

    'Myth and Meaning in Petronius', *Latomus* 29 (1970), 397-425.

COFFEY, M.: *Roman Satire*, London and New York 1976.

COLLIGNON, A.: *Étude sur Pétrone*, Paris 1892.

COURTNEY, E.: 'Parody and Allusion in Menippean Satire', *Philo-
    logus* 106 (1962), 86-100.

GEORGE, P.A.: 'Style and Character in the *Satyricon*', *Arion* 5
    (1966), 336-358.

    'Petronius and Lucan *de Bello Civili*', *CQ N.S.* 24 (1974),
    119-133.

GILL, C.: 'The Sexual Episodes in the *Satyricon*', *CP* 68 (1973),
    172-185.

GRIMAL, P.: *La Guerre Civile de Pétrone dans ses rapports avec
    la Pharsale*, Paris 1977.

GUIDO, G.: *Dal Satyricon: Il Bellum Civile*, Bologna 1976.

HEINZE, R.: 'Petronius und der griechische Roman', *Hermes* 34
    (1899), 494-519 (= *Vom Geiste des Römertums*³, Darmstadt 1960,
    417-439.

HIGHET, G.: 'Petronius the Moralist', *TAPA* 72 (1941), 176-194.

KENNEDY, G.: 'Encolpius and Agamemnon in Petronius, *AJP* 99 (1978),
    171-178.

LUCK, G.: 'On Petronius' *Bellum Civile*', *AJP* 93 (1972), 133-141.

MARTIN, R.: 'Quelques remarques concernant la date du *Satiricon*',
    REL 53 (1975), 182-224.

PETERSMANN, H.: *Petrons urbane Prosa: Untersuchungen zu Sprache
    und Text (Syntax), Sitzungsberichte der Oesterreichischen
    Akademie der Wissenschaften, Phil.-Hist. Klasse* 323, 1977.

PIANO, C.: 'La moralità epicurea del Satyricon', *Rendiconti dell'
    Accademia di Archeologie, Lettere e Belle Arti dei Napoli* 51
    (1976), 3-30.

RANKIN, H.D.: 'Petronius, Priapus and Priapeum LXVIII', *C&M* 27
    (1966), 225-242 (= *Petronius the Artist, Essays on the
    Satyricon and its author*, The Hague 1971, 52-67).

    'Some Themes of Concealment and Pretence in Petronius'
    Satyricon', *Latomus* 28 (1969), 99-119 (= *Petronius the
    Artist* 32-51).

    'Eating People is Right: Petronius 141 and a *Topos*',*Hermes*
    197 (1969), 381-384 (= *Petronius the Artist* 100-105).

ROSENBLUETH, M.: *Beiträge zur Quellenkunde von Petronius' Satiren*,
    Berlin 1909.

SANDY, G.: 'Satire in the Satyricon', *AJP* 90 (1969), 293-303.

    'Scaenica Petroniana', *TAPA* 104 (1974), 329-346.

SOCHATOFF, A.F.: 'The Purpose of Petronius' *Bellum civile*: A Re-
    examination', *TAPA* 93 (1962), 449-458.

STOECKER, C.: *Humor bei Petron*, Diss. Erlangen 1969.

STUBBE, H.: *Die Verseinlagen im Petron, Philologus* Suppl. 25
    (1933).

VEYNE, P.: 'Le 'je' dans le *Satyricon*', *REL* 42 (1964), 301-324.

WALSH, P.G.: 'Lucius *Madaurensis*', *Phoenix* 22 (1968), 143-157.

    'Eumolpus, The *Halosis Troiae*, and the *De Bello Civili*', *CP*
    63 (1968), 208-212.

    'Was Petronius a moralist?', *G&R* 21 (1974), 181-190.

WRIGHT, J.: 'Disintegrated assurances. The contemporary American
    response to the *Satyricon*', *G&R* 23 (1976), 32-39.

ZEITLIN, F.I.: 'Petronius as Paradox: Anarchy and Artistic Integ-
    rity', *TAPA* 102 (1971), 631-684.

'*Romanus Petronius*: A Study of the *Troiae Halosis* and the *Bellum Civile*', *Latomus* 30 (1971), 56-82.

Apuleius:

BEAUJEU, J.: 'Sérieux et frivolité au IIe siècle de notre ère: Apulée', *Bulletin de l'association Guillaume Budé* 4 (1975), 83-97.

ENK, P.J.: 'A propos d'Apulée', *Acta Classica* 1 (1958), 85-88.

FEHLING, D.: *Amor und Psyche, Die Schöpfung der Apuleius und ihre Einwirkung auf das Märchen: eine Kritik der romantischen Märchentheorie, Akademie der Wissenschaften und der Literatur* (Mainz), *Abhandlungen der Geistes und Sozialwissenschaftlichen Klasse* 9, Wiesbaden 1977.

FELDBRUGGE, F.J.J.: *Het schertsende karakter van Apuleius' Metamorphosen*, Diss. Nijmegen 1938, Utrecht 1939.

HEINE, R.: 'Picaresque Novel versus Allegory', in Hijmans-van der Paardt, *infra* 25-42.

HELM, R.: 'Das "Märchen" von Amor und Psyche', *NJklAlt* 33 (1914), 170-209 (= Binder-Merkelbach, *Amor und Psyche*, Darmstadt, 1968, 175-234).

HIJMANS, B.L. Jnr., and van der PAARDT, R.Th., (edd.): Aspects of Apuleius' *Golden Ass*, Groningen 1978.

NORWOOD, F.: 'The Magic Pilgrimage of Apuleius', *Phoenix* 10 (1956), 1-12.

MASON, H.J.: '*Fabula Graecanica*: Apuleius and his Greek Sources', in Hijmans-van der Paardt *supra* 1-15.

MERKELBACH, R.: 'Eros und Psyche', *Philologus* 102 (1958), 103-116 (= Binder-Merkelbach, *Amor und Psyche*, Darmstadt, 1968, 392-407).

PFISTER, F.: Review of Riefstahl, *infra*, *PhW* 60 (1940), 539-541.

REITZENSTEIN, R.: *Das Märchen von Amor und Psyche bei Apuleius*, Leipzig 1912 (= Binder-Merkelbach, *Amor und Psyche*, Darmstadt 1968, 87-158).

RIEFSTAHL, H.: *Der Roman des Apuleius, Frankfurter Studien zur Religion und Kunst der Antike* 15.2, Frankfurt 1938.

SANDY, G.: '*Serviles Voluptates* in Apuleius' *Metamorphoses*', *Phoenix* 28 (1974), 234-244.

SCAZZOSO, P.: *Le Metamorfosi di Apuleio*, Studio critico sul significato del romanzo, Milan 1951.

SCHLAM, C.: '*Platonica* in the *Metamorphoses* of Apuleius', *TAPA* 101 (1970), 477-487.

SMITH, W.S. Jnr.: 'The Narrative Voice in Apuleius', *TAPA* 103 (1972), 513-534.

TATUM, J.: 'The Tales in Apuleius' *Metamorphoses*', *TAPA* 100 (1969), 487-527.

Apuleius and The Golden Ass, Ithaca and London 1979.

THIBAU, R.: 'Les Métamorphoses d'Apulée et la théorie platonici- enne de l'Éros', *Studia philosophica Gandensia* 3 (1965), 89-144.

WLOSOK, A.: 'Zur Einheit der Metamorphosen des Apuleius', *Philo- logus* 113 (1969), 68-84.

General:

BERGSON, H.: *Le Rire, Essai sur la signification du comique*, Paris 1901.

CÈBE, J.-Ph.: *La caricature et la parodie dans le monde romain antique des origines à Juvenal*, Paris 1966.

DECKER, A.F.: *Ironie in de Odyssee*, Leyden 1955.

DUCKWORTH, G.: *The Nature of Roman Comedy*, Princeton 1952 (repr. 1971).

FRECAUT, J.M.: *L'Esprit et L'Humour chez Ovide*, Grenoble 1972.

GRANT, M.: *Ancient Rhetorical Theories of the Laughable, Univers- ity of Wisconsin Studies in Language and Literature* 21, Madison 1924.

HAURY, A.: *L'Ironie et l'humour chez Ciceron*, Leyden 1955.

HORSTMANN, A.E.-A.: *Ironie und Humor bei Theokrit, Beiträge zur klassischen Philologie* 67, Meisenheim am Glan 1976.

HUIZINGA, J.: *Homo Ludens. A study of the play-element in Culture*, English translation by R.F.C. Bull, London 1949.

LEGRAND, Ph.-E.: *Daos*, Paris 1911.

MADER, M.: *Das Problem des Lachens und der Komödie bei Platon, Tübinger Beiträge zur Altertumswissenschaft* 47 (1977).

RADERMACHER, L.: *Weinen und Lachen, Studien über antikes Lebens- gefühl*, Vienna 1947.

SUESS, W.: *Lachen, Komik und Witz in der Antike*, Zurich/Stuttgart 1969.

SNELL, B.: 'Ueber das Spielerische bei Kallimachos' in *Die Ent- deckung des Geistes*[3], Hamburg 1955, 353-370.

ZUNTZ, G.: 'On Euripides' *Helena*: Theology and Irony', *Entretiens sur l'Antiquité Classique* VI, Vandoeuvres-Genève 1960, 201-242.

INDEX LOCORUM

INDEX OF PERSONS AND PLACES

(Adjectival and nominal forms of towns
and countries are indexed together.)

ADDITIONAL NOTE

While this monograph was in press I made a number of
discoveries which alter my views on the literary intentions of
the Greek novels in a few small particulars. But they alter much
more substantially the context of literary history in which any
future views must be formulated: the origins of the Greek novel
can at last be established rather than conjectured. The standard
plots, and not just the eccentric *Tefnut* or *Nectanebus*, can be
pointed out in oriental tales of demonstrably greater antiquity
than any likely Greek sources. The final proof comes in a group
of Sumerian texts much closer to the contents of *Daphnis and Chloe*
than Barnes' Egyptian specimens were to any of the then known
novels. We can now point to a text in which the Shepherd Dumuzi,
and his sister Inanna form a *Liebespaar*, and Dumuzi escapes time
after time from ominous intruders.[1] Better still, in a related
text[2] Dumuzi tries to seduce Inanna by showing her the sexual
behaviour of his flock. To this Sumerian *Daphnis and Chloe* we can
add a genuinely 'Phoenician' *Phoenicica*. The Ras Shamra text of
the Aquat story can be paired with the tale of *The Porter and the
Three Girls of Baghdad* in the *Arabian Nights* to show that Lollianus
was using material which appears elsewhere as separate tales,
including variants of 'doomed prince' and Satni-Khammuas stories.
Similarly, the *captatio*-episode in Petronius can be related to a
tale found in the Sultanpepe tablets (*The poor man of Nippur*) and
its development in the *Arabian Nights* tale of *Ma'aruf the Cobbler*
(which may even give us the clue to how Eumolpus got away). After
all this it is no surprise to be able to relate the *Onos*-complex
to versions of the Semiramis-story and kindred material, though
it has other surprises in store: we can now conjecture what the
roses really were the cure for. Most spectacular of all:
Iamblichus' claims to be using genuine oriental material are
vindicated: a long line of development can be drawn through variants of the Sesonchosis-story and the *Babyloniaca* to the Medieval
Georgian *Visramiani*. What emerges is an oriental branch of the
Tristan Romance - not surprising company for the oriental version
of the Grail Legend traceable from the (*Genesis*) Joseph-legends
through the *Acts of Thomas* to the Arabic story of Judar. Such is
a small sample of the relationships which have emerged. I shall
provide the appropriate documentation in a book shortly to be

published by Croom Helm, provisionally entitled *Ancient Fiction*.

1   The so-called Dumuzi's Dream. A translation is provided in the edition by B. Alster, Copenhagen 1972.

2   *Cuneiform Texts from Babylonian Tablets* XV 28-29.